PHYSICS
SUCCESS
in 20 Minutes
a Day

PHYSICS
SUCCESS
in 20 Minutes
a Day

Valentina Tobos
Laurentiu Tobos

LEARNINGEXPRESS®

NEW YORK

Copyright © 2006 LearningExpress, LLC.

All rights reserved under International and Pan-American Copyright Conventions.
Published in the United States by LearningExpress, LLC, New York.

Library of Congress Cataloging-in-Publication Data:
Tobos, Valentina.
   Physics success in 20 minutes a day / Valentina Tobos, Laurentiu Tobos.
      p. cm.
      ISBN 1-57685-497-3
   1. Physics—Programmed instruction. I. Tobos, Laurentiu. II.Title. III. Title: Physics success in twenty
minutes a day.
QC21.3.T63 2005
530'.07—dc22   2005020315

Printed in the United States of America

9 8 7 6 5 4 3 2 1

ISBN 1-57685-497-3

For information on LearningExpress, other LearningExpress products, or bulk sales, please write to us at:
   LearningExpress
   55 Broadway
   8th Floor
   New York, NY 10006

Or visit us at:
   www.learnatest.com

About the Authors

Valentina Tobos

Valentina Tobos is an assistant professor of physics at Lawrence Technological University, Southfield, Michigan. During her teaching career, she was involved with all levels of teaching physics, from elementary school level to advanced physics classes. This combination keeps her in close contact with all the facets of teaching and learning physics. She likes to say "Every challenge in learning will only *exercise* your mind."

Laurentiu Tobos

Laurentiu Tobos is a physicist engineer working at the National Superconducting Cyclotron of Michigan State University in Lansing, Michigan. He has exercised his "teaching charisma" at the University of Bucharest, Romania, and Western Michigan University in the Physics and Electrical Engineering departments. His interest in physics is surpassed only by his interest in mathematics and computers.

Contents

CONTENTS

Introduction ▶

If you have never taken a physics course and now find that you need to know physics, this is the book for you. If you have already taken a physics course but felt that you never understood what the teacher was trying to tell you, this book can teach you what you need to know. If it has been a while since you have taken a physics course and you need to refresh your skills, this book will review the basics and reteach you the skills you may have forgotten. Whatever your reason for needing to know physics, *Physics Success* will teach you what you need to know. It gives you the basics of a Physics I course in clear and straightforward lessons that you can do at your own pace.

▶ How to Use This Book

Physics Success teaches basic physics concepts in 20 self-paced lessons. The book includes a pretest, a posttest, a glossary to help you recognize and remember the key physics concepts, conversion factors and constants tables, and a section with additional resources, in case you would like to enhance your physics knowledge beyond the skills you will have learned in this book. Before you begin Lesson 1, take the pretest. The pretest will assess your current physics abilities. This will be helpful in determining your strengths and weaknesses. You'll find the answer immediately following the pretest.

After taking the pretest, move on to Lesson 1. Each lesson offers detailed explanations of a new concept. Numerous examples are given with step-by-step solutions. As you proceed through a lesson, you will find tips and shortcuts that will help you learn a concept. Each new concept is followed by a set of practice problems. The answers to the practice problems are in the answer key located at the end of the book.

When you have completed all 20 lessons, take the posttest. The posttest has the same format as the pretest, but the questions are different. Compare the results of the posttest with the results of the pretest you took before you began Lesson 1. What are your strengths? Do you have weak areas? Do you need to spend more time on some concepts, or are you ready to go to the next level?

▶ Make a Commitment

Success does not come without effort. If you truly want to be successful, make a commitment to spend the time you need to improve your physics skills. When you achieve physics success, you have laid the foundation for future challenges and opportunities.

So sharpen your pencils and get ready to begin the pretest!

PHYSICS SUCCESS
in 20 Minutes
a Day

▶ Pretest

Before you begin Lesson 1, you may want to get an idea of what you know and what you need to learn. The pretest will answer some of these questions for you. The pretest is 30 multiple-choice questions covering the topics in this book. While 30 questions can't cover every concept, skill, or shortcut taught in this book, your performance on the pretest will give you a good indication of your strengths and weaknesses. Keep in mind the pretest does not test all the skills taught in this book.

If you score high on the pretest, you have a good foundation and should be able to work your way through the book quickly. If you score low on the pretest, don't despair. This book will take you through the physics concepts, step by step. If you get a low score, you may need to take more than 20 minutes a day to work through a lesson. However, this is a self-paced program, so you can spend as much time on a lesson as you need. You decide when you fully comprehend the lesson and are ready to go on to the next one.

Take as much time as you need to do the pretest. When you are finished, check your answers with the answer key at the end of the book. Along with each answer is a number that tells you which lesson of this book teaches you about the physics skills needed for that question. You will find the level of difficulty increases as you work your way through the pretest.

1.	ⓐ	ⓑ	ⓒ	ⓓ	11.	ⓐ	ⓑ	ⓒ	ⓓ	21.	ⓐ	ⓑ	ⓒ	ⓓ
2.	ⓐ	ⓑ	ⓒ	ⓓ	12.	ⓐ	ⓑ	ⓒ	ⓓ	22.	ⓐ	ⓑ	ⓒ	ⓓ
3.	ⓐ	ⓑ	ⓒ	ⓓ	13.	ⓐ	ⓑ	ⓒ	ⓓ	23.	ⓐ	ⓑ	ⓒ	ⓓ
4.	ⓐ	ⓑ	ⓒ	ⓓ	14.	ⓐ	ⓑ	ⓒ	ⓓ	24.	ⓐ	ⓑ	ⓒ	ⓓ
5.	ⓐ	ⓑ	ⓒ	ⓓ	15.	ⓐ	ⓑ	ⓒ	ⓓ	25.	ⓐ	ⓑ	ⓒ	ⓓ
6.	ⓐ	ⓑ	ⓒ	ⓓ	16.	ⓐ	ⓑ	ⓒ	ⓓ	26.	ⓐ	ⓑ	ⓒ	ⓓ
7.	ⓐ	ⓑ	ⓒ	ⓓ	17.	ⓐ	ⓑ	ⓒ	ⓓ	27.	ⓐ	ⓑ	ⓒ	ⓓ
8.	ⓐ	ⓑ	ⓒ	ⓓ	18.	ⓐ	ⓑ	ⓒ	ⓓ	28.	ⓐ	ⓑ	ⓒ	ⓓ
9.	ⓐ	ⓑ	ⓒ	ⓓ	19.	ⓐ	ⓑ	ⓒ	ⓓ	29.	ⓐ	ⓑ	ⓒ	ⓓ
10.	ⓐ	ⓑ	ⓒ	ⓓ	20.	ⓐ	ⓑ	ⓒ	ⓓ	30.	ⓐ	ⓑ	ⓒ	ⓓ

1. Consider the following conversion: 1 yd = 3 ft and 1 yd = 91.44 cm. The Millau Viaduct in France measures 1,222 feet and is 53 feet taller than the Eiffel tower. Find the size of both the Viaduct and the Eiffel tower in yards and in meters.
   a. 337 yards and 305 meters; 16 yards and 14 meters
   b. 441 yards and 403 meters; 18 yards and 16 meters
   c. 754 yards and 308 meters; 17 yards and 12 meters
   d. 312 yards and 142 meters; 12 yards and 14 meters

2. How many quartz are in a 2 liter bottle?
   a. 2.11
   b. 3.21
   c. 2.31
   d. 1.32

3. There are 250,000.00 miles between Earth and the moon. What is this distance in meters?
   a. 250,000.00 meters
   b. 250,000.00 kilomets
   c. $4.0225 \cdot 10^8$ kilometers
   d. $4.0225 \cdot 10^8$ meters

4. The largest speed known to us is the speed of light: $3 \cdot 10^8$ miles/second. Convert this speed to miles/hour.
   a. $7 \cdot 10^8$ miles/hour
   b. $3 \cdot 10^8$ miles/hour
   c. $3 \cdot 10^8$ miles/second
   d. $7 \cdot 10^8$ miles/second

5. Light emitted by the sun takes 8.0 minutes to reach us at a speed of $3 \cdot 10^8$ meters/second. Find the distance in meters it travels in that time.
   a. $3 \cdot 10^{11}$ meters
   b. $1.4 \cdot 10^{11}$ kilometers
   c. $1.4 \cdot 10^{11}$ meters
   d. $1.4 \cdot 10^8$ meters

6. You have measured the size of an object's diameter seven times, and you have the following values: 3.5, 3.5, 3.4, 3.3, 3.2, 3.1, and 3.6 cm. What is the average measurement expressed with the correct number of significant figures?
   a. 3.2 cm
   b. 3.6 cm
   c. 3.4 cm
   d. 3 cm

7. Write the following quantities in scientific notation: 0.034 kg, 123.34 in, 1,500.0 N, $1.013 \cdot 10^5$ N/m^2
   a. $3.4 \cdot 10^{-2}$ kg, $1.234 \cdot 10^2$ in, $1.5 \cdot 10^3$ N, $0.1013 \cdot 10^6$ N/m^2
   b. $3.4 \cdot 10^{-2}$ kg, $1.234 \cdot 10^2$ in, $1.5 \cdot 10^3$ N, $1.013 \cdot 10^5$ N/m^2
   c. $3.4 \cdot 10^{-2}$ kg, $12.34 \cdot 10^1$ in, $1.5 \cdot 10^3$ N, $1.013 \cdot 10^5$ N/m^2
   d. $0.34 \cdot 10^{-1}$ kg, $1.234 \cdot 10^2$ in, $1.5 \cdot 10^3$ N, $1.013 \cdot 10^5$ N/m^2

8. Perform the following additions to the correct number of significant figures: 75.20 + 0.135 + 1,254.25 + 101.05 = ? And 1,234.56 + 0.32 = ?
   a. 1,430.6 and 1,234.88
   b. 1,430.63 and 1,235
   c. 1,430.635 and 1,234.88
   d. 1,430.63 and 1,234.88

9. In a three-dimensional system, the vector represented by the following coordinates (second set of numbers is the tip of the vector) $(3, -2, 5)$ and $(6, 0, 5)$ is:

a.

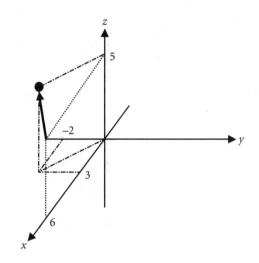

b.

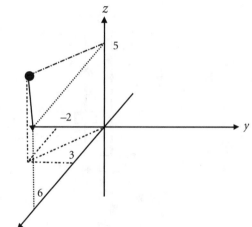

c.

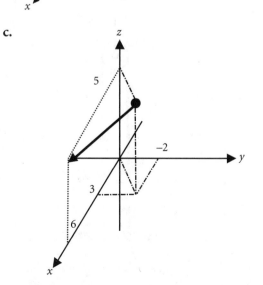

10. Draw the following vectors and find their resultant $(R = A + B)$ graphically and quantitatively: $A = (3,3)$ and $B = (-6, -5)$.

a. $R = 6.3$

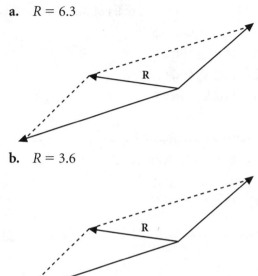

b. $R = 3.6$

c. $R = 3.6$

11. Consider two objects acted on by the same force and their final accelerations 2.00 m/s^2 and 4.00 m/s^2. If the mass of the first object is 3.25 kg, find the force and the mass of the second object.

   a. 1.62 kg and 6.5 N

   b. 16.2 kg and 6.5 N

   c. 1.62 kg and 65 N

   d. 1.62 kg and 0.65 N

12. A small object is acted upon by a force of 2.24 N and accelerates with 12.0 m/s^2. What is the mass of the object?

   a. 187 kg

   b. 18.7 kg

   c. 1.87 kg

   d. 0.187 kg

13. A car of mass 1,500 kilograms starts from rest and travels 10 meters in 2 seconds. What are the values of the acceleration, assuming uniform acceleration, and of the net force?

   a. 10 m/s^2 and 7,500 N

   b. 5 m/s^2 and 9,500 N

   c. 5 m/s^2 and 7,500 N

   d. 5 m/s^2 and 75 N

14. A book is sitting on a table. The book has a mass of 553 g. Find the weight and the normal force.

   a. $W = 0$ N and $N = 5.5$ N

   b. $W = 5.5$ N and $N = 0$ N

   c. $W = N = 5.5$ N

   d. $W = 5.5$ N and $N = 10$ N

15. Which of the free body diagrams below fully represents the forces acting on the two objects? The pulley and string are considered of negligible mass.

   a.

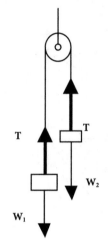

   b.

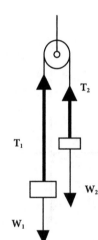

   c.

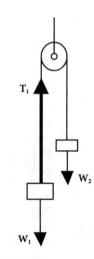

16. An object of 50 g mass moves on a surface with the coefficient of kinetic friction of 0.3. Find the force of friction acting on the object.
   a. 1.5 N
   b. 15 N
   c. 0.15 N
   d. 0.015 N

17. Two different objects have the same momentum, but one object is ten times larger in mass than the other ($m_1 > m_2$). How do the two velocities compare? Consider one-dimensional motion.
   a. $m_1/m_2 = v_1/v_2 = 10$
   b. $m_2/m_1 = v_2/v_1 = 10$
   c. $m_1/m_2 = v_2/v_1 = 1$
   d. $m_1/m_2 = v_2/v_1 = 10$

18. A car comes to a complete stop in 20 seconds. Considering the mass of the car to be 1,500 kg and the initial speed 18 m/s, find out the average breaking force.
   a. 1,350 N
   b. 1.350 N
   c. 135.0 N
   d. 13.5 N

19. Two objects of masses 25 and 5 kg collide perfectly elastically and head on. Object 1, which is heavier, is at rest initially, and object 2 is moving at a speed of 1.5 m/s. After collision, object 2 will recoil at a speed of 1.2 m/s. What is the speed of the heavy object? There is no external force acting on the system.
   a. 54 m/s
   b. 0.54 m/s
   c. 0 m/s
   d. 540 m/s

20. Consider a car collision in which one car is driving north at a 11 m/s speed and the other is moving east at 9 m/s. The cars are of similar mass. Find the velocity immediately after the collision if the cars get entangled and move together before they stop.
   a. $\mathbf{v} = \dfrac{1}{2}(9\,\mathbf{j})$
   b. $\mathbf{v} = \dfrac{1}{2}(11\,\mathbf{k})$
   c. $\mathbf{v} = \dfrac{1}{2}(11\,\mathbf{k} + 9\,\mathbf{j})$ m/s
   d. 0 m/s

21. Find the work done by the weight of an object (300.0 N) if the object moves a distance of 240.0 cm on the horizontal.
   a. 720 J
   b. 700 J
   c. 0 J
   d. 72,000 J

22. A work of $W = -(50 \cdot m)$ J, where m is the mass of the object, is done on an object. Find the change in kinetic energy.
   a. $\Delta KE = W = -(50 \cdot m)$ J
   b. $\Delta KE = 0$ J
   c. $\Delta KE = -50$ J
   d. $\Delta KE = -(50 \cdot m)$ J

23. Find the centripetal acceleration on a car taking a curve at a speed of 60 miles/hour if the curvature of the road has a radius of 50 meters.
   a. 14.14 m/s
   b. 14.14 m/s^2
   c. 14.14 m/s^3
   d. 0 m/s^2

24. Find the pressure exerted by a layer of water 5 feet deep on the bottom of a pool.

   a. $0 \cdot 10^3$ Pa

   b. $5 \cdot 10^1$ Pa

   c. $5 \cdot 10^3$ atm

   d. $5 \cdot 10^3$ Pa

25. Water has a very large specific heat. Around the ocean shore or seaside, is the weather heating up fast? Why?

   a. No, the large heat capacity means that the temperature changes little with heat exchange.

   b. Yes, the water makes it feel colder.

   c. No, because there are winds blowing all the time.

   d. There is no connection between water and the temperature change.

26. Consider the PV diagram below. Find the work for the process.

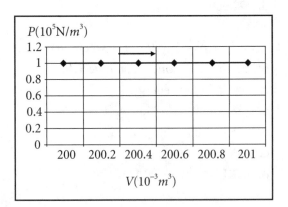

   a. -10^2 J

   b. 0 J

   c. 10^2 J

   d. -10^5 J

27. Consider two objects, one made of rubber and the other made of nylon, both initially electrically neutral. You rub the two objects together, and the rubber becomes charged with $-2.88 \cdot 10^{-16}$ Coulombs. What is the nylon's charge and how many electrons have been shifted to the rubber from the nylon in the process?

   a. $-2.88 \cdot 10^{-16}$ Coulombs; 1,800 protons

   b. $+2.88 \cdot 10^{-16}$ Coulombs; 1,800 protons

   c. $-2.88 \cdot 10^{-16}$ Coulombs; 1,800 electrons

   d. $+2.88 \cdot 10^{-16}$ Coulombs; 1,800 electrons

28. A current passes through a wire. What is the ratio of the magnetic fields produced at a distance of r and $4 \cdot r$ from the wire?

   a. 1

   b. 2

   c. 4

   d. 16

29. Light travels from air to a medium with an index of refraction 1.55. What is the speed of light in that medium?

   a. $1.94 \cdot 10^8$ km/s

   b. $1.94 \cdot 10^8$ m/s

   c. 1.94 m/s

   d. 10^8 m/s

30. An object is placed in front of two mirrors that make a 90° angle. The positions of the images formed by the two-mirror system are:

a.

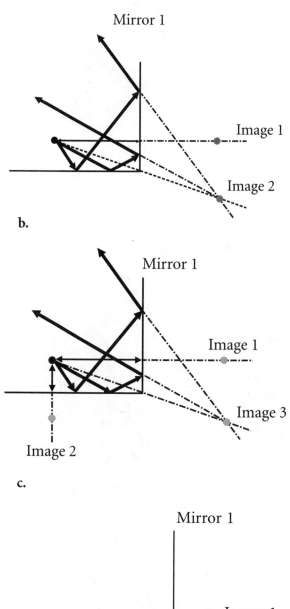

b.

c.

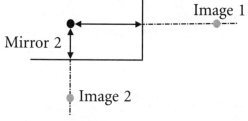

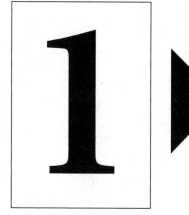

LESSON

Units and Prefixes

LESSON SUMMARY

Measurements and observations form the base of our scientific knowledge of the world. Some quantities we measure can be calculated in terms of others, while some cannot; those that cannot are the most fundamental quantities. The *International System of Units* (SI) is based on seven fundamental units from which we can express all other units. Sometimes, we deal in practice with quantities much larger or much smaller than the defined unit. In such cases, it is convenient to use prefixes. Last but not least, we look at significant figures and guidelines for their use in computations and the scientific notation.

▶ Fundamental and Derived Units

Physics is exciting when it can predict how nature will behave in one situation on the basis of data obtained in another situation. Therefore, a great deal of effort goes into making measurements as accurate and reproducible as possible in a given situation.

For example, the *atomic mass unit* u has a value of one-twelfth ($1/12$) the mass of the carbon isotope C^{12}. As long as we stay within the boundaries of atomic physics, the picture is nice and clear: The hydrogen atom has (approximately) a one-unit mass, 1 u; the oxygen atom has a mass of 16 u; and so forth. And these data

Choosing a unit for a particular quantity is a highly subjective exercise; choosing a good one will allow accurate measurements that are easily accessible and reproducible so that everybody understands when we document our observations.

can be obtained from nice atomic collision measurements. The ugly part (due to our somewhat arbitrary definition of u) comes when we want to link this to another mass standard, such as the kilogram. We find the following:

$$1 \text{ u} = 1.66067 \cdot 10^{-27} \text{kg}$$

and all our nice atomic data transform into strings carrying four or five decimals. It can make us wonder why the kilogram is the only one of the seven fundamental units still defined in terms of a physical platinum-iridium cylinder artifact kept in Paris.

Often, it is possible to split the units of measurement into simpler units. For example, a unit of area, say, a square foot, may be actually the area of a square that is 1 foot long by 1 foot wide. In other words, we can reduce the area measurement to a length measurement.

But there are times when this trick is not possible anymore. For example, to measure the length, we need to actually perform a direct comparison to a convenient unit of length. We call length a *fundamental quantity* and the unit of length a *fundamental unit*. Other well-known fundamental units are the ones measuring time and mass. We should think of these base units as some of the building blocks that we use in our dimensional puzzle to get units for other important physical quantities such as speed, force, or energy.

▶ Practice

1. You want to measure the volume of your microwave oven. What do you need and how do you proceed? Is volume a fundamental or a derived quantity?
2. We define the density of a substance as the mass of the unit volume of that substance. Would the density unit be a fundamental or a derived unit?
3. One of the units initially used to express values for the atmospheric pressure was the length of a vertical mercury column balanced by the surrounding pressure, as in Figure 1.1. Without knowing anything about what pressure is, can you tell if it is a fundamental quantity or not?

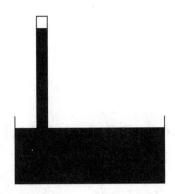

Figure 1.1

4. When you buy a lightbulb at the store, you may choose one that is rated at 25W, 60W, 100W, and so on. Is this a good measure for the light you get

from your bulb? Remember, a good unit is accessible, universal, and reproducible. Why do you think some manufacturers of "eco-bulbs" use units such as lumens on their packaging when they advertise their bulbs?

5. The radian is the angle spanned on a circle's circumference by an arc of length equal to the radius of that circle. Look at Figure 1.2 and decide if this angular measure is a fundamental quantity?

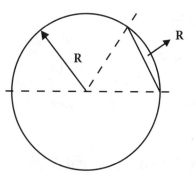

Figure 1.2

▶ International System of Units (SI)

Revolutionary times call for revolutionary units! The main ideas for an international system of units were born out of the French Revolution, when the metric system and the kilogram were introduced to measure lengths and weights. Another revolution, and a New World, had already adopted a decimal system—you guessed it, in the United States, where a dime has ten cents, a dollar has ten dimes, and so forth. But the United States fell short of putting Thomas Jefferson's decimal idea in practice outside the financial system.

Eventually, these revolutionary ideas prevailed and took over the world, when in 1960, the *International System of Units* (SI) was adopted by the 11th General Conference on Weights and Measurements.

This system defines seven fundamental quantities and their associated units: length and meter, mass and kilogram, time and second, electric current and ampere, temperature and degree Kelvin, luminous intensity and candela, and, last but not least, the amount of substance and the mole. All other units can be consistently derived from these seven *fundamental units.*

The metric system had a strong influence on the scientific community. Therefore, eventually the first coherent system of units and a precursor to SI showed up in the 1860s as the *CGS system.* It defined the *centimeter, gram, and second* (or CGS) as fundamental units for length, mass, and time. Another hundred years had to pass for us to fully realize we needed another four more fundamental units to get the whole picture, that is, so that we could derive any other measurement in terms of these seven fundamental quantities.

A coherent system of units enforces a certain set of rules for manipulating the results of the actual measurements. To get sensible results, only quantities with the same unit can be added or subtracted.

When listing data and performing calculations, do the following:

- Write down the units explicitly, convert everything to the same unit, and use the same prefixes throughout a calculation.
- Treat all units as algebraic quantities. In particular, when identical units are divided, they cancel each other out.
- Use conversion factors between different unit systems. For instance, the conversion factor of 1 lb = 0.4536 kg might be used to go back and forth between SI and British units of mass.
- Check to see that your calculations are correct by verifying that the units combine algebraically to give the desired unit for the answer. Remember, only quantities with the same units can be added or subtracted.

Some usual practical conversion factors between different units in the SI and the U.S. or British system are as follows:

1 inch = 2.54 centimeters

1 yard = 3 feet = 36 inches = 91.44 centimeters

1 mile = 1.609 kilometers

1 pound (lb) = 0.4536 kilograms

1 quart = 946 milliliters = 0.946 liters

Example

You travel to Canada where the highway posted speed limit is 100 km/h. How fast are you allowed to go in mi/h?

Solution

Obviously, your car speedometer shows you values in miles per hour, so we have to figure out this km/h value. Reversing the relation 1 mi = 1.609 km, we get:

1 km = 0.621 mi

Therefore:

100 km/h = 100 · (1 km/1 h) = 100 · (0.621 mi/1 h) = 62.1 mi/h

100 km/h = 62.1 mi/h

▶ Practice

Use the conversion factors to work the following practice problems.

6. If you are to measure the mass of the earth, you will end up with $5.98 \cdot 10^{24}$ kg. Find the mass in pounds and in ounces.

7. How many liters of engine oil do you need to buy if your car engine capacity is 3.5 quarts?

8. A room is 10.0 feet long by 8.5 feet wide. What is the area of the room in m^2?

9. In the previous practice problem, the room is 12 feet tall. What is the volume in m^3?

10. What is the SI unit for temperature? What is the unit for mass?

11. How many ounces of pudding are there in a 300-gram serving? Use the fact that 1 pound has 16 ounces.

12. You buy a European car that uses 14 liters of gas for 100 kilometers. How many gallons of gas do you need to travel 62.1 miles?

13. In problem 12, how many miles can your car go using just one gallon of gas?

▶ Unit Prefixes and Use

We already mentioned that SI is a decimal-based system, where each unit may be divided or multiplied by 10 to form the next subunit or multiple units. Initially, it was decided that multiples would use root words coming from Greek: *deka* for 10, *hecto* for 100, *kilo* for 1,000. And submultiples would use Latin root words: *deci* for one-tenth, *centi* for one-hundredth, *milli* for one-thousandth, and so on. Eventually, our needs expanded so much that now there are 20 usual *prefixes* used to form multiples and submultiples of SI units, and the initial rules were relaxed somehow. Here are the 12 most usual of these prefixes.

Table 1.1 Prefixes

MULTIPLE UNITS	SUBUNITS
$10^{12} =$ tera $=$ T	$10^{-12} =$ pico $=$ p
$10^9 =$ giga $=$ G	$10^{-9} =$ nano $=$ n
$10^6 =$ mega $=$ M	$10^{-6} =$ micro $= \mu$
$10^3 =$ kilo $=$ k	$10^{-3} =$ milli $=$ m
$10^2 =$ hecto $=$ h	$10^{-2} =$ centi $=$ c
$10^1 =$ deka $=$ da	$10^{-1} =$ deci $=$ d

A few rules on the use of prefixes follow:

- A prefix should always be followed by the unit that it divides or multiplies.
- Prefixes cannot be combined: We use pm (picometer) and not $\mu\mu$m (micro-micro-meter).
- The only SI unit that has a prefix already in its name is the kilogram. In this case, the prefix names are used with the name *gram* and the symbol *g*. Another exception of the previously mentioned rule exists: It is also usual to say *kton* (kiloton) instead of *megagram*.

The use of prefixes allows us to conveniently scale up or scale down our units to the task at hand and for simplifying the calculations involving our measurements. It is more convenient to use centimeters when measuring the circumference of your waist or the length of your arm (if you are a tailor, for example) and to use kilometers when measuring the distance between two cities than the other way around.

▶ Practice

14. The root word *centi* means 100 in which language?
  a. Greek
  b. Latin
  c. Spanish

15. Which metric prefix means one-thousandth?
  a. kilo
  b. centi
  c. milli

16. A time of 5 milliseconds is equal to which of the following?
  a. 0.0005 s
  b. 0.005 s
  c. 0.05 s

17. Twenty-five kilometers is equal to which of the following?
  a. 250,000 m
  b. 25,000 m
  c. 250 m

18. What do you call 2.5×10^3 kg of steel?
  a. 250,000 g
  b. 25,000 g
  c. 2.5 tons

19. 1×10^{-3} kg is equal to which of the following?
  a. 1 milligram
  b. 1 gram
  c. 1 milikilogram
  d. all of the above

▶ Significant Figures

We explore and know our world by making a subjective use of our five senses (vision, touch, hearing, smell, and taste). This is one of the reasons that there is no such thing as an exact or absolute measurement. In our measurements, we are sometimes held back by the quality of the tools we use, by our own skills, or by the methods we use to gather our data. To overcome some of these limitations, a simple solution exists: Repeat the measurement several times, and then somehow figure out which of the measurements we get as our results are significant. For a single direct measurement, the

As a rule: The last digit we keep (the 6 in bold) is rounded up to the next value (in this case, it would be 7) if the first of the insignificant figures being dropped is 5 or greater; if it's less than 5, we leave it unchanged (which is the case here).

rule of thumb is that we can accurately (precisely) estimate by up to half of the smallest division on the scale of our instrument, and we can take a best guess up to one-tenth of this smallest division. For example, using a *vernier caliper* that can measure exactly to one-tenth of a millimeter to find the diameter of a rod, the best-case estimate of our precision would be 0.01 mm. We choose to accept a result of 3.23 mm for the diameter. But given our tool, if someone tells us he or she measured the rod diameter to be 3.22778 mm, we would have to be very skeptical about the last three digits. We say in this case our measurement has only three *significant figures*, because only these first three figures are known with a certain degree of confidence. And certainly, the last digit is the least accurate; this is where our confidence is somewhat lower than for the other digits.

Example

You measure the mass of a small crucible on a precision electronic balance that is rated to measure down to one-tenth of a milligram. You get the following results when you perform this measurement three times: 3.0757 g, 3.0754 g, and 3.0758 g. What are the significant figures in your results?

Solution

From these data, it is clear that even if you claim to have a very precise instrument, something happens during the measuring process that limits your precision to only milligrams. Maybe you lean on the bench where the balance sits, or air currents affect your experiment, or some hardware problem exists with your balance. Averaging your measurements, you can say that your crucible has 3.0756333 g. But wait: Your balance can measure only up to a tenth of a milligram; in other words, we can have only five significant figures in our measurement. We have to somehow limit our answer to only five digits.

Therefore, we quote our result for the crucible weight as 3.0756 g. From these figures, we know for sure the first four digits are more accurate than the last one, which is just an estimate—a best effort to guess the exact value.

To get more accurate data, we could do the following:

- Try to be more careful when taking the actual data, and see if this helps.
- Repeat the experiment more than ten times, and use mathematics (statistics) to get a best-guess average of the result (which is beyond the scope of this text).
- Try both of the previous suggestions.
- Upgrade your hardware. Buy a more expensive balance that has an even better precision.

An important rule to be observed when we use experimental data to further calculate other quantities is that the worst precision of our measurements propagates to the result: The result has as many significant figures as the member with the least number of significant figures.

Example

What is the area of a room that is 9.66 feet by 5.2 feet?

Solution

The area is the product of the two measured dimensions. If we keep the unit *feet* and look only for the significant figures after multiplication, we find the area is 50.232 square feet. However, because one of the factors has only two significant figures, we have to limit our result to only two figures as well. Therefore, we say that the area of the room is 50 square feet.

▶ Introduce Rule

Rule for addition and subtraction: the result of addition and subtraction has the same number of decimal places as the least number of decimal places of the original numbers.

30.25 + 2.01089 = 32.26 (only second decmial place is considered)

Rule for multiplication and division: the result of multiplication or division has the same number of significant figures the least number of significant figures in any of the original numbers.

30.25 × 2.01089 = 60.83 (only four significant figures are considered)

▶ Practice

20. You have an electronic balance with a five-digit display, and you measure a crucible to have a weight of 5.2546 g. Then, using the same balance, you measure the oven that will be used to heat up that crucible and find that it is 78.236 g. What is the mass of the crucible and oven assembly?

21. What factor is limiting your precision in the case of the previous problem measurements?

22. You measure the size of your microwave oven to be 28.6 cm × 27.9 cm × 20.8 cm. What is the volume of the oven in cm³? How many significant figures does your result have?

23. The voltage across one of the elements of a voltage divider is 97.2 volts and is 13.758 volts across the other element. What is the result of adding these two voltages together? How many significant figures does the result have?

24. Assume that 1 pound has an exact mass of 453.59237 g. To three significant figures, this is which of the following?
   a. 453.6 g
   b. 454 g
   c. 0.45359 kg

25. Assume that 1 pound has an exact mass of 453.59237 g. To two significant figures, this is equal to which of the following?
   a. 453 g
   b. 454 g
   c. 0.45 kg

▶ Scientific Notation

One way to express more elegantly very small (atomic size) or very large (astronomic size) numbers is to use a notation that allows us to multiply a standard number (say, between 1 and 10) with a multiple. This format is called *scientific notation.*

The usefulness can be seen also in expressing results with the correct number of significant figures, as discussed in the previous section.

Example

A long rod has a radius of 5.2 mm and a length of 1.20 m. Express the volume in scientific notation.

Solution

We first convert the data to the same unit of length.

$r = 5.2$ mm $= 5.2$ mm $\cdot 10^{-3}$ m/1 mm $= 5.2 \cdot 10^{-3}$ m

$L = 1.20$ m

$V = A \cdot L = ?$

$V = \pi \cdot r^2 \cdot L = \pi \cdot (5.2 \cdot 10^{-3}$ m$)^2 \cdot 1.20$ m $= 32 \cdot 10^{-6}$ m^3

And to finish the problem, we must express this result in scientific notation:

$V = 32 \cdot 10^{-6}$ m$^3 = 3.2 \cdot 10^{-5}$ m^3

$V = 3.2 \cdot 10^{-5}$ m^3

▶ Practice

26. Write the following numbers in scientific notation:

1 kg = 0.6852 slug

1 mi/h = 1,609 m/h

1 N = 0.2448 lb

Planck's constant $= 0.0006626 \cdot 10^{-30}$ J $\cdot$ s

Acceleration due to gravity $= 32.2$ ft/s^2

Sun's mass $= 199 \cdot 10^{28}$ kg

27. Is it true that if you use scientific notation, you do not have to worry about significant figures? Explain briefly.

28. The atomic mass of the chemical element niobium (Nb) is 92.90638 u. Convert this mass into kilograms using only three significant figures. Use scientific notation to express your answer.

L E S S O N

2 ▶ Scalars and Vectors

LESSON SUMMARY

We start this chapter by briefly considering a reference frame and the coordinates of a point-like object relative to it. Next, we make a distinction between scalar and vector quantities, and present examples of both. At the end of the chapter, we take a quick look at the properties of vectors.

▶ Coordinates

In order to be able to locate a point-like object on a line, on a surface, or in space, we need to choose a reference position called an *origin* and then give directions regarding how to get to the object starting from the origin.

A *reference frame* consists of an origin through which one or more axes specifying some given directions are passing. *Coordinates* are sets of numbers that uniquely specify the position of a point-like object with respect to this certain reference frame. These coordinates measure certain properties of the path from the origin to the object when we follow these axes according to some given instructions.

The simplest case is the one-dimensional motion, along a straight line. In this case, the line is also the only reference axis we need. In order to completely specify the position of an object, we have to choose a fixed point as our origin, and then find the distance from the object to the origin using some convenient units. Because our object may be either to the left or to the right of the origin, we consider by convention that the distance is positive if the object lies to the right of the origin and negative if it lies to the left. This distance and the corresponding sign is what we call the coordinate of the object with respect to our frame of reference. The distance between two points in this case is just the difference between their coordinates. In Figure 2.1, the distance from P to Q is PQ; then $PQ = [4.5 - (-2.5)] = 7$ units.

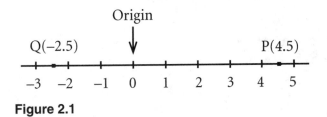

Figure 2.1

In the two-dimensional case, a frame of reference is specified by an origin and a set of two axes passing through that origin. To get to the position of a given object at point P, we may say: Start from the origin and follow x-axis for a length of three units; then follow the direction of y-axis (that is, follow a parallel to the y-axis) for another four units. That is, our object has an x-coordinate of 3 and a y-coordinate of 4 (see Figure 2.2).

If the two axes are perpendicular to each other, we can find the distance from the origin to point P by applying Pythagoras' theorem:

$$d^2 = x^2 + y^2$$
$$d^2 = 3^2 + 4^2$$
$$d^2 = 25$$
$$d = 5$$

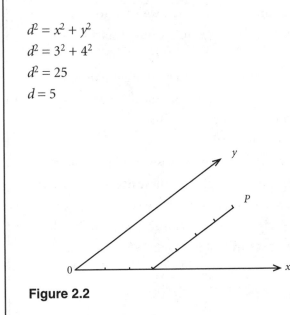

Figure 2.2

The most widely known two-dimensional (2-D) system of coordinates or reference frames is the *Cartesian* one, when the two axes are perpendicular to each other. Given any point P, we draw parallel lines to the axes. The distance from where these lines intercept the axes to the origin are the two coordinates (x, y) of point P. This way of labeling points is known as the Cartesian system, in honor of the French mathematician and philosopher Renee Descartes (1596–1650), who was the first to think of this system.

A quick reference to Pythagoras's theorem gives the distance between two points with coordinates (x_1, y_1) and (x_2, y_2) as:

$$d^2 = (x_1 - x_2)^2 + (y_1 - y_2)^2$$

Another widely used way of specifying a point's position on a plane surface is by using its so-called *polar coordinates* (r, θ) with $r > 0$.

One coordinate is the *length r of the segment OP* from the origin of the reference frame to the point, and the other is the angle θ that this segment OP makes with a reference axis Ox. This angle θ gives the *direction* to the point P, and r gives the *distance to the origin*. See Figure 2.3.

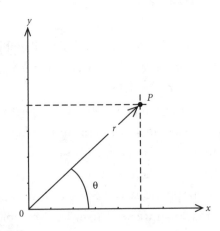

Figure 2.3

If the origin and the x-axis of the two representations are the same, then we can relate these sets of coordinates by the following relations:

$x = r \cdot \cos \theta$

$y = r \cdot \sin \theta$

and consequently:

$r^2 = x^2 + y^2$

Depending on the symmetry of the problem we try to solve, it may be easier to use one or the other of these two representations.

Example

The following Cartesian coordinates characterize a point: $x = 7.0$ and $y = 2.0$. Find the polar coordinates of this point.

Solution

Considering the previous explanation for polar coordinates, we can first find the distance to the point in polar coordinates, r, and then, applying trigonometric functions, we can determine the angle θ.

$x = 7.0$

$y = -2.0$

$r = ?$

$\theta = ?$

$r^2 = x^2 + y^2$

$r^2 = 7^2 + (-2)^2$

$r^2 = 53$

$r = \mathbf{7.3}$

$\sin \theta = -2.0/7.3$

$\theta = \mathbf{-16°}$

Both these two-dimensional systems of coordinates may be extended to three dimensions by adding a z-axis perpendicular to the plane, and we get the 3-D Cartesian and, respectively, the *cylindrical coordinates systems*.

For a 3-D Cartesian system of reference, the distance r of point $P(x_0, y_0, z_0)$ having coordinates x_0, y_0, and z_0 to the origin is given by:

$R^2 = x_0^2 + y_0^2 + z_0^2$

To go from this to the 3-D cylindrical system, we use the same relationship between (x,y) and (r,θ) in the horizontal plane, and the height z is the same: (r, θ, z).

Example

Find the cylindrical system coordinates of point Q of (Cartesian) coordinates (3,4,6) units.

Solution

We have:

$r^2 = x^2 + y^2$

$r^2 = 3^2 + 4^2 = 25$

and therefore:

$r = 5$

$\sin \theta = $ component on y/r

$\sin \theta = 4/5 = 0.8$

and therefore:

$\theta = 53°$

Point Q coordinates in the cylindrical system are $(5, 53°, 6)$.

▶ Practice

1. Find the polar coordinates r and θ of a point P having Cartesian coordinates $x = 3$ and $y = 6$.
2. What is the distance between point P having Cartesian coordinates (2,5) and point Q having coordinates (5,9)?

3. What are the polar coordinates of point Q in the previous question?

4. What angle does the segment PQ make with the axis Ox in the previous question?

5. What is the distance from the origin to point Q in practice problem 2?

6. A point P has the following coordinates in a cylindrical system: $(3,30°,5)$. Find the coordinates in a Cartesian 3-D system.

7. What is the distance from point P to the origin in practice problem 6?

8. A point P in a horizontal plane has coordinates $(-3.50,6.20)$ meters. Find the polar coordinates of this point.

▶ Scalars and Vectors

Each of the physical quantities we may encounter in physics can be categorized as either *scalars* or *vectors*. A quantity that is completely specified only by its magnitude using a certain unit is called a *scalar* quantity. When you say, "I bought 3 lbs of tomatoes," you have pretty much specified all the relevant information about your purchase. Therefore, mass is a scalar quantity. Other examples of scalar quantities include temperature, volume, pressure, density, and time. When you say that the temperature outside is 55° F, you do not need to specify a direction. Scalar quantities can be used in regular arithmetic computations with the only precaution being to express them using the same units.

At other times, in order to fully characterize a physical quantity, we need to specify both a magnitude and a direction. For example, in order to get from Lansing, Michigan, to Detroit, Michigan, you have to travel approximately 70 miles due east. Going in the wrong direction will take you to Grand Rapids or maybe Jackson, instead of Detroit.

A vector quantity therefore has both a magnitude and a direction. In the previous example, we say that *displacement* is a vector. We usually draw a vector as an arrow. The direction of the arrow gives the direction of the vector, and its length is usually scaled proportionally to the magnitude of the vector, using appropriate units. The magnitude of a vector is always a positive number. A vector symbol is a bold letter, for instance, **A**.

For a 3-D Cartesian system, we define a *unit vector* along each one of the axes; we do so by making a vector along the axis, pointing it in the positive direction, and making it have a unit length. The usual notation is **i** for the unit vector along the x-axis, **j** for the unit vector along the y-axis, and **k** for the unit vector along the z-axis.

$$|\mathbf{i}| = |\mathbf{j}| = |\mathbf{k}| = 1$$

Unit vectors are used to specify the directions of the reference axes. We also define a vector's components $\mathbf{A}_x$, $\mathbf{A}_y$, and $\mathbf{A}_z$ as the difference of its starting point and end tip coordinates (see Figure 2.4).

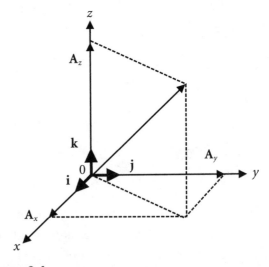

Figure 2.4

Then, we may represent the vector as:

$$\mathbf{A} = \mathbf{i}\, A_x + \mathbf{j}\, A_y + \mathbf{k}\, A_z$$

Assuming the starting point of vector **A** is $P(x_s, y_s, z_s)$ and the end tip is at point $Q(x_t, y_t, z_t)$ then:

$$A_x = x_t - x_s \quad A_y = y_t - y_s \quad A_z = z_t - z_s$$

The magnitude of a vector is:

$$A^2 = A_x^2 + A_y^2 + A_z^2$$

▶ Practice

9. Find the magnitude of the following vectors: $(3.0, -5.0, 6.0)$ meters and $(20, 45, -30)$ N.

10. Is it possible for a vector to have zero magnitude but nonzero components? Explain.

▶ Vector Properties

Vectors enjoy certain properties that can make their handling easier. For example, the components of any vector can be used in place of the vector itself in any calculation where it is convenient to do so.

Two vectors are equal if they have the same magnitude and the same direction. As the direction is specified by a whole bundle of parallel lines to each other, this allows us most of the time to move a vector parallel to itself without affecting the outcome of the problem.

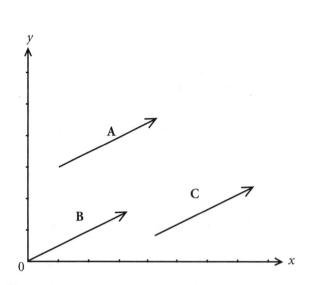

Figure 2.5

Example

All three vectors **A**, **B**, and **C** in Figure 2.5 are equal to one another. Their directions are parallel, and their magnitudes are equal.

We define the sum of two vectors as a *new vector*, also called a *resultant vector*.

One method to obtain the resultant vector is by moving one of the vectors parallel to itself until its starting point coincides with the end of the first one. The resultant vector starts at the tail of the first vector and ends at the end tip of the second vector.

We write the resultant vector as:

$$\mathbf{R} = \mathbf{A} + \mathbf{B}$$

Without any loss of generality, we can limit ourselves to the two-dimensional case of vectors in the same plane.

Example

Show graphically the addition of two vectors **A** and **B**.

Solution

As defined previously, we move the second vector parallel to itself so that its tail intersects the tip of the first

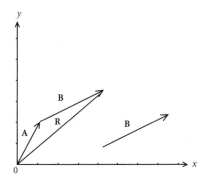

Figure 2.6

Figure 2.8

vector (see Figure 2.6). If the two vectors being added have components (A_x, A_y, A_z) and (B_x, B_y, B_z), the sum or resultant can be easily seen to have the components (R_x, R_y, R_z) given by:

$$R_x = A_x + B_x$$

$$R_y = A_y + B_y$$

$$R_z = A_z + B_z$$

and the magnitude of the resultant is:

$$R^2 = R_x^2 + R_y^2 + R_z^2$$

While the resultant vector can be written as:

$$\mathbf{R} = \mathbf{i} \cdot R_x + \mathbf{j} \cdot R_y + \mathbf{k} \cdot R_z$$

The opposite of a vector $\mathbf{A}$ is a vector $-\mathbf{A}$, having the same magnitude, but oriented in the opposite sense relative to the initial vector (see Figure 2.7).

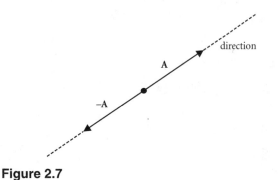

Figure 2.7

This allows us to define the difference of two vectors by means of adding one of the vectors with the opposite of the other.

$$\mathbf{A} - \mathbf{B} = \mathbf{A} + (-\mathbf{B})$$

In Figure 2.8, the resultant vector of $\mathbf{A} - \mathbf{A} = \mathbf{A} + (-\mathbf{A}) = 0$ is demonstrated. The two vectors have intentionally not been perfectly superimposed as an aid to the eye.

Example

Find the magnitude of the resultant vector of the following vectors: $(3, -5, -2)$ m and $(-2, 0, 8)$ m, and of the difference of the same vectors.

Solution

The components of the resultant are:

$$R_x = A_x + B_x = 3 - 2 = 1 \text{ m}$$

$$R_y = A_y + B_y = -5 + 0 = -5 \text{ m}$$

$$R_z = A_z + B_z = -2 + 8 = 6 \text{ m}$$

Therefore:

$$R^2 = 1 + 25 + 36 = 62 \text{ m}^2$$

and the magnitude of the resultant vector is:

$$R = 7.9 \text{ m}$$

For the difference:

$$\mathbf{A} - \mathbf{B} = \mathbf{A} + (-\mathbf{B})$$

and the components of the $\mathbf{A} + (-\mathbf{B})$ are:

$$R_x = A_x + (-B_x) =$$

$$3 + [-(-2)] = 5 \, \text{m}$$

$$R_y = A_y + (-B_y) = -5 + 0 = -5 \, \text{m}$$

$$R_z = A_z + (-B_z) =$$

$$-2 + (-8) = -10 \, \text{m}$$

Therefore:

$$R^2 = 25 + 25 + 100 = 150 \, \text{m}^2$$

and the magnitude of the resultant vector is:

$$R = 12 \, \text{m}$$

We call the *scalar product* (or *dot product*) of two vectors $\mathbf{A}$ and $\mathbf{B}$ a scalar quantity. $\mathbf{A} \cdot \mathbf{B}$ is obtained by multiplying the magnitudes of the two vectors and the cosine of the angle made by their directions (see Figure 2.9).

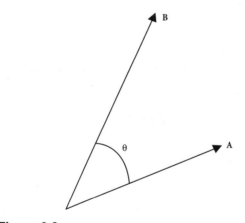

Figure 2.9

$$\mathbf{A} \cdot \mathbf{B} = \mathbf{A} \cdot \mathbf{B} \cdot \cos\theta$$

Example

What is the angle between two vectors that have a scalar product equal to zero?

Solution

When the scalar product of two vectors of nonzero magnitude is zero:

$$\mathbf{A} \cdot \mathbf{B} = 0$$

It follows that the cosine of the angle made by their directions should be zero, and therefore, the two vectors must be perpendicular to each other.

$$\cos\theta = 0$$

$$\theta = \pi/2$$

For the scalar product, the order of multiplication is not important: $\mathbf{A} \cdot \mathbf{B} = \mathbf{B} \cdot \mathbf{A}$ (scalar product is commutative). We apply the previous definition to both sides of the equality:

$$\mathbf{A} \cdot \mathbf{B} = \mathbf{A} \cdot \mathbf{B} \cdot \cos\theta$$
and

$$\mathbf{B} \cdot \mathbf{A} = \mathbf{B} \cdot \mathbf{A} \cdot \cos(-\theta)$$

But A and B are numbers, so $A \cdot B$ will equal $B \cdot A$, and the cosine function is symmetric: $\cos\theta = \cos(-\theta)$. Hence, both sides yield the same answer.

We call the vector product (or *cross product*) of two vectors $\mathbf{A}$ and $\mathbf{B}$ a vector quantity: $\mathbf{A} \times \mathbf{B}$ with a magnitude obtained by multiplying the magnitudes of the two vectors and the sine of the angle made by their directions. The direction of the resultant vector is perpendicular on the plane defined by these two vectors (see Figure 2.10).

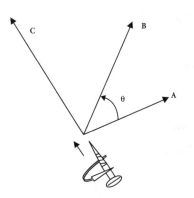

Figure 2.10

$$C = A \times B$$

$$C = A \cdot B \cdot \sin\theta$$

The direction of the resultant vector is given by the *right-hand rule* (also known as the *corkscrew rule*). If you position the right hand around the direction of the angle between the two vectors such that the fingers point in the direction of moving the first vector on top of the second vector, and you extend your thumb, the direction of the resultant vector is given by the thumb. Also, for the corkscrew rule: If we rotate the corkscrew such that the first vector advances on top of the second vector, the direction of advance of the screw is the direction of the resultant vector. The two rules are identical, so whichever you find less weird and are able to apply to your problem should bring you to the same result.

For the vector product, the order of multiplication is important because the result is a vector. Vector product is not commutative:

$$A \times B = -B \times A$$

We apply the above definition to both sides of the equality:

$$|A \times B| = A \cdot B \cdot \sin\theta$$

and

$$|B \times A| = B \cdot A \cdot \sin(-\theta)$$

But *A* and *B* are numbers, so $A \cdot B = B \cdot A$, and the sine function is antisymmetric: $\sin\theta = -\sin(-\theta)$. Hence, although the magnitude is the same, the direction is opposite:

$$|A \times B| = A \cdot B \cdot \sin\theta$$

$$|B \times A| = -B \cdot A \cdot \sin\theta$$

The vector product is distributive. This means that when having three vectors, the following equality holds true:

$$(A + B) \times C = A \times C + B \times C$$

We should also note the following remarkable identities between the unit vectors **i**, **j**, and **k**:

$$i \cdot i = j \cdot j = k \cdot k = 1$$

$$i \cdot j = j \cdot k = k \cdot i = 0$$

$$i \times j = k, j \times k = i, \text{and } k \times i = j$$

Using these identities and the other properties of vectors, we can calculate the scalar and vector product of any two vectors when we know their *x*, *y*, and *z* components.

Example

Show that $i \times j = k$.

Solution

First, we will show the magnitudes of the left-hand side and right-hand side to be equal:

$$|i \times j| = 1 \cdot 1 \cdot \sin 90° = 1$$

$$|k| = 1$$

For the orientation, we can show through a diagram the orientation of the $i \times j$ vector. In Figure 2.11, we see the screw rotating from **i** unit vector toward the **j** unit vector in the direction of the angel, and the screw advances upward in the direction of **k**.

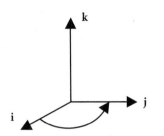

Figure 2.11

▶ Practice

11. In Figure 2.12, which vectors are equal? Explain.

12. Let **A** = 2.0 **i** + 3.0 **j** and **B** = 3.0 **i** − 2.0 **j**. Using the properties of unit vectors **i**, **j**, and **k**, find the components of the vector **C** = **A** × **B**.

13. Calculate **A** · **B** for the vectors in problem 12. What can you say about the directions of **A** and **B**?

14. Calculate **A** · **C** and **B** · **C** for the vectors in problem 12. What can you say about their directions?

15. For the vectors in problem 12, calculate **A** + **B** and **B** − **A**. What are the magnitudes of these two new vectors?

16. What can you say about the directions of the vectors calculated in problem 15?

17. Calculate the magnitude of vector **C** in problem 12.

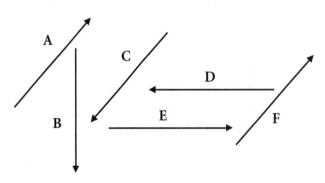

Figure 2.12

3 ▶ Motion in One Dimension

LESSON SUMMARY

We start the chapter by defining the notions of displacement, velocity, speed, and acceleration. Then we look into graphical representation of motion as a way of describing the motion of an object or particle. We consider a special case of unidimensional motion where the acceleration is constant and show an application to the free fall of objects in the gravity field of Earth.

▶ Displacement, Velocity, and Acceleration

Motion involves an object changing its position during some finite time interval with respect to a given reference frame. For most of the time, the object's position may be associated with just one set of coordinates at a time—that would be just one coordinate in the case of a one-dimensional motion. Also, motion is a relative notion: You may be sitting still in a car, so you do not move, but the car may be speeding on the highway, and therefore, you are in fast motion with respect to the road.

We say that displacement is the change in position of a particle or object with respect to a given reference frame. Because the position is a vector, the displacement is also a vector: It points from the initial to the final position and has a magnitude equal to the distance between the two positions. We can always associate both a direction and a size with a displacement.

For a particle moving along a straight line in one dimension, the displacement can be expressed in terms of the initial and final coordinates as:

$$\Delta x = x_f - x_i$$

If x_f is greater than x_i, then we have a positive displacement; otherwise, the displacement is negative.

For any object in motion for a finite duration of time, we can define an average speed as the ratio of the distance traveled over the time elapsed:

$$v = \frac{d}{t} = \frac{x_f - x_i}{t_f - t_i}$$

This formula assumes our moving object starts at the time zero at some point P and then moves a distance d during a time interval t.

Example

You can go from Lansing to Detroit, Michigan, in, say, 2 hours, but out of these 2 hours, you spend 1 hour going 60 miles from Lansing to Novi and the next hour going the rest of 40 miles from Novi to Detroit (mostly stuck in traffic). Find the average speed from Lansing to Novi, the average speed from Novi to Detroit, and the overall average speed from Lansing to Detroit.

Solution

Since all quantities are given in miles and hours, we will keep these units instead of using SI units.

Your average speed from Lansing to Novi is 60 miles per hour. From Novi to Detroit, as you are stuck in traffic, your average speed is only 40 miles per hour. The overall average speed from Lansing to Detroit is:

$$\frac{100 \text{ mi}}{2 \text{ h}} = 50 \text{ mi/h}$$

We note that for calculating the average speed, only the total distance traveled and the total time are important. The example also shows that during a long time interval, we may at times move faster and at other times slower; the overall average speed gives us an idea of the rate at which we move *on average* during the whole trip.

Now let's look for a moment at what happens when the time interval t is made almost zero. In this case, the distance traveled d also becomes very small (for normal-range finite speed values). Therefore, the start point and the end point are very close to each other. Our average speed is calculated over a very small space interval around the point P. In this case, our average velocity is a very close approximation to the *instantaneous speed* at point P.

Back to our example, a good practical approximation of the car's instantaneous speed at every moment of time during the trip from Lansing to Detroit is the value we read on the car's speedometer.

Let's note that speed is always a positive quantity. The SI unit for measuring speed follows from its definition: meter per second. Other convenient units may be miles per hour or kilometers per hour.

As far as the direction of the movement is concerned, we need to extend the speed to the concept of *velocity*. We can reach this by replacing the "distance" in the definition of the average speed with the "displacement" vector. The *instantaneous velocity* is a vector obtained by taking the ratio of the displacement vector d to the time t elapsed for that displacement to occur, when the time interval is very small:

$$\mathbf{v} = \frac{\mathbf{d}}{t}$$

Therefore, the instantaneous velocity indicates how fast the car moves and the direction of motion at each instant of time.

For the case of motion in one dimension along a straight line, the distance and the magnitude of the displacement are the same, and therefore, *the speed is the magnitude of the velocity*. This statement remains

Instantaneous velocity indicates how fast the car moves and the direction of motion at each instant of time.

true in the general case of an arbitrary motion in two or three dimensions. The proof is a trivial exercise of infinitesimal calculus. Is it really a surprise that Sir Isaac Newton is, at the same time, one of the inventors of the infinitesimal calculus and the famous father of the laws of mechanics?

As the velocity shows the change in an object's position, the acceleration shows how the velocity of the object changes. As the velocity is a vector, it can change either its magnitude or its direction. In either case, the object will feel an acceleration a given by:

$$a = \frac{v_f - v_i}{t_f - t_i}$$

Therefore, in the International System, or SI, unit for acceleration is m/s^2.

Example

Suppose a car starts from rest. The car accelerates straight down the road and at $t = 30$ s attains a speed of $v = 30$ km/h. Determine the average acceleration of the car.

Solution

(30 km/h − 0 km/h)/(30 s − 0 s) = 1.0(km/h)/s
= 1,000 m/3,600 s$^2 \cong 0.28$ m/s^2

Similar to the case of velocity, we start by defining an *average acceleration* over a finite time interval Δt and then get to the concept of *instantaneous acceleration*, taking this time interval to zero:

$$a(t) = \lim_{\Delta t \to 0} \frac{v(t + \Delta t) - v(t)}{\Delta t}$$

Whenever the acceleration and velocity vectors have opposite directions, the object slows down and is said to be *decelerating*.

▶ Practice

1. A jogger runs with a constant 2.2 m/s speed for 15 minutes. What distance does she travel during that time?

2. After 15 minutes, the jogger in problem 1 gets tired, and during the next 2 seconds, she reduces her speed to 1.8 m/s. What was her average acceleration during these 2 seconds?

3. Assuming she moves during these 5 seconds with an average speed of 2.0 m/s, what distance does she travel while decelerating?

4. Add the results in problems 1 and 3, and using the total time of the motion, 15 minutes and 5 seconds, find the overall average speed of the jogger.

5. What is the acceleration of a tennis ball if initially it comes toward the player's racquet at 20 m/s, and it leaves in the opposite direction at 24 m/s? A high-speed camera indicates the time of impact of 4.0 ms.

6. How long does it take the ball in problem 5 to travel 15 meters after being played? Neglect the gravitational effect, and suppose the ball travels along a straight line and assume a speed of 24 m/s.

7. A racecar driver steps on the gas, and his car travels 16 meters in 2 seconds, starting from rest. What is the average velocity in m/s and in km/h?

8. What is the average acceleration of the racecar in problem 7 in m/s²?

▶ Graphs and Motion

An easy and clear method of quickly analyzing relationships among large quantities of numerical data is to plot the experimental data as a function of time or of some other variable. Straight lines on a graph can be easily recognized and interpreted, and they play an important role in graphically analyzing experimental data.

By far, the most usual kind of graph is the Cartesian one, where both axes have linear scales. The horizontal axis is also called *abscissa*, and the vertical axis is called *ordinate*. The graph shows the dependency of the quantity, which is represented as the ordinate on the quantity, which is represented as the abscissa.

We define the *slope* of a straight line on the graph by choosing any two points on the line and taking the ratio of the ordinate separation of these two points to their abscissas separation. If the graph is not made up of straight lines, then we can define a slope at any point along the curve by drawing a tangent to the curve and calculating the slope of this tangent, using the slope definition for a straight line.

In the case of position versus time graphs, the slope of the graph at a certain time is immediately associated with the instantaneous velocity at that time, as the ratio of position coordinate difference versus the time interval to go from the initial position to the other is an exact reformulation of the definition of speed. By similar reasoning, the slope of a velocity versus time graph is associated with the instantaneous acceleration of the object at that time.

Example

The two graphs in Figure 3.1 show the position versus time for two swimmers racing across a 35-meter pool. Interpret the information in the graphs.

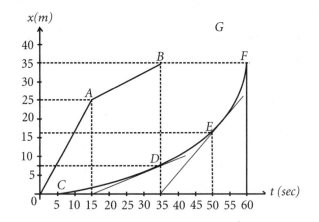

Figure 3.1

Solution

There is a lot of information we can read from these graphs.

The first athlete starts at time $t = 0$ and swims the first 25 meters of the race at constant speed $v_0 = 25$ m/15 s $= 1.6$ m/s. He gets tired and goes the last 10 meters of the race at a much slower pace, at a speed $v = 10$ m/20 s $= 0.5$ m/s.

The second athlete starts with a handicap of 5 seconds and initially goes slowly. For example, from point C to point D, his speed is almost constant. His speed at point D, after 35 seconds from the beginning of the race, is given by the slope of the tangent and is $v_D = 7.5$ m/25 s $= 0.3$ m/s. But at point E, 50 seconds after the beginning of the race, his instantaneous speed increased to $v_E = 16.5$ m/15 s $= 1.1$ m/s. The last 10 seconds of the race, he rides Flipper the dolphin, and at point F, his final speed is around 2.8 m/s. This reminds us somewhat of the *Hare and Tortoise* fable but with an aquatic spin!

▶ Practice

Refer to Figure 3.1 for numerical values needed to solve the following problems.

9. Find the overall average speed of swimmer number one during the race.

10. Find the overall average speed of the second swimmer from the time he starts swimming until he ends his race.

11. What is the instantaneous speed of the second swimmer at time $t = 25$ s during the race?

12. What is the average acceleration of the second swimmer during the time interval starting at $t_i = 25$ s and ending at $t_f = 50$ s?

13. What is the average acceleration of the second swimmer during the time interval starting at $t_i = 25$ s and ending at $t_f = 35$ s?

14. What is the average acceleration of the first swimmer during the time interval starting at $t_i = 10$ s and ending at $t_f = 30$ s?

▶ Motion with Constant Acceleration

Let's examine now the case of *constant acceleration motion*. This is an important kind of motion encountered in frequent approximations to real situations. An object sliding down an incline or multiple objects falling near the surface of the earth when we neglect air resistance are both situations where we encounter constant acceleration motion.

As the acceleration is constant, the instantaneous and average accelerations are equal, and we can invert the definition to get:

$$\Delta \mathbf{v} = \mathbf{a} \, \Delta t$$

If we consider that at time $t = 0$, the initial velocity is v_0, we can write this as:

$$\mathbf{v}(t) = \mathbf{v}_0 + \mathbf{a} \cdot t$$

For the case of the one-dimensional motion, this becomes a scalar relation between speeds, with a positive acceleration a when it is directed in the sense of the motion, and a negative acceleration a when its direction is against the direction of the motion.

If we consider that at the initial time $t = 0$, there is an initial displacement x_0, then the position at time t is given by:

$$x(t) = x_0 + v_0 \cdot t + \tfrac{1}{2} a \cdot t^2$$

Solving for t in the velocity equation and inserting the result in the displacement equation, we obtain another useful relation that is independent of time:

$$v^2 = v_0^2 + 2a\Delta x$$

▶ Practice

15. A car brakes from 60 mi/h to a full stop in 4 seconds. Find the acceleration of the car during this time interval in m/s^2.

16. What distance did the car in problem 15 travel in the time since first applying the brakes?

17. A cheetah resting in the savanna sees her prey and accelerates from rest to 70 mi/h in 6.2 seconds. Assuming she moves with a constant acceleration, find this acceleration and the distance she ran when she first reaches 30 mi/h.

18. After what distance did the cheetah reach 70 mi/h?

▶ Freely Falling Objects

Any object found in the neighborhood of the surface of the earth suffers a gravitational pull with a downward acceleration g = 9.80 m/s². The exact value slightly varies depending on various factors such as the latitude and the mineral composition of the earth's crust, which finally affects the mass distribution of the earth. But for the purpose of most calculations, we may assume all objects fall down with a constant acceleration g = 9.80 m/s². The direction is always *downward*, actually toward the center (or mass—for pedantic eyes) of the earth.

The main experimental result for the freely falling motion was obtained by Galileo hundreds of years ago and states that when we can neglect air resistance, all bodies fall at the same rate, no matter how heavy or light they are. He reached this conclusion by dropping at the same time different objects from the top of the Tower of Pisa and observing that they always hit the ground almost at the same time. If the experiment could be done so that there is no air drag, such as in a vacuum tube, the times of the falls would certainly be identical, and they would hit the ground *exactly* at the same time. And that is exactly what Robert Boyle (1627–1691) did when he perfected his vacuum pumps in the mid-1600s and had a golden opportunity to test Galileo's work for the first time.

This may sound counterintuitive at some point: If we drop a quarter and a sheet of paper from the same height at the same time, the quarter quickly reaches the floor, while the paper still slowly flutters through air for a period of time. But if we crush the paper into a wrinkled ball and therefore cut its air drag without changing its weight, it will hit the ground almost at the same time as the quarter.

In general, for a body moving along the vertical plane near the surface of Earth, we can apply the rules of constant acceleration motion. Considering the direction of motion is positive from the surface of Earth upward, the acceleration will be $a = g = -9.80$ m/s² for an ascending body, and $a = +9.80$ m/s² for a falling body. NOTE: The direction of the acceleration due to gravity is always directed toward the center of Earth.

Example

A bullet blasts from the barrel of a gun upward in the vertical direction with an initial speed of 700 m/s. Find the maximum altitude reached by this bullet and the time needed to reach it.

Solution

At the highest point of its path, the bullet reverses direction from moving upward to falling downward. Therefore, at this point, its instant velocity (and speed) should be zero. Using the formula linking square speeds to acceleration and distance, we find:

$$0^2 = v_o^2 + 2(-g)\,h = 700^2\,\text{m}^2/\text{s}^2$$

$$- \; 2 \cdot 9.8\,\text{m/s}^2 \cdot h$$

Solving for h, we find:

$$h = 25{,}000\,\text{m} = 25\,\text{km}$$

To find the time needed to reach that altitude, we simply use:

$$v = v_o + a \cdot t$$

or, plugging in the numbers:

$$0 = 700\,\text{m/s} - 9.8\,\text{m/s}^2 \cdot t$$

Solving for the time t, we find:

$$t = 71.43\,\text{s}$$

► Practice

19. Find the fall time for an object dropped from an altitude of 25,000 meters, neglecting air drag (i.e., the time it takes the bullet in the previous example to return to the starting point, from the time it reached its maximum height).

20. Suppose the bullet is still effective in piercing sheet metal at a speed of 100 m/s. What is the maximum altitude at which you could still use this bullet to fight an aerial attack?

21. To find the depth of a well, you drop a small pebble and time its fall until you hear the splash of the pebble on the water surface below. What is the depth of the well if the time you got is 3.25 seconds? Consider that sound propagates almost instantaneously from the surface of the water to your ear.

22. What is the depth of the well if we take into account the finite sound speed in air of 334 m/s?

23. A mouse is dropped from an eagle's claws starting at an altitude of 150 meters. What distance does it fall in the first second after it is dropped?

24. What distance does the mouse in problem 23 travel in the third second of its free fall?

25. At what speed does the mouse in problem 23 hit the ground?

4 ▶ Motion in Two Dimensions

LESSON SUMMARY

In this lesson, we will continue the study of important motion quantities and learn about motion in two dimensions, relative velocity, and projectile motion.

▶ Two-Dimensional Motion

In the last lesson, we were concerned with motion on a line and equations that have been drawn from the time dependence of the position of an object. Our definitions were based on vector quantities, and as we remember from Lesson 2, a vector can represent behavior over three separate directions x, y, and z. The same concepts of displacement, average and instantaneous velocity, and average and instantaneous acceleration will apply to motion in two dimensions. The major difference is that we will work with formulas containing only one variable at a time: x or y or z. This is a real advantage, as in separate directions, different interactions might predominate, and therefore, the source of interaction (and the specific force) will be considered for separate directions.

The displacement vector is the segment that connects the initial and final positions, and is directed toward the final position:

$$\Delta r = r_f - b_i$$

In this case, the vector position for each of the initial and final positions is determined by two coordinates: x and y.

$$\Delta x = x_f - x_i$$

$$\Delta y = y_f - y_i$$

And from these components, the displacement of the vector is:

$$\Delta r = (\Delta x, \Delta y)$$

Or:

$$\Delta r = \Delta x + \Delta y$$

Example

A toy car starts from the corner of the classroom and travels to a new position of coordinates (5,6) meters away from the corner. Draw the displacement and find the magnitude.

Solution

We can see that the two measurements in the problems are expressed in meters, so no conversion is necessary. We will draw a system of coordinates, and we will place the car in the origin of the system at the beginning of motion. This is the initial position. The final position is given by the problem. We will construct the displacement as the vector that connects the initial and final position and then find the magnitude by using the components.

Now the problem becomes a one-dimensional problem because we can write the equations for motion on the separate axis (see Figure 4.1):

$$(x_i, y_i) = (0,0) \text{ m}$$

and

$$(x_f, y_f) = (5,6) \text{ m}$$

$$\Delta x = x_f - x_i$$

$$\Delta x = 5 - 0 = 5 \text{ m}$$

$$\Delta y = y_f - y_i$$

$$\Delta y = 6 - 0 = 6 \text{ m}$$

$$\Delta r = (5,6) \text{ m}$$

$$\Delta r = (5^2 + 6^2)^{1/2} = 8 \text{ m}$$

If the motion is more complicated (for example, a nonlinear trajectory), then we would have cases where the distance traveled is not necessarily the same as the displacement. For example, in the case shown in Figure 4.2, the distance is larger than the displacement.

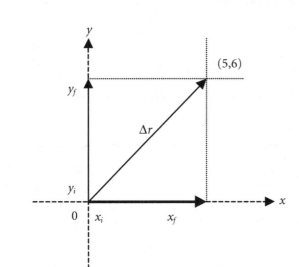

Figure 4.1

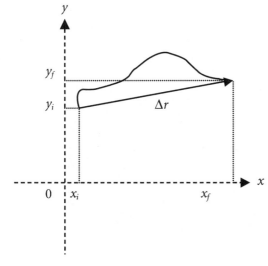

Figure 4.2

Example

A car travels 40 miles to the west and then another 30 miles to the north. Draw the displacement, calculate the magnitude and direction of the displacement, and compare to the distance traveled.

Solution

As the single values of this problem are in miles and no other requirement exists for conversion in the prob-

lem, we can keep the solution in miles. If we are asked to convert to SI, we would multiply each of the two distances with the conversion factor 1,609 meters/1 mile to determine the result in meters.

$$\Delta \mathbf{r}_i = 40 \text{ miles W}$$

$$\Delta \mathbf{r}_f = 30 \text{ miles N}$$

$$\Delta \mathbf{r}_{total} = ?$$

$$\text{distance} = ?$$

The distance traveled by the car is the sum of the two distances:

$$\text{Distance} = 40 \text{ miles} + 30 \text{ miles} = 70 \text{ miles}$$

The total displacement has to take into account each of the displacements, but we cannot simply add the two numbers because their vector expressions put them in different directions. Let us draw a motion diagram. We will consider east as the positive x-axis and north as the positive y-axis (see Figure 4.3).

$$(\Delta r_{total})^2 = (\Delta r_i)^2 + (\Delta r_f)^2$$

$$\Delta r_{total} = [(\Delta r_i)^2 + (\Delta r_f)^2]^{1/2}$$

$$\Delta r_{total} = 50 \text{ miles}$$

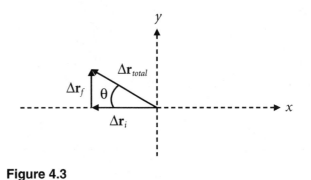

Figure 4.3

Average velocity is the time rate of change of displacement:

$$v_{average} = \frac{\Delta r}{\Delta t}$$

The direction is the angle θ, and it can be calculated from the geometry of the problem:

$$\sin \theta = r_f / r_{total} = 30 \text{ miles} / 50 \text{ miles}$$

$$\theta = \sin^{-1}(0.6) = 37°$$

Hence, displacement is $\Delta r_{total} = 50$ miles at 37° north of west or (40 miles, 30 miles) by the x and y components.

It can be seen that the distance is larger compared to the displacement, as shown in the figure (the two sides of the triangle added together are larger than the hypotenuse).

Based on the definition of displacement, we introduce also the average velocity.

When the time interval is very small (approaching zero, or $\Delta t \to 0$), the definition of the average velocity becomes the definition of the instantaneous velocity.

If the motion is such that *velocity is constant* (both in magnitude and direction), then the average speed and the instantaneous velocities are the same.

Example

A toy car starts moving at a constant speed for 10 seconds. Show with vectors, at two separate positions, the average and instantaneous velocities.

Solution

We will represent the car in a two-dimensional motion by using a point-like object and drawing the two velocities. They are equal vectors (this means that both direction and magnitude are the same). See Figure 4.4.

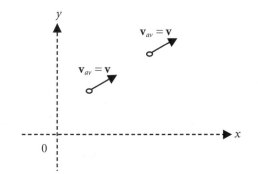

Figure 4.4

When the trajectory is nonlinear, instantaneous velocity is a vector always *tangent* to the trajectory as shown in Figure 4.5.

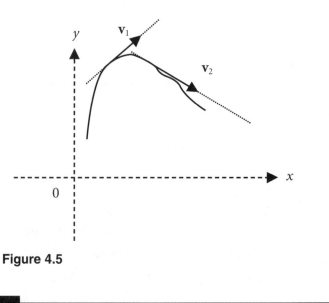

Figure 4.5

Instantaneous velocity is velocity at a certain time:

$$v = \frac{\Delta r}{\Delta t}; \text{ when } \Delta t \to 0$$

Example

Use a diagram to show the displacement of a car that moves between the following positions: (50,30) meters to (−40,40) meters in 4 seconds, and then calculate displacement and the average velocity, both expressed with their coordinates and magnitude and angle.

Solution

All units are expressed in SI. In order to calculate the average velocity, we need to determine displacement. Figure 4.6 shows the initial and final positions.

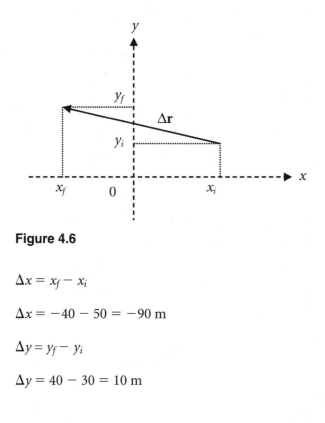

Figure 4.6

$\Delta x = x_f - x_i$

$\Delta x = -40 - 50 = -90$ m

$\Delta y = y_f - y_i$

$\Delta y = 40 - 30 = 10$ m

$\Delta r = (-90, 10)$ m

$\Delta r = (90^2 + 10^2)^{1/2} = 91$ m

$\tan \theta = \Delta y / \Delta x = 10 \text{ m}/(-90 \text{ m}) = -1/9$

$\theta = \tan^{-1}(1/9) = -6°$

Therefore, displacement is 91 meters at an angle of 6° north of west.

Average velocity is:

$$\mathbf{v}_{average} = \frac{\Delta \mathbf{r}}{\Delta t}$$

$$\mathbf{v}_{average} = \frac{(-90, 10) \text{ m}}{4 \text{ s}} = (-22.5, 2.5) \text{ m/s}$$

Or:

$$\mathbf{v}_{average} = (22.5^2 + 2.5^2)^{1/2} = 23 \text{ m/s}$$

$$\theta = \tan^{-1}(-2.5/22.5) = -6°$$

Or average velocity is 23 m/s (also = 91 m/4 s) at an angle of 6° north of west.

We can see that the average velocity and displacement are in the same direction. As noted previously, the instantaneous velocity will be tangent to the trajectory at every point but not necessarily in the same direction as displacement and average velocity.

If the motion is made with changing velocity, then acceleration can be defined.

Similar to the average and instantaneous velocity, starting with the definition just given, when the time

Average acceleration is the time rate of change of velocity:

$$a_{average} = \frac{\Delta v}{\Delta t}$$

interval approaches zero, one can define instantaneous acceleration.

As seen in both these definitions, the vector acceleration has the direction of the change in velocity, and that can be determined by either change in magnitude or change in direction.

Example

Consider an object moving on a curve as shown in Figure 4.7. Draw the vector average acceleration based on the information in the graph.

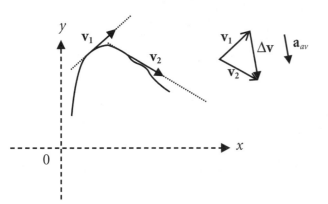

Figure 4.7

Solution

Start by constructing the vector Δv and then draw the average acceleration $a_{average}$ based on this direction.

Because average acceleration is nothing else, then by dividing a vector (Δv) by a scalar (Δt), there will be no change in direction. Only magnitude will be increased or decreased, depending on the size of the denominator.

▶ Practice

1. In your daily travels, you leave home in the morning, go to school and then to volleyball practice, and return home 8 hours later. During this entire trip, compare the distance and the displacement.

2. During a board game, you move a piece first 10 cm toward the east and then 8 cm toward the northeast. Find the total displacement of the piece as a vector.

3. In the previous practice problem, compare displacement with the distance traveled by the piece.

4. When the speed of an object is constant, does that mean that its velocity is constant also?

5. Show on a diagram the displacement of a car that moves between the following positions: (20,20) meters to (60,50) meters in 2.5 seconds, and then calculate displacement and the average velocity, both expressed with their coordinates and magnitude and angle.

6. Consider a rock held by a string and rotated in a circle. Choosing two positions on the trajectory, draw the instantaneous velocity at those points and then draw the average acceleration.

Instantaneous acceleration is acceleration at a certain time:

$$a = \frac{\Delta v}{\Delta t}; \text{ when } \Delta t \rightarrow 0$$

▶ Relative Motion

As you have probably started to notice, a lot in mechanics is *relative*. All measurements start with distance and time, neither of which have an absolute origin that can be easily applied to all sorts of motion. So, what solution do we have for this issue? The answer is to consider our own reference frames and origins of space and time. You have considered a simple, one-axis system of reference in linear motion. In this chapter, we worked on a reference system composed of two perpendicular axes: *x* and *y*. In real space, a need exists for a third axis—*height*, or the *z*-axis. And even more, some consider that *time* be represented by a fourth coordinate, because motion spans not only in space but also in time. Depending on the axes of reference, motion looks different. Imagine yourself in space, far away from any cosmic object. Is your ship moving or not? If the engines are quiet, and there is no acceleration, you will not be able to tell your motion if you are not looking at your sensors. But if an alien species is watching you with deep space sensors from a far away planet, they will be able to tell if you are moving and how are you moving. So, who is right? Sure enough, the answer is *both observants:* the alien species and you. The difference is that each of you relates to different frames: Your frame moves with you, so evidently, you cannot determine whether you are at rest or not, while the aliens analyze your motion relative to a different system and see that you are in motion with respect to

their system. This is why for more down-to-earth motion, we define *relative velocity*.

The *fixed frame reference* for most of our problems will be Earth. We will not consider Earth's motion around its own axis or around the sun when we are considering an apple falling from a tree or a car or boat traveling for some distance. In other cases, such as for space travel, a distant star can be considered as a fixed position. Although this is not completely true (the distant star is moving), if the stellar object is far enough away, the motion during the experiment might be negligible compared to the motion of the analyzed system.

Example

While biking, you keep your velocity at a constant 12 m/s magnitude directed east with respect to the earth. The wind starts blowing toward the west with a speed of 5 m/s, with respect to the earth. What is your resultant speed with respect to the earth at the time the wind starts blowing.

Relative velocity is the resultant vector measuring the velocity of an object in a fixed frame.

$$\mathbf{v_r} = \mathbf{v_1} - \mathbf{v_2}$$

Where $\mathbf{v_1}$ is the speed of an object with respect to a moving frame and $\mathbf{v_2}$ is the speed of the frame with respect to a fixed frame.

Solution

We will draw a diagram to show the two velocities. The resultant velocity is the vector sum of the two velocities considered in the problem. We will consider east to be the positive *x*-axis direction (see Figure 4.8).

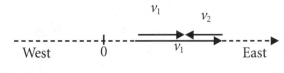

Figure 4.8

Hence, the resultant speed is:

$$\mathbf{v_r} = \mathbf{v_1} - \mathbf{v_2}$$

$$\mathbf{v_r} = \mathbf{v_1} - \mathbf{v_2}$$

$$\mathbf{v_r} = 12 - 5 = 7 \text{ m/s}$$

$\mathbf{v_r}$ is 7 m/s in the east direction.

▶ Practice

7. An airplane travels with a velocity of 34 m/s relative to air due north, and the wind blows at 7 m/s due north. What is the relative velocity of the airplane relative to Earth?
8. A boat's engine develops a velocity of 11.0 m/s when the boat is moving across the river and the water current is 2.00 m/s downstream. Find the relative speed of the boat with respect to an observer on the shore.
9. A drop of rain moves downward at a velocity of 5 m/s and hits a car window that moves due east at 28 m/s. Find the angle of the mark the raindrop leaves on the window.

▶ Projectile Motion

A classic case of two-dimensional motion is *projectile motion.* Imagine you throw an object horizontally, as in skipping a rock. In a gravity-free and friction-free world, the rock will move horizontally until it interacts with an obstacle as shown in Figure 4.9. The diagram shows the constant velocity (magnitude and direction).

If we consider the friction with the air, the rock will use energy through conversion to heat during its path and it will slow down. Figure 4.10 shows the velocity and the acceleration (constant acceleration).

Figure 4.9

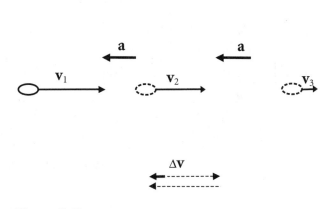

Figure 4.10

If we consider no friction but an acceleration downward, as in the case of the acceleration due to gravity, $g = 9.8$ m/s^2, what happens to the velocity? You might surmise the answer from everyday happenings, but this is a good place to use what we learned and to learn something new. The graph in Figure 4.11 shows the object moving down, and then acceleration due to gravity is also down. As we have seen before, the acceleration is in the same direction as the change in velocity, hence the change in velocity, $\Delta\mathbf{v}$, has to be also downward. But $\Delta\mathbf{v} = \mathbf{v}_2 - \mathbf{v}_1$ and that means according to the diagram that $\mathbf{v}_2$ has to be the same direction as $\mathbf{v}_1$ and larger than $\mathbf{v}_1$.

Hence, we will complete the diagram in Figure 4.11 with the vector velocity at other positions (see Figure 4.12).

What will happen if the object moves up? Then the acceleration is opposite to the initial velocity, and we have a case similar to the previous one with friction. The object will slow down.

In the previous discussion, we separated the horizontal and vertical motion, and we examined different motion. What happens if we consider a more complex motion on both x and y direction? We will be able then to add the x and y components of displacement, velocity, and acceleration and then fully characterize the two-dimensional motion: We obtain *projectile motion*.

Example

A rock is thrown with a speed of 10 m/s at an angle of 30 degrees from the horizontal. Draw a diagram of motion and show in a few places, both when the rock is ascending and descending, the velocity, and the acceleration.

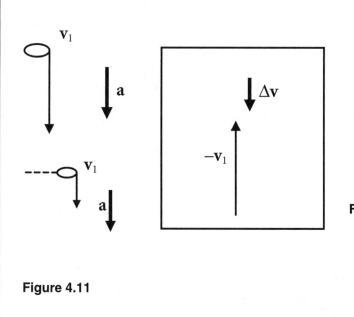

Figure 4.11

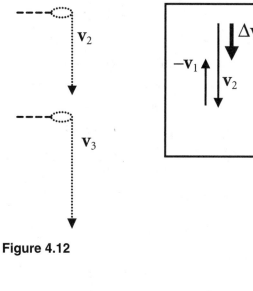

Figure 4.12

Solution

$v_0 = 10 \text{ m/s}$

$\alpha = 30°$

We will consider a two-dimensional frame and a friction-free motion.

On the horizontal x-axis, the object moves with constant velocity (v_x = constant and $v_x = 0 \text{ m/s}^2$) because there is no friction and no other interaction. Also, if the object does not start from the origin of the reference frame, an offset has to be considered, x_0:

$x = x_0 + v_x \cdot \Delta t$

and v_x is the component of the speed on the x-axis (see Figure 4.13).

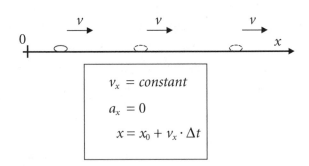

$$v_x = constant$$
$$a_x = 0$$
$$x = x_0 + v_x \cdot \Delta t$$

Figure 4.13

In the vertical direction, the object moves up decelerating (slowing down), stops at the top of the trajectory, and then returns down accelerating (see Figure 4.14). All this motion is determined by the constant acceleration due to gravity.

The initial components of the velocity can be found from the data in Figure 4.15.

$v_{0x} = v_0 \cdot \cos \alpha$

$v_{0y} = v_0 \cdot \sin \alpha$

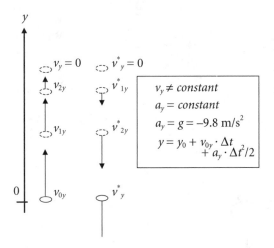

$$v_y \neq constant$$
$$a_y = constant$$
$$a_y = g = -9.8 \text{ m/s}^2$$
$$y = y_0 + v_{0y} \cdot \Delta t + a_y \cdot \Delta t^2/2$$

Figure 4.14

With all this information, the x-y graphical description of the previous motion is shown in Figure 4.16.

The maximum height (vertical) and distance (horizontal) the object reaches is based on the initial speed and the angle of throw. The horizontal distance for a symmetric projectile motion as in this previous example (the projectile starts and finishes at the same y position) is called *range*. To summarize the equation of motion for the x- and y-axis are:

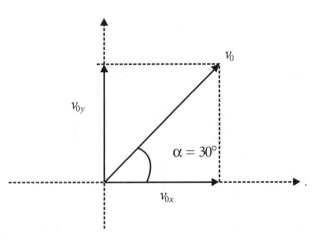

Figure 4.15

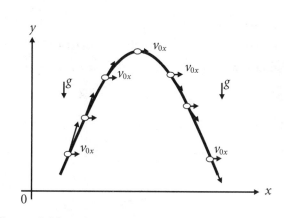

Figure 4.16

x-axis

$$v_{0x} = v_0 \cdot \cos \alpha = \text{constant}$$

$$x = x_0 + v_0 \cdot \cos \alpha \Delta t$$

$$a_x = 0 \text{ m/s}^2$$

y-axis

$$v_{0y} = v_0 \cdot \sin \alpha$$

$$y = y_0 + v_{0y} \cdot \Delta t + a_y \cdot \Delta t^2/2$$

$$a_y = \text{constant}$$

If we eliminate the time dependence from both $x(t)$ and $y(t)$, then we get the $y(x)$ dependence:

$$y = y_0 + (\tan \alpha) \cdot x - \frac{g}{2 \cdot v_0^2 \cdot \cos^2 a} \cdot x^2$$

And we can determine the *range* and the *maximum height* to be:

$$R = \frac{2 \cdot v_0^2 \cdot \sin \alpha \cdot \cos a}{g}$$

$$h = \frac{(v_0 \cdot \sin \theta)^2}{2 \cdot g}$$

In these equations, the initial position is considered to be the origin:

$$x_0 = 0$$

$$y_0 = 0$$

The time it takes the object to describe this trajectory is called *time of flight* and can be calculated to be:

$$t = \frac{2 \cdot v_0 \cdot \sin \theta}{g}$$

Figure 4.17 shows the different paths an object takes for a fixed speed with different throwing angles. The longest path (maximum range at a given speed) is for the 45°.

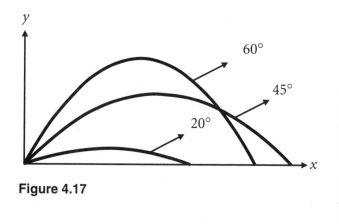

Figure 4.17

▶ Practice

10. At the top of the trajectory, is the velocity of the object moving in a projectile motion equal to zero or nonzero? Describe.

11. A rock is thrown with an initial speed and at an angle with respect to the horizontal. At what time is the acceleration zero?

12. Find the range and the maximum height if a rock is thrown with an initial velocity of 10.0 m/s first at an angle of 20.0° and then at an angle of 45.0°.

LESSON

5 ▶ Newton's Mechanics: The Laws and the Forces

LESSON SUMMARY

From the previous chapters on physical quantities and their corresponding units, you now know that the unit for mass, *kilogram*, is a *fundamental unit*. Mass might also be called a *fundamental quantity*. It relates to motion, forces, and energy, and therefore basically to the whole field of physics. In the following lesson, we will discuss inertia, Newton's laws of classical mechanics that connect motion to forces, and conditions for an equilibrium or nonequilibrium situation when an object is subjected to two or more forces at the same time.

▶ Inertia

Imagine a situation where you have to push some furniture around, for example, if you are moving to a new home. Although you might think that taking clothes out of the dresser drawers before moving the dresser is a waste of time, the reality is that the amount of effort you put into unloading the dresser is much less than the effort you would use to move the full dresser. What opposition do we encounter in the two processes of moving the furniture? It is the mass that makes the difference; it is the mass that causes the resistance. This resistance that an object has to motion is something we call *inertia*. *Mass* is the quantity that measures inertia, and the fundamental unit for mass is the *kilogram* (kg).

Motion on a straight trajectory is called *linear motion*. Later, we will study objects moving in a *circular trajectory*, and they too will exhibit inertia; in this case, called *rotational inertia*.

Newton's first law of motion, or the law of inertia, states that an object continues to stay at rest or move in a uniform linear motion as long as there is no resultant (net) action on it.

▶ Practice

Use the conversion table and the prefixes to work the following examples.

1. If you are to measure the mass of the earth, you will end up with $5.98 \cdot 10^{24}$ kg. Rewrite the mass in grams.
2. Does a 40 kg piece of furniture have more or less inertia than a 10 kg one? Explain briefly.
3. Does a 4,000 μg object have more or less inertia than a 10 kg object? Explain briefly.

▶ Newton's First, Second, and Third Laws of Motion

The idea of resistance to motion was formulated by Newton into what we now call the *first law of motion* or the *law of inertia.*

There are two important words in this definition: *continues* and *resultant.* To understand this law, you must work with these two words together. *Resultant (net) action* refers to the idea that there might be an action on the object, or two, or more. The importance is not in individual actions but in the total effect on the object. The other word, *continues,* refers to one of the two situations: rest or uniform linear motion. That is, the object will maintain, or continue, an identical state of rest or motion at all times if there is no external action.

▶ Practice

4. A car starts from a traffic light and accelerates about 1 minute. Is this a uniform linear motion? Explain briefly.
5. In the example in the previous problem, is there a resultant force on the object? Explain briefly.
6. While driving on the highway with constant speed, the net force on your car is zero. Will your car remain at uniform linear motion if you turn off the engine?

Most objects around us, when left to act independently of engines, will not continue their uniform linear motion. Also, objects that might be at rest at one time can change their state and accelerate. The motion is a result of interaction, and the objects accelerate (speed up) or decelerate (slow down). The change in the state of motion is due to a resultant force. The relationship among the resultant force, the mass, and the acceleration is the subject of the *second law of motion.*

As you may remember, physical quantities can be scalars or vectors. In this case, mass is a scalar, but both acceleration and force are vector quantities. Therefore, the second law does not refer only to the proportionality but also to the direction of the acceleration, telling us that the acceleration and the resultant force are in the same direction. The expression of the second law is as follows:

$$\mathbf{a} = \frac{\sum \mathbf{F}}{m}, \text{ or } \sum \mathbf{F} = m \cdot \mathbf{a}$$

Newton's Second Law of Motion

The acceleration of an object is directly proportional to the resultant (net) force and inversely proportional to the mass of the object.

where **a** is the vector acceleration, $\Sigma\mathbf{F}$ is the vector representing the resultant force, and m is the mass of the object. This equation defines also the unit for force: a *newton*, or N. As we replace the unit for acceleration (m/s²) and for mass (kg), we can find the unit for force to be $kg \cdot m/s^2 = 1$ N.

As with all vectors, force will be completely defined by value, unit, and direction. The direction of the net force will also give the type of acceleration; if $a > 0$ (a positive number is considered to be the direction of motion), then the object is accelerated, and if $a < 0$ (opposite to motion), then the object is decelerated (slowed down).

Example

A 1,000 kg car starts from a traffic light and moves accelerated in the NE direction with an acceleration of 0.45 m/s². Find out the resultant force on the car.

Solution

We need to find the value of the resultant force because the direction will be the same as that of the acceleration, northeast.

$\mathbf{a} = 4.5$ m/s² in NE direction

$\mathbf{F} = m \cdot \mathbf{a}$

$1{,}000$ kg $\cdot \, 0.45$ m/s² $= 450$ N

$\mathbf{F} = 450$ N in NE direction

Example

A 2-D force with components $F_x = 100$ N and $F_y = 45$ N accelerates an object of mass 5 kg. If this force is the net force on the object, find the value of the acceleration and its direction relative to the x-axis.

Solution

According to the second law of motion, we need to divide the force in each direction to the mass of the object to find the two components of the acceleration.

$F_x = 100$ N

$F_y = 45$ N

$m = 5.0$ kg

$a_x = \dfrac{F_x}{m} = \dfrac{100 \text{ N}}{5 \text{ kg}} = 20$ m/s²

$a_y = \dfrac{F_y}{m} = \dfrac{45 \text{ N}}{5 \text{ kg}} = 9$ m/s²

Because the two components are 90° apart, we can apply *Pitagora's theorem* to find the acceleration:

$a = \sqrt{a_x^2 + a_y^2} = \sqrt{20^2 + 9^2} = 22$ m/s²

To find the direction relative to x-axis, α, we calculate the tangent of the angle and find the angle.

$\tan \alpha = \dfrac{\text{opposite}}{\text{adjacent}} = \dfrac{a_y}{a_x} = 0.45$

$\alpha = 24°$

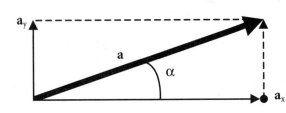

Figure 5.1

So, acceleration can be written in two ways:

$\mathbf{a} = (20,9)$ m/s^2 for each component, or

$\mathbf{a} = 22$ m/s^2 at 24° north of east

▶ Practice

7. If the acceleration of an object is zero, does it mean there are no forces acting on the object? Explain briefly.

8. If the net force on an object is zero, can the object move with increasing speed? Explain briefly.

9. If the net force on an object is zero, is the object necessarily moving in a uniform linear motion? Explain briefly.

10. If the net force on an object is directed to the northwest, can we assume that the velocity is also in the NW direction at all times? Explain briefly.

11. For a given net force, can we assume that the larger the mass of an object means the larger the acceleration will be? Explain briefly.

12. A car of mass 2,000 kg starts from rest and travels 10 m in 2 s. What are the values of the acceleration, assuming uniform acceleration, and of the net force?

13. An object moves in the xy plane with an acceleration having components of $a_x = 1.00$ m/s^2 and $a_y = 9.80$ m/s^2. What are the components of the net force if the object has a 0.500 kg mass?

14. In practice problem 8, find the acceleration and resultant force.

15. In practice problem 8, find the angle of the net force with respect to the y direction.

16. Consider two different objects acted upon by the same net force, but one object has a mass $\frac{3}{4}$ the mass of the second object. Find the ratio of the acceleration of the first object with respect to the second object.

17. Is it possible to have an object accelerated by a net force in the NW direction while there is a force acting in the SW direction? Explain briefly.

18. Consider a puck on the ice (low to no friction) and two hockey players trying to push the puck in opposite directions, with forces of 190 N in the x direction and 250 N in the $-x$ direction. If the puck's mass is 200.0 grams, find the net force and the acceleration.

19. The hockey puck in practice problem 18 is launched by the players and now slides across the ice with constant velocity. What are the net force and acceleration in this example?

20. Consider a battery-operated toy car. If the battery dies, the car will decrease its speed at a rate of 10 cm/s every second (we will consider in this example uniform accelerated motion). Find out the acceleration on the object and the net force if the car's mass is 150 g.

The net force described by Newton's second law or any other force is, by definition, a measure of the interaction. Whenever you interact with an object, you will feel the effect of the interaction yourself. When you kick a ball, the ball will react (due to the interaction) by shooting into the air, but your foot will "feel" the interaction also. This effect is described by the *third law of motion*.

If you act with a force on an object, the object will react with a force equal and opposite on the first object.

In this case, one force is called *action* and the other one *reaction*. As a **very important note**: The two forces are acting on different objects and so, although equal and opposite, they still have an effect on the system.

Example

Consider a car moving on a road. Determine the action and reaction forces on each tire.

Solution

Let's look at the situation for one tire, and the same can be repeated for the remaining tires. The car's left tire acts on the road with a force that we call *action*, and the road reacts with an equal and opposite force on the tire called *reaction*. That is how the car can move.

reaction   action

Figure 5.2

▶ Practice

21. If a student pulls on a string with a force of 25 N, identify the force of action, the force of reaction, and the value of the two forces. Make sure to explain on which object each of these forces acts.

22. Imagine the solar system. Earth acts on the moon with a force we call gravitational force. Does the moon act on the earth? And with what force?

▶ Weight

Let's put to work the knowledge we've accumulated and define some important types of forces in classical mechanics, one of which is *weight*. Whenever two objects are in proximity, they interact through a force. If you consider Earth and an apple that is about to fall from a tree, the apple is attracted by Earth with the force of *gravity*, so it will accelerate toward the earth for as long as it falls (if we do not consider other forces present such as friction with air). Because the gravity is the only force on the apple, it will be the only component in the net force. According to the second law, this force is also proportional to the mass of the apple and the acceleration, and we call it *weight*. The expression of the weight of an object of mass *m* is:

$$W = m \cdot g$$

The symbols in the expression are: W is weight, m is mass, and g is the acceleration. It is **very important to note** that this expression gives us the argument to answer the question: Are mass and weight the same quantity? The answer is No! Weight is a force, and mass is a scalar quantity that gives a measure of the inertia of the object. In the previous example, the apple falling down due to gravity is in a *free fall*, and the acceleration of fall, which is the same for all objects at the same place on the earth, is called *acceleration due to gravity, g*. Although the acceleration due to gravity varies with the mass of the planet and the distance from an object to the center of the planet, for most purposes herein, we will take the acceleration due to gravity on Earth to be g = 9.8 m/s^2. Another and last **very important note** for this section is that weight is a vector always pointing toward the center of Earth.

Example

Consider the apple falling freely toward Earth. Why is Earth not falling toward the apple?

Solution

The third law of motion says that every action has an equal and opposite reaction, so the apple is acted on by gravity, and hence, Earth has to be acted on by an equal and opposite force. The reason the earth does not start moving toward the apple is that the same force acting on a huge object (Earth) has a negligible effect while having a definite effect on a smaller object (the apple).

▶ Practice

23. A solid object and a feather have equal masses. Do they reach the ground in the same amount of time? Explain briefly.
24. The two objects in the previous question move, now in vacuum. Do they reach the ground in the same amount of time? Explain briefly.
25. Do the two objects in practice problem 23 have to be of equal mass to reach the ground in the same amount of time?

26. Consider playing with a medicine ball and you let it fall freely. (These balls can be anywhere between 1 kg and 10 kg. We will consider ours to be 2,500 g.) Draw a diagram for this problem including the vector corresponding to the weight, and then find the value of the weight.

    Note: Remember, all vectors are symbolized as arrows pointing in the direction of the motion. An object moving with a constant velocity toward north (consider north to be at the top of the page) will be represented as in Figure 5.3.

27. The weight of the same spaceship is different if you measure it on Earth or on another planet by 3:2 ratio. Find out the acceleration due to gravity on the other planet compared with the acceleration due to gravity on Earth.

Figure 5.3

▶ Normal Force

The fact is that not all objects fall or fly; most of them are at rest or moving in contact with different surfaces. In such a case, we have an action, weight, and a reaction from the surface toward the object, and we call that a *normal force*, with a symbol *N*. In the simplest case, an object sits on a horizontal surface and pushes down only with its own weight; the surface responds with an equal and opposite force as shown in Figure 5.4. A drawing that includes all the forces acting on an object is called a *free-body diagram*.

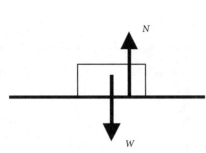

Figure 5.4

When the surface is no longer horizontal, part of the weight will not act on the supporting surface, so the normal force of the object is now smaller than the weight of the object as seen in Figure 5.5. In this case, the component of the weight, called W_x, is the one acting on the surface, and normally is:

$$W_x = -N$$

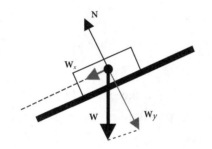

Figure 5.5

The other component of the weight is not equalized by any other force in this case, and therefore, the object will accelerate toward the bottom of the plane. In real-life applications, there will be at least one other force acting. Yes, you guessed it: *friction*. But we will talk about this later.

In many real-life applications, you will have to take into consideration other forces acting on the object: pushes, pulls, and so on. In these cases, the free-body diagram will be more complex, and the calculation of the normal force can result in amounts smaller or larger than the weight, as we will show in the following example.

Example

Set a book on a table (a mass of 1,000 g) and exert a pushing force on the book of 10.0 N. Now draw the object's free-body diagram and calculate the reaction of the table.

Solution

Start by drawing the free-body diagram that will show the three forces acting in the problem: the weight of the book on the table, the pushing force, and the reaction of the table (normal).

$$m_{book} = 1,000 \text{ g} = 1.00 \text{ kg}$$

$$F_{push} = 10.0 \text{ N}$$

$$N = ?$$

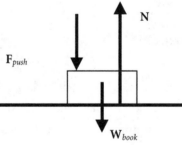

Figure 5.6

The weight of the book is:

$$W_{book} = m \cdot g = 1 \text{ kg} \cdot 9.8 \text{ m/s}^2 = 9.8 \text{ N}$$

The total force on the table is then:

$$F = W_{book} + F_{push} = 19.8 \text{ N}$$

And the reaction of the table according to the third law of motion is a force equal and opposite of F:

$$N = 19.8 \text{ N upward}$$

As you can see, this force is larger than the weight of the object.

► Practice

28. Consider that a friend is moving. You stack a couple of boxes and would like to find out what is the normal force. One box has a mass of 8 kg and the other has a mass of 12 kg. Draw a free-body diagram and find the normal force.

29. Neglecting friction, consider an object on an inclined plane. Also consider pushing down on the object (perpendicular to the surface of the plane). Draw a free-body diagram of the object.

30. Consider an object of mass $m = 15.0$ kg that is pushed by a 20.0 N force at a 30.0° angle with the positive x-axis. Find out the normal force on the object. We will neglect friction.

► Tension

In the process of moving small or large objects, we often use tools. One of these tools is a simple string and is the base of more complex machines such as *pulleys*. A string in a pulley is used to transfer forces from the source of force to the object(s), to reduce the load on the string, and also to change the direction of motion. In the simplest case, it is considered that the string has no mass, hence no energy is needed to accelerate the string (there is no net force on the rope itself).

Example
Consider the following situation for which the free-body diagram needs to be determined.

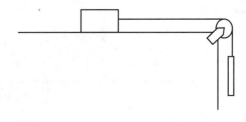

Figure 5.7

Solution
The hanging body is acted upon only by its weight and the tension in the rope, which is the reaction of the force on the rope as it can be seen in Figure 5.8.

Figure 5.8

The object on the surface is acted upon by the tension in the rope and on the vertical by the weight and the normal force.

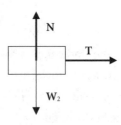

Figure 5.9

On the pulley, we have tension from both ends of the rope. (This is similar to a rubber band when you try to pull it down by putting your finger inside it and pulling on it; you can feel each part of the elastic band pulling on your finger.) Also, we have the reaction of the table to which the pulley is attached.

The magnitude f_k of the kinetic frictional force is proportional to the normal force N and to the coefficient of kinetic friction:

$$f_k = \mu_k \cdot N$$

where μ_k is the coefficient of kinetic friction and is a dimensionless quantity.

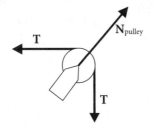

Figure 5.10

So, the free-body diagram treats the system of objects as independent objects, the connection between them being the tension force (the interaction force).

▶ Friction

So, what happens then in terms of interaction between the object and the surface if we cannot neglect friction? At an atomic level, even the smoothest surface shows some roughness, and so if two such surfaces come into contact, there is a resistance to motion, which we call *friction.*

The forces of friction are classified in the following ways: (1) *static* frictional force can have a value of zero up to a maximum frictional force, f_S^{MAX}, and has a value dependent on the applied force, and (2) *kinetic* frictional force, which acts when the object is in motion and is directly opposite to the direction of motion.

Example

Consider a hockey puck of 500 g mass sliding on ice. If the puck's normal force is equal only to the weight of the object, what are the frictional force and the acceleration of the object if the coefficient of kinetic friction is 0.3? In the horizontal plane, consider only the frictional force.

Solution

In order to find the acceleration, construct a free-body diagram and calculate the frictional force. We know:

$$m = 500 \text{ g} = 0.5 \text{ kg}$$

$$\mu_k = 0.3$$

$$W = N$$

Then we calculate the normal force (see Figure 5.11):

$$N = m \cdot g = 0.5 \cdot 9.8 = 4.9 \text{ N}$$

$$f_k = \mu_k \cdot N = 0.3 \cdot 4.9 = 1.5 \text{ N}$$

$$f_k = 1.5 \text{ N}$$

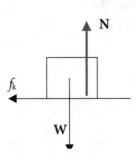

Figure 5.11

And because there is no other interaction, the second law of mechanics will give us the acceleration of motion. But before calculating acceleration, we determine that forces in the direction of motion will be considered positive and forces opposite to the motion will be negative.

$$\Sigma F = m \cdot a$$

$$\Sigma F = f_k = m \cdot a$$

$$f_k = m \cdot a$$

Because the motion is in one direction, we can neglect the vector sign and write:

$$-\mu_k \cdot N = m \cdot a$$

$$a = -\mu_k \cdot N/m = -\mu_k \cdot m \cdot g/m =$$

$$-\mu_k \cdot g = -3 \, \text{m/s}^2$$

$$a = -3 \, \text{m/s}^2$$

This value of the acceleration tells us that the object is slowing down.

The problem can also be solved numerically using the value of $f_k = 1.5 \, N$ and applying the second law of motion:

$$a = -f_k/m = -1.5 \, N/0.5 \, \text{kg} = -3 \, \text{m/s}^2$$

▶ Static Equilibrium

An object is in equilibrium when it has zero acceleration. The condition of equilibrium can be expressed as:

$$\sum F_x = 0$$

$$\sum F_y = 0$$

These conditions are equivalent to the fact that all forces acting on the object must balance. Then, in the nonequilibrium state, acceleration is nonzero:

$$\sum F_x = m \, a_x$$

$$\sum F_y = m \, a_y$$

Example
Consider an object accelerating and decelerating due to gravity on an inclined plane that has a kinetic frictional coefficient μ_k. Find the expression of the acceleration along the plane in the two cases mentioned.

Solution
Start with the free-body diagram for the first case, applying the conditions of equilibrium appropriate to each direction and then calculate the acceleration (see Figure 5.12).

Then find out the components of the weight along the plane and perpendicular to the plane: W_x and W_y.

$$W_x = W \sin \alpha = m \, g \sin \alpha$$

$$W_y = W \cos \alpha = m \, g \cos \alpha$$

Then write Newton's second law for directions along the plane and perpendicular to the plane. Again,

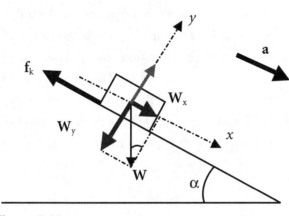

Figure 5.12

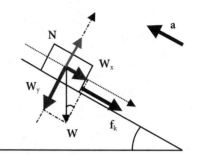

Figure 5.13

we will work with each direction so we can use a scalar equation.

y-axis

$$a_y = 0$$

$$m\, a_y = N - W_y$$

$$0 = N - W_y$$

$$N = W_y = m\, g \cos \alpha$$

x-axis

$$m\, a_x = W_x - f_k = W_x - \mu_k N$$

$$m\, a_x = m\, g \sin \alpha - \mu_k m\, g \cos \alpha$$

The acceleration is:

$$a_{x\,DOWN} = g(\sin \alpha - \mu_k \cos \alpha)$$

In the second case, when the object is moving up the inclined plane, we have a different free-body diagram. In order for the object to move up, imagine you gave it an intial push. All forces are the same except the fricitonal force, which acts against motion. Then apply Newton's second law along the plane and perpendicular to the plane as follows:

y-axis

$$a_y = 0$$

$$m\, a_y = N - W_y$$

$$0 = N - W_y$$

$$N = W_y = m\, g \cos \alpha$$

x-axis

$$-m \cdot a_x = W_x + f_k = W_x + \mu_k N$$

$$-m \cdot a_x = m\, g \sin \alpha + \mu_k m\, g \cos \alpha$$

And the acceleration is:

$$a_{x\,UP} = -g(\sin \alpha + \mu_k \cos \alpha)$$

▶ Practice

31. In all cases, the normal force exerted by a surface on an object will be equal to the weight of the object? Explain briefly.

32. Consider a simple pulley like the one in Figure 5.14. Show all forces acting on the two masses and the pulley. The mass on the left is larger than the mass on the right, and there is no friction

Figure 5.14

between the pulley and the string. The string has negligible mass.

33. Consider an object of mass $m_1 = 2.00$ kg on an inclined plane of angle 60.0°. There is no friction with the plane. The object is connected with another object through a massless string and a pulley, as in Figure 5.15. Draw the free-body diagram and find the acceleration of the objects for the following cases: (a) $m_2 = 2$ kg; (b) $m_2 = 1$ kg; and (c) $m_2 = 0.5$ kg.

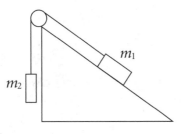

Figure 5.15

34. Consider case (a) in the previous problem and imagine you try to help raise the box up the hill by pushing with a horizontal force on the box of mass m_1, as shown in Figure 5.16. What is the new state of motion of the system of the two objects?

35. You plan to hang a framed picture on the wall, and, because it is a precious family heirloom, you want to take all precautions and find out if the string you have will hold it. The picture has a mass of 2,500 g, and the string can hold up to a tension of 20 N. Considering the final setup similar to the one in Figure 5.17 ($\alpha = 45°$), find out if your string will have enough strength to support the picture.

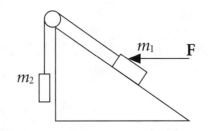

Figure 5.16

36. You are moving again, and have two boxes side by side and want to push them out of your way. There is friction with the floor of about 0.8 coefficient of kinetic friction, and the boxes are 12 and 18 kg. You are pushing with a 500 N force horizontally. Find out the acceleration of the system.

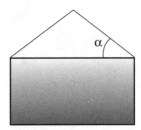

Figure 5.17

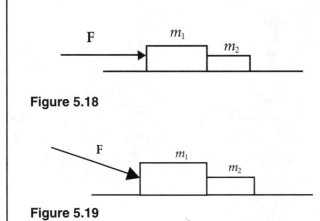

Figure 5.18

Figure 5.19

37. While you are pushing boxes, your back starts hurting, so you proceede to change the position of your body. In the diagram in Figure 5.18, you now apply the force at an angle of 60° with the vertical (see Figure 5.19). Calculate once again the acceleration of the boxes.

6▶ Linear Momentum

LESSON SUMMARY

In the previous lesson, we introduced interactions as measured and controlled by forces. In this lesson, we will be studying objects in motion from the point of view of the velocity and mass they carry. This concept we call *momentum*. One more time we will find a connection between motion and interaction; in this case, a more complex concept—*impulse*. Based on this knowledge, we will discuss an important law of conservation—momentum conservation—and apply it to elastic and perfect inelastic collisions.

▶ Linear Momentum

From driving, biking, rollerblading, or any other motion-related activities, you might recall that a heavier object and a lighter object collide with other objects in different ways. If I recall my first lesson in bowling: You have to let go of the bowling ball while you are moving instead of while you are simply standing, because the ball will have more *momentum*. Do you think I had a good teacher? We define momentum as the product of the mass and its velocity at one time, and we say that momentum measures inertia for an object in motion.

$$\mathbf{p} = m \cdot \mathbf{v}$$

This quantity is a vector and its direction is the same direction as the velocity. Also, the unit for momentum is kg · m/s.

Example

Two different objects have the same momentum, but one object is ten times larger in mass than the other. How do the two velocities compare? Consider one-dimensional motion.

Solution

The assumption suggested by the problem refers to the expression of the momentum where both momentum and velocity are vectors. If we consider a 1-D motion, then the significance of the vector sign disappears.

$$m_1 = 10 \cdot m_2$$

$$p_1 = p_2$$

$$v_1/v_2 = ?$$

$$p_1 = m_1 \cdot v_1$$

$$p_2 = m_2 \cdot v_2$$

$$\frac{p_1}{p_2} = \frac{m_1 \cdot v_1}{m_2 \cdot v_2}$$

$$1 = \frac{m_1 \cdot v_1}{m_2 \cdot v_2}$$

$$1 = \frac{10 \cdot v_1}{v_2}$$

$$\frac{v_1}{v_2} = \frac{1}{10}$$

So, the second object having a smaller mass moves faster at the same momentum.

▶ Practice

1. Does a larger mass necessarily mean a larger momentum? Explain briefly.
2. In what conditions can an object have zero momentum? Explain briefly.
3. Can an object have negative momentum? Explain briefly.

▶ Impulse

In order to move an object, a net force applied to the object is necessary. The *magnitude* of the force and the *interval of time* that the force acts on the object are important in determining the effect. Figure 6.1 shows a measurement of the time dependence of force in two separate collisions.

On the left, the effect on the object is much larger than on the right, because for the same interval of time, the average force applied is larger.

In order to fully characterize this process, a quantity called *impulse* is introduced and the *impulse of a force, J*, is proportional to the product of the average force acting on the object and the interval of time of contact between the two:

$$J = F \cdot \Delta t$$

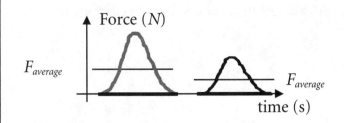

Figure 6.1

The direction of the impulse is the same as the direction of the average force, and the unit for impulse is N · seconds. Note that because the force is time dependent, we cannot consider any random point on the curve, but must use an average for the entire time interval instead.

Example

Consider a soccer player hitting a ball with an average force of about 0.80 kN. Find the impulse if the contact between the ball and the player's foot extends to about 6.0 ms.

Solution

Consider first the data given in the problem and the units of the data. Then a simple replacement of the quantities in the expression of impulse will yield the answer.

$$F_{average} = 0.80 \, \text{kN} = 800 \, \text{N}$$

$$\Delta t = 6.0 \, \text{ms} = 6.0 \cdot 10^{-3} \, \text{s}$$

$$J = ?$$

According to the definition, the impulse is the product of the average force and the time interval:

$$J = F \cdot \Delta t$$

$$J = 800 \, \text{N} \cdot 6.0 \cdot 10^{-3} \, \text{s}$$

$$J = 4.8 \, \text{Ns}$$

The direction of the impulse is the same as the direction of the force.

▶ Practice

4. What is the connection between the unit for impulse and for momentum?
5. Are impulse and force measuring the same quantity? Explain briefly.
6. Does a large force always produce a large impulse? Explain briefly.
7. Consider the time dependence for a force such as the one in Figure 6.2. Based on the data given, estimate the impulse.

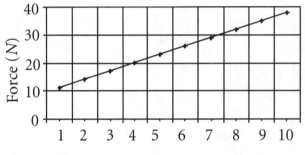

Figure 6.2

▶ Impulse-Momentum Theorem

Newton's second law of motion can be used to reveal the connection between the impulse and the momentum. When the application of an external net force changes the object's speed, the equation of motion is:

$$v = v_0 + a \cdot t$$

Momentum theorem says that when a net force acts on an object the impulse of the force is equal to the change in momentum:

$$J = \Delta p$$

In this expression, both the momentum and the impulse are vector quantities.

Then, the uniform acceleration can be found to be:

$$a = (v - v_0)/t$$

But, according to Newton's second law, the net force on the object is proportional to the acceleration and the mass of the object:

$$F = m \cdot a$$

$$F = m \cdot (v - v_0)/t$$

$$F = (m \cdot v - m \cdot v_0)/t$$

$$F = (p - p_0)/t$$

$$F = \Delta p/t$$

$$F \cdot t = \Delta p$$

$$J = \Delta p$$

As one can see, the momentum measures the state of motion at one moment, whereas when defining impulse, we talk about a change in the motion of the object. If the object is at rest or moving with constant velocity, impulse is zero because momentum does not change.

Example

Consider the previous example with the soccer ball and imagine you are again in a case where motion is one dimension. Your ball is directed toward a fence and in the process of interacting with the fence, the ball changes its direction of motion and returns toward you with less speed: The ball moves away with 0.8 m/s and returns to you with 0.6 m/s. Find out the impulse if the ball's mass is 810 g.

Solution

Setting the equation right means to look for the clues, and in this problem, we include the 1-D motion, which means we can give up the vector signs. The second factor is the motion of the ball itself: Going away will be a positive number while returning will be a negative number.

$$v_0 = 0.80 \text{ m/s}$$

$$v = -0.60 \text{ m/s}$$

$$m = 810 \text{ g} = 0.81 \text{ kg}$$

$$J = ?$$

According to the impulse momentum theorem:

$$J = \Delta p$$

$$J = m \cdot (v - v_0)$$

$$J = 0.81 \, \text{kg} \cdot (-0.60 - 0.80) \, \text{m/s}$$

$$J = -1.1 \, \text{N} \cdot \text{s}$$

▶ Practice

8. If you are to receive a hit from a ball, would you rather make it last a longer or a shorter time?

9. Why do some brittle objects break when they hit a hard floor but survive a fall on a carpeted floor? Explain briefly.

10. Is it correct to say that momentum and impulse measure the same quantity? Explain briefly.

11. In which case is the impulse greater: when an object slows down to half of the speed or when it stops completely? Explain briefly.

12. Is it possible for an object to move and have zero impulse? Explain briefly.

13. A car comes to a complete stop in 15 seconds. Consider the mass of the car to be 1,500 kg and the initial speed to be 18 m/s. Find the average breaking force.

▶ Conservation of Momentum

Two types of forces can act on a system:

- *Internal* forces (within the system)
- *External* forces (outside the system)

When we discuss internal forces, we talk about the interaction between the atomic components and chemical bonds, whereas for external forces, we talk about tension, friction, and different types of push and pull forces. There are also systems we call *isolated systems*. A system for which the result of all the external forces is zero is called an *isolated system*. For these systems, the principle of conservation of linear momentum says that the total linear momentum of an isolated system remains constant, and at different times, the momentum of the system has the same value.

Example

Now consider yourself on rollerblades. You hold a ball in your hands. Your mass and the ball's is 75 kg, while the mass of the rollerblades is 3.5 kg. There is no friction with the asphalt. You step down on the rollerblades with a speed of 0.50 m/s, and the rollerblade starts moving in the opposite direction. Find the speed of the rollerblade immediately after your descent.

Solution

First, we need to see what is given, check units, and then try to solve for the unknown, which is the speed of the blade (see Figure 6.3).

$$m = 3.5 \, \text{kg}$$

$$m_{you} = 75 \, \text{kg}$$

$$v_{you} = +0.50 \, \text{m/s}$$

$$v_{blade} = ?$$

Because there is no friction or other external force acting on the system, the linear momentum for this system (you and rollerblades) is conserved. So before and after you step down, there will be the same momentum:

$$\mathbf{p}_{total} = \mathbf{p} + \mathbf{p}_{blade} = \text{constant}$$

As long as there is no net external force acting on the system, the linear momentum before and after the collision will be the same.

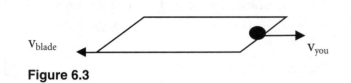

Figure 6.3

This is a vectorial relationship. The total momentum stays the same for the system, and because the system starts at rest, velocity is 0, then momentum is also 0. After you step down, the total momentum should be found to be 0:

Before jump:

$$p_{total} = 0$$

After jump:

$$p_{total} = m\, v_{blade} + m_{you}\, v_{you}$$

Then the final equation is:

$$p_{total} = 0$$

$$0 = m\, v_{blade} + m_{you}\, v_{you}$$

$$m\, v_{blade} = -m_{you}\, v_{you}$$

$$v_{blade} = -(m_{you}/m)\, v_{you}$$

$$v_{blade} = -11 \text{ m/s}$$

▶ Practice

14. What difference in the conservation of momentum does it make that the momentum is a vector quantity? Explain briefly.

15. Can you have *three* objects moving and have the total momentum of the three-body system zero? Explain briefly.

16. In the previous example with the rollerblades, how can you start moving without stepping down (remember, you are holding the ball in your arms)? Explain briefly.

17. Would it help more if the ball was a medicinal ball, say of mass 10 kg, rather than a soccer ball that you can throw at the same speed? Why or why not?

▶ Elastic and Perfectly Inelastic Collisions

The following two types of collisions can be considered:

- *Elastic* collisions: the collisions in which the total energy of motion (which we will call kinetic) of the system before collision equals the total kinetic energy after the collision (conservation of kinetic energy).
- Perfectly *inelastic* collisions: the collisions in which the kinetic energy before and after collision is different. This happens when the two objects stick together after the collision.

Example

Consider two objects in an elastic collision (one of mass 25 kg and the other of mass 5 kg). Also, let's say that object 1 is at rest and object 2 is moving at a speed of 1.5 m/s. The two objects will collide head on, and the second object will recoil at a speed of 1.2 m/s. What is the speed of the heavy object? There is no external force acting on the system. See Figure 6.4.

Solution

In this case, both the energy and momentum are conserved.

$$m_1 = 25 \text{ kg}$$

$$m_2 = 5.0 \text{ kg}$$

$$v_{1 \text{ initial}} = 0 \text{ m/s}$$

$$v_{2 \text{ initial}} = 1.5 \text{ m/s}$$

$$v_{1 \text{ final}} = ?$$

$$v_{2 \text{ final}} = -1.2 \text{ m/s (minus at } v_{2 \text{ final}} \text{ because we are}$$

told that it recoils)

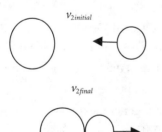

Figure 6.4

The momentum equation is:

$$m_1 v_{1 \text{ initial}} + m_2 v_{2 \text{ initial}} = m_1 v_{1 \text{ final}} + m_2 v_{2 \text{ final}}$$

$$25 \cdot 0 + 5 \cdot 1.5 = 25 \cdot v_{1 \text{ final}} + 5 \cdot (-1.2)$$

$$v_{1 \text{ final}} = 0.54 \text{ m/s}$$

Example

A ball of clay moving on a horizontal plane with a momentum of 0.8 kg · m/s hits a plastic ball, head on. The plastic ball has a mass larger than the mass of the clayball with 0.2 kg. Find out the initial speed of the plastic ball if, after the perfect inelastic collision, the system moves at a speed of 0.5 m/s in the same direction as the incoming clay ball. We are also able to calculate that the final momentum is 1.6 times smaller than the momentum of the clay ball. Determine the mass of the two balls.

Solution

All quantities in the example are expressed in SI. To calculate the speed and the two masses, we have to identify the type of collision and the given information. This is a case of a perfectly inelastic collision, so after the collision, the two objects move as one. We will use a subscript 1 for the clay ball and 2 for the plastic ball.

$$p_{\text{initial clayball}} = m_1 v_{1 \text{initial}} = +0.8 \text{ kg} \cdot \text{m/s}$$
(we'llconsider this object moving to the right)

$$m_2 = 0.2 \text{ kg} + m_1$$

$$v_{\text{final}} = 0.5 \text{ m/s}$$

$$p_{\text{final}} = p_{\text{initial clay ball}} / 1.6 =$$

$$+0.8 \text{ kg} \cdot \text{m/s} \div 1.6 = +0.5 \text{ kg} \cdot \text{m/s}$$

$$v_{2 \text{ initial}} = ?$$

We apply the principle of conservation of momentum principle and write:

$$m_1 v_{1 \text{ initial}} + m_2 v_{2 \text{ initial}} = (m_1 + m_2) v_{\text{final}}$$

$0.8 \text{ kg} \cdot \text{m/s} + (0.2 \text{ kg} + m_1) \cdot v_{2 \text{ initial}} =$

$(m_1 + 0.2 \text{ kg} + m_1) \cdot 0.5 \text{ m/s}$

But the left-hand side of the previous equation is the final momentum, which is given to us as:

$(m_1 + 0.2 \text{ kg} + m_1) \cdot 0.5 \text{ m/s} =$

$+ 0.5 \text{ kg} \cdot \text{m/s}$

And so we can calculate first for the mass m_1 by dividing both sides by 0.5:

$(m_1 + 0.2 \text{ kg} + m_1) = 1$

$2 \cdot m_1 + 0.2 \text{ kg} = 1$

$2 \cdot m_1 = 0.8 \text{ kg}$

$m_1 = 0.4 \text{ kg}$

$m_2 = 0.6 \text{ kg}$

Returning to the principle of conservation of momentum, we have now:

$0.8 \text{ kg} \cdot \text{m/s} + 0.6 \text{ kg} \cdot v_{2 \text{ initial}} = 0.5 \text{ kg} \cdot \text{m/s}$

$0.6 \text{ kg} \cdot v_{2 \text{ initial}} = -0.3 \text{ kg} \cdot \text{m/s}$

$v_{2 \text{ initial}} = -(0.3/0.6) \text{ m/s}$

$v_{2 \text{ initial}} = -0.5 \text{ m/s}$

The minus sign tells us that the motion of the second ball is in the opposite direction to the motion of the clay ball.

▶ Practice

18. A ball suffers a horizontal collision with a (non-moving) wall. Are the vector interpretations of momentum and impulse important in this case? Why or why not?

19. Two identical objects, 1 and 2, headed in the same direction collide perfectly elastically. After the collision, object 1 comes to a rest. Compare the velocity of object 2 after the collision with that of object 1 before the collision (is it equal, larger, smaller?).

20. Two equal-mass atomic particles move in the same direction with speed v_1 and v_2. One catches up with the second, and they collide perfectly inelastically. What is the speed of the system after the collision compared to before the collision as a function of v_1 and v_2?

21. A small piece of clay is thrown at a moving bike, and the clay sticks to the bike. What happens to the speed of the bike if the mass of the clay is much smaller than the mass of the bike?

▶ 2-D Collisions

Collisions do not always happen in one dimension. In most real-life applications, the encounter is at least a 2-D collision. The need for the vectorial interpretation of velocity, momentum, and impulse is made evident by such cases. This applies to collisions at the atomic level (e.g., between nuclear particles) and at the macroscopic level (e.g., planetary motion).

The most general expression of the principle of conservation of momentum is one that considers the vectors velocity for the objects involved in the collision. Take two objects of masses m_1 and m_2 colliding perfectly elastically:

$m_1 \cdot v_{1 \text{ initial}} + m_2 \cdot v_{2 \text{ initial}} =$

$m_1 \cdot v_{1 \text{ final}} + m_2 \cdot v_{2 \text{ final}}$

$$m_1 \cdot v_{1x\,initial} + m_2 \cdot v_{2x\,initial} =$$

$$m_1 \cdot v_{1x\,final} + m_2 \cdot v_{2x\,final}$$

While for a perfectly inelastic collision:

$$m_1 \cdot v_{1\,initial} + m_2 \cdot v_{2\,initial} = (m_1 + m_2) \cdot v_{final}$$

The simplification comes from the fact that we can treat independently the equations for each of the three rectangular axes: x, y, and z.

And the same expressions can be written for the y and the z direction.

Example

Consider a car collision in which one car is driving north at a speed of 16 m/s and the other is moving east at 14 m/s. The cars are of similar mass, 1,500 kg. Find the velocity immediately after the collision if the cars get entangled and move together.

Solution

The units for the data given in the problem are in SI, so there is no need to convert. This is a two-dimensional perfectly inelastic collision, so consider the vector components of the velocities of the two cars.

$$m_1 = m_2 = 1{,}500 \text{ kg}$$

$v_{1\,initial} = (0,16)$ m/s or 16 m/s moving north (we consider positive y direction north and positive x direction east)

$v_{2\,initial} = (14,0)$ m/s or 14 m/s moving east

$\mathbf{v}_{final} = ?$

$\mathbf{p}_{final} = ?$

The expressions for the conservation of momentum for the two directions are:

$$m_1 \cdot v_{1x\,initial} + m_2 \cdot v_{2x\,initial} = (m_1 + m_2) \cdot v_{x\,final}$$

$$m_1 \cdot v_{1y\,initial} + m_2 \cdot v_{2y\,initial} = (m_1 + m_2) \cdot v_{y\,final}$$

Because the masses are all the same, they cancel out in both equations, leaving a factor 2 on the right-hand side:

$$v_{1x\,initial} + v_{2x\,initial} = 2 \cdot v_{x\,final}$$

$$v_{1y\,initial} + v_{2y\,initial} = 2 \cdot v_{y\,final}$$

And replacing the known values of the x and y components of the velocity, we get:

$$0 + 14 \text{ m/s} = 2 \cdot v_{x\,final}$$

$$16 \text{ m/s} + 0 = 2 \cdot v_{y\,final}$$

And the results are:

$$v_{x\,final} = 7 \text{ m/s}$$

$$v_{y\,final} = 8 \text{ m/s}$$

or:

$$\mathbf{v}_{final} = (7,8) \text{ m/s}$$

$$m_1 \cdot v_{1x\,initial} + m_2 \cdot v_{2x\,initial} = (m_1 + m_2) \cdot v_{x\,final}$$

Or, using Pythagoras's theorem for the sides of the right triangle:

$$v_{final} =$$

$$\sqrt{v_{x\,final}^2 + v_{y\,final}^2} =$$

$$\sqrt{7^2 + 8^2} = 9 \text{ m/s}$$

And the direction is given by the angle with x- or y-axes.

$$\tan \alpha = \frac{v_y}{v_x} = \frac{8}{7} = 1.1$$

$$\alpha = 48°$$

So the final velocity is:

$$\mathbf{v}_{final} = 9 \text{ m/s at } \alpha = 48° \text{ with the } +x\text{--axis.}$$

▶ Practice

22. A firecracker set on the ground splits into two pieces of equal sizes that spread in two opposite directions. How do the speeds of the two pieces compare?

23. In practice problem 22, how do the velocities compare? Why?

24. Two cars approaching from different directions (say east and north) collide. Is it possible for the momentum to be zero immediately after collision? Explain.

25. What if the cars in practice problem 24 collide head on? Is it possible for the momentum to be zero immediately after the collision? Explain.

26. Consider again the firecracker in practice problem 22, but in this case moving upward in the NW direction with a speed of 15 m/s. If the mass of the firecracker is 800 g and it splits in three pieces of mass $m_3 = 2 \cdot m_2 = 10 \cdot m_1$, with the second piece flying after collision in the west direction at 10 m/s, and the third piece flying north at 12 m/s, find the x and y component of the velocity for the first piece.

27. Write each velocity in practice problem 26 as a vector quantity. Use both the component form with (a_x, a_y) and the value + angle form.

28. What is the mass of each of the three pieces in practice problem 24?

Mechanical Energy

LESSON SUMMARY

In the previous chapters, we discussed important concepts such as mass, motion, and forces. We will pull all that knowledge together in a concept that, while very abstract, is at the essence of science and nature — energy. In this lesson, we will concentrate on a form of energy that characterizes mechanical properties. We will define mechanical energy and its two forms: kinetic and potential. We will wrap up our lesson with a study of the law of conservation of energy in a mechanical system.

▶ Work

Work is a quantity that measures the effect of moving an object when a force is applied. When a constant force (no variation in time or space) is exerted but the object does not move, as in the case when you would push against a wall, we say that no work has been done.

To summarize in an expression the definition of work, we have:

$$W = (F \cdot \cos \alpha) \cdot d$$

Work is proportional to the product of the distance over which an object is moved, the displacement, and the constant force along that direction.

The unit for work is Newtons times meters (N · m) and is known as a *Joule* (in honor of James Joule 1818–1889). Work is a scalar quantity although it is the result of two vectors—force and displacement. In other words: The most general expression of the work done is the dot product of force and displacement; and the result of a dot product, although starting with two vectors, is a scalar.

Example

Your car needs to be moved for a short distance, but it has no gas in the tank, so it will need to be pushed. You apply a force of 1,000 N and move it for about 180 cm. What is the work done?

Solution

First, convert the units into SI (remember, 1 m = 100 cm). Next, construct a diagram of the problem, and then proceed to find the answer.

$d = 180 \text{ cm} = 180 \text{ cm} \cdot 1 \text{ m}/100 \text{ cm} = 1.8 \text{ m}$

$F = 1,000 \text{ N}$

$W = ?$

As Figure 7.1 shows, the force and the displacement are in the same direction, so then the angle between F and d is zero. Since $\cos 0° = 1$, the expression of the work becomes:

$W = (F \cdot \cos \alpha) \cdot d = (F \cdot \cos 0°) \cdot d = F \cdot d$

$W = 1,000 \text{ N} \cdot 1.8 \text{ m} = 1,800 \text{ J} = 1.8 \text{ kJ}$

Example

Now imagine we are using the same force to push a big

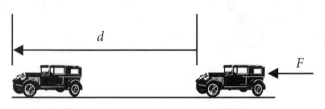

Figure 7.1

pile of boxes around, but the force is exerted so that the angle with the horizontal is 60°. Find out the work performed on the boxes by the force of 1,000 N in a distance of 180 cm.

Solution

First, we convert the units to SI (1 m = 100 cm). Next, construct a diagram of the problem, and then proceed to find the answer.

As Figure 7.2 shows, the force and the displacement are not in the same direction, but they make an angle of 60°. Because $\cos 60° = 0.5$, the expression of the work becomes:

$W = (F \cdot \cos \alpha) \cdot d =$

$(F \cdot \cos 60°) \cdot d = F \cdot d/2$

$W = 1,000 \text{ N} \cdot 1.8 \text{ m}/2 = 900 \text{ J} = 0.9 \text{ kJ}$

▶ Practice

1. Find the work done by a force of 300.0 N exerted on an object to lift it vertically to a distance of 240.0 cm above the ground.
2. Find the work done by the force of friction of 100 N on an object moving on a horizontal surface along a distance of 2 km.

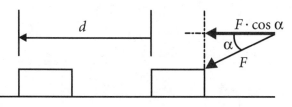

Figure 7.2

3. An object of mass 450 g moves along a horizontal surface with constant velocity due to a force that pulls the object (traction force). Find the work done by the net force and the force of friction over a distance of 2 m if the coefficient of kinetic friction is 0.6.
4. In practice problem 3, find the work done by the weight, and the work done by the force of friction.

▶ Power

Any amount of work done can be performed in different intervals of time, and that will have an effect on how we perceive the total work done. How can we take this into account? Imagine you are taking the stairs up to the second level of a building and you take your time to go up. You are in no hurry, and if you run up the stairs, you will experience more tiredness. So, the shorter time you take to go up the stairs, the more your muscles work. So, how can you characterize this situation? We must define a new quantity: *power*.

There are other units that you might encounter for power, but the one referred to most often is *horsepower* (hp).

1 horsepower =

550 feet · pounds/seconds = 745.7 watts

Another way to determine power is through the expression of the work: For a constant force acting along the direction of the displacement, the previous definition becomes:

$$P = \frac{W}{\Delta t} = \frac{F \cdot \cos 0° \cdot d}{\Delta t} = \frac{F \cdot d}{\Delta t} = F \cdot \bar{v}$$

where the time rate of change of displacement defines the average speed:

$$\frac{d}{\Delta t} = \bar{v}$$

$$\bar{v} = \frac{v + v_0}{2}$$

and v_0 is the initial speed, where v is the final speed.

Power

Power is proportional to the work performed on an object and inversely proportional to the time taken to perform the work:

$$P = \frac{W}{\Delta t}$$

P stands for power and Δt for the interval of time. The unit for power is called a *watt* and is equal to joules per second ($W = J/s$), in honor of James Watt, 1736–1819. One watt is the power needed to perform one joule of work in a time of 1 second.

Example

Consider a car of 1,500 kg starting from the stop light and accelerating for a distance of 25 m with an acceleration of 3.5 m/s². Calculate the average power generated by the force producing the acceleration.

Solution

First, check to see that the quantities are expressed in SI. Next, list the known data.

$m = 1,500 \text{ kg}$

$a = 3.5 \text{ m/s}^2$

$d = 25 \text{ m}$

$P = ?$

We can use the second expression of the power because we can determine the accelerating force and the average speed using Newton's second law for the first one, and we can use the equations of motion for the second quantity.

$F = m \cdot a = 1,500 \text{ kg} \cdot 3.5 \text{ m/s}^2 = 5.2 \cdot 10^3 \text{ N}$

Now, to find the average speed, although we are given displacement, we do not have the time, so we have to use the equations of motion (Lesson 3) to make the connection between average speed, acceleration, and displacement.

$$\bar{v} = \frac{v + v_0}{2} = \frac{a \cdot \Delta t + v_0}{2} = \frac{a \cdot \Delta t}{2}$$

By raising to the second power, we have:

$$v^2 = \frac{a^2 \cdot \Delta t^2}{4}$$

And we can also write the displacement as:

$$d = v_0 \cdot \Delta t + \frac{a \cdot \Delta t^2}{2} =$$

$$\frac{a \cdot \Delta t^2}{2} = \frac{2}{a} \cdot \left(\frac{a^2 \cdot \Delta t^2}{4} \right) = \frac{2}{a} \cdot \bar{v}^2$$

And then the expression for the average speed becomes:

$$\bar{v}^2 = \frac{ad}{2}$$

And the average speed is:

$$\bar{v} = \sqrt{\frac{a \cdot d}{2}} = \sqrt{3.5 \frac{\text{m}}{\text{s}^2} \cdot \frac{25}{2} \text{m}} = 6.6 \frac{\text{m}}{\text{s}}$$

We can now calculate the power done by the force of acceleration to be:

$$P = F \cdot \bar{v} = 5.25 \cdot 10^3 \, \text{N} \cdot 6.6 \, \frac{\text{m}}{\text{s}} = 35 \cdot 10^3 \, \text{watts}$$

▶ Practice

5. At a construction site, a plank of mass 425 kg is lifted to a height of 11.2 m above the ground by a constant force in 1.00 minute. The plank is lifted at a steady pace. Find the power needed to produce this displacement.

6. The same power is applied to two spinning wheels: One has a radius of 25 cm and the other has a radius of 10 cm. On which wheel is the applied force greater if they both describe a complete rotation in 30 s? The force on each wheel is always perpendicular to the radius as shown in Figure 7.3. This is similar to the construction of a bicycle with multiple speeds! Explain.

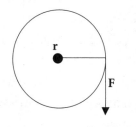

Figure 7.3

7. Consider two engines working the same amount of time. Can you conclude that one engine is doing twice the work if it is generating twice the power?

8. A regular light bulb has a power of 60 watts. If you are to give the number in horsepower, how much would you end up with?

▶ Kinetic Energy

One result of doing work on objects, as we have seen in the examples before, might be motion, or it might be change in position. So, how are we characterizing the difference between these two situations—between motion and change in position? When an object is accelerated or decelerated because of work performed on it, we will measure the energy of motion known as the *kinetic energy*. Consider an accelerating force (net force) that changes the way an object moves. According to Newton's second law:

$$F = m \cdot a$$

The force is acting over a distance d and along the displacement ($\alpha = 0°$), then the work is:

$$W = F \cdot d = m \cdot a \cdot d$$

From Lesson 3, we also know that:

$$v^2 - v_0^2 = 2 \cdot a \cdot d$$

Then multiplying both sides with the mass m:

$$m \cdot (v^2 - v_0^2) = m \cdot 2 \cdot a \cdot d$$

And then dividing by 2:

$$\frac{m \cdot (v^2 - v_0^2)}{2} = m \cdot a \cdot d$$

Or:

$$\frac{m \cdot v^2}{2} - \frac{m \cdot v_0^2}{2} = m \cdot a \cdot d$$

And again:

$$\frac{m \cdot v^2}{2} - \frac{m \cdot v_0^2}{2} = W$$

The kinetic energy of an object of mass m and speed v is defined by:

$$KE = \frac{m \cdot v^2}{2}$$

With the definition of kinetic energy, the expression of the work can also be written as:

$$KE - KE_0 = W$$

$$\Delta KE = W$$

This formula is called the *work-energy theorem* and expresses the fact that when a net external force does work on an object, the work is equal to the change in kinetic energy. This equation also defines the unit for kinetic energy, which is a joule, because the two quantities—work and the change in kinetic energy—are not only proportional but equal. Note that the work-energy theorem does not apply to individual forces but only to net external forces.

▶ Practice

9. If the initial kinetic energy is larger than the final kinetic energy, what significance does the minus sign have on the work? Explain briefly.
10. An object is slowing down to a final speed three times smaller than the initial speed. What is the ratio of the final and initial kinetic energies?
11. Is it possible for a small object to have a large kinetic energy? Explain briefly.
12. An object is moving with constant speed, overcoming friction. What is the work performed by the net force on the object?

13. An object is moving up on an inclined plane until it stops. Find the speed at the bottom of the plane if the work done on the object is $W = -(50 \cdot m)$ J, where m is the mass of the object.
14. An object is kicked and starts moving with a speed of 3.0 m/s on a surface with a coefficient of kinetic friction of 0.80. Find the distance over which the object will stop.

▶ Gravitational Potential Energy

Consider a body being launched up an inclined plane, and suppose the friction is so small that we can neglect it altogether. If one calculates the work done to raise the object on the inclined plane, one has to consider only the work done by the force along the direction of the plane. That is $-W \cdot \sin \alpha$, where α is the angle the inclined plane makes with the horizontal, and W is the weight of the object (the minus shows that although they are on the same axis, the displacement and the force are in opposite directions). To avoid confusion, we will use the expression of the weight with respect to mass: $W = m \cdot g$. Therefore, the force performing work is (see Figure 7.4):

$$-m \cdot g \cdot \sin \alpha$$

The gravitational potential energy of an object of mass m is defined by:

$$PE = m \cdot g \cdot h$$

where h is the distance from the surface of the earth that is considered zero potential energy.

And the displacement on the plane is $h/\sin \alpha$. Hence, the work done by the weight on the object is:

$$W = F \cdot d =$$

$$-m \cdot g \cdot \sin \alpha \cdot (h/\sin \alpha) = -m \cdot g \cdot h$$

We can also write this expression as:

$$W = 0 - m \cdot g \cdot h$$

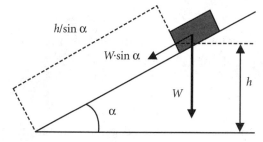

$h/\sin \alpha$

$W \cdot \sin \alpha$

W

h

α

Figure 7.4

Or:

$$W = -(m \cdot g \cdot h - 0) =$$

$$-(m \cdot g \cdot h - m \cdot g \cdot 0)$$

This helps us define a new form of energy that is not related to motion, or to speed, but to the position from the ground—*height* (h).

We can now rewrite the expression of the work as the negative of the change in potential energy:

$$W = -(m \cdot g \cdot h - m \cdot g \cdot h_0)$$

$$W = -(PE - PE_0)$$

$$W = -\Delta PE$$

In Figure 7.4, you can see that the same result can be obtained if you find the work done, by weight, on raising the object directly on the vertical:

$$W = m \cdot g \cdot h$$

In this case, the work performed is independent of the chosen path. This is called a *conservative force*. A conservative force is also defined as the force that determines zero work when it acts on a closed path. An example of a nonconservative force is friction.

Example

The first swing of a pendulum raises the ball at the end of a string 30.0 cm long at an angle of 60.0° with the vertical. Find the potential energy at the top of the swing if the mass of the ball is 0.25 kg.

Solution

The data given in the problem is in SI units. List the known data and draw a diagram of the problem (see Figure 7.5).

$$l = 30.0 \text{ cm}$$

$$\alpha = 60.0°$$

$$m = 0.25 \text{ kg}$$

$$PE = ?$$

Because the problem does not specify, the choice of the ground level is ours. So, we will consider 0 level as the position where the ball starts moving. At that

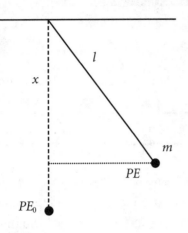

Figure 7.5

level, the potential energy is also 0: $PE_0 = 0$ J. The final potential energy will be given by the distance with respect to this ground level.

$$PE = m \cdot g \cdot h$$

From the diagram in Figure 7.5, we can see that the height of the ball with respect to the ground is $l - x$. So, we need to find x first and then final *potential energy* (PE).

$$x = l \cdot \cos \alpha$$

$$h = l - l \cdot \cos \alpha = l \cdot (1 - \cos \cdot \alpha)$$

$$PE = m \cdot g \cdot l \cdot (1 - \cos \alpha) = 37 \text{ J}$$

▶ Practice

15. An object has a potential energy relative to Earth of 1,200 J. If the potential energy reduces to 800.0 J by dropping for 20.0 m, find the mass and the weight of the object.

16. An object has been raised on an inclined plane free of friction to a distance *d* with respect to the bottom of the plane where the potential energy is 1,200 J. If the component of the weight along the plane is 600 N, find the distance *d*.

▶ Conservation of Mechanical Energy

The forms of energy discussed previously give the *mechanical energy* of an object and encompass both the energy of motion and the potential energy:

$$E = KE + PE$$

And considering the work-energy theorem discussed previously, we have:

$$W = \Delta KE$$

$$W = -\Delta PE$$

Then:

$$\Delta KE = -\Delta PE$$

$$KE - KE_0 = -(PE - PE_0)$$

And rearranging the terms so that each side contains only initial or final states, we write:

$$KE_0 + PE_0 = KE + PE$$

In other words, the initial and final mechanical energies are equal as long as there are no nonconservative forces in the process or if the work they perform is zero. This establishes the principle of *conservation of mechanical energy.*

Example

Consider an object falling freely from a height of 22 m and stopping on a cliff at a distance of 10 m from the starting point. Find out the speed of the object when it lands on the cliff.

Solution

All data is given in the SI units. Therefore, list the data and draw a diagram for this example.

$$h_0 = 22 \text{ m}$$

$$h = 22 \text{ m} - 10 \text{ m} = 12 \text{ m}$$

The total mechanical energy of an object remains constant provided that the net work done by the external nonconservative forces is zero.

$$E_{initial} = E_{final}$$

Because the object moved 100 m away from where it was released, it must be closer to the earth.

$v = ?$

And because this is a conservative process, the energy is conserved, and the mechanical energy at the top and at the time the object hits the cliff are equal. And finally, because the object is falling freely, it means that it started with zero speed:

$v_0 = 0 \text{ m/s}$

$m \cdot g \cdot h_0 + m \cdot v_0^2/2 = m \cdot g \cdot h + m \cdot v^2/2$

$m \cdot g \cdot h_0 = m \cdot g \cdot h + m \cdot v^2/2$

The mass can be canceled out through the entire expression:

$g \cdot h_0 = g \cdot h + v^2/2$

And we need to solve for v:

$v^2/2 = g \cdot h_0 - g \cdot h$

$v^2 = 2 \cdot g \cdot (h_0 - h)$

$v^2 = 2 \cdot g \cdot (22 - 12)$

$v = 14 \text{ m/s}$

▶ Practice

17. Consider a process in which the mechanical energy is conserved. What happens to the kinetic energy when the potential energy is increasing?

18. Does an increase of the kinetic energy of an object necessarily mean an increase of mechanical energy for that specific object?

19. An object is slowing down due to friction with the surface on which it is moving. In this case, is the total mechanical energy conserved? Explain briefly.

20. An object is placed on a kitchen table. What do you have to do in order to reduce the potential energy of the object? Explain briefly.

21. The first swing of a pendulum raises the ball at the end of a string 30.0 cm long at an angle of 60.0° with the vertical. Find the kinetic energy when the ball returns to the bottom of the swing if the mass of the ball is 0.25 kg and the ball is released at the maximum angle.

22. An object is thrown perfectly vertically from the surface of Earth, with an initial speed of 15.0 m/s. Assuming no air resistance and using the principle of conservation of mechanical energy, find the maximum height reached by the object.

23. A volleyball of mass of 450 g at 1.8 m above ground is served so that it has an initial velocity of 15 m/s directed at an angle of 60° above the horizontal. Find the kinetic, potential, and mechanical energies at the beginning of the trajectory.

24. In practice problem 23, assume there is no friction with air, and find the maximum height reached by the ball.

25. A 0.750 kg ball is dropped from rest at a point 0.80 m above the floor. There is no air resistance, and the floor is at zero potential energy. Find the potential and the mechanical energy at the highest point.

26. For practice problem 25, find the velocity of the ball when it reaches the floor.

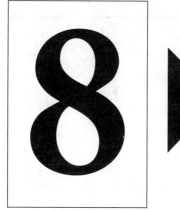

8 ▶ Uniform Rotational Motion

LESSON SUMMARY

In Lesson 2, we talked about motion in one dimension and introduced concepts such as displacement, speed and velocity, and acceleration. We will be following the same concepts, but in this case, for a circular trajectory. We will end the lesson by studying the centripetal force, acceleration, and the origins of both.

▶ Uniform Circular Motion

First, let us look at the new type of trajectory, a circle, and define some fundamental quantities. We will define uniform circular motion as the motion of an object traveling at a constant speed on a circular path. One rotation around the trajectory is called a *revolution*.

Uniform circular motion is the motion of an object traveling at a constant speed on a circular path.

▶ Practice

1. In a uniform circular motion, is the velocity constant also? Explain briefly.
2. Considering the answer to practice problem 1, will there be an acceleration associated with this motion? Explain briefly.
3. Is uniform circular motion a uniform linear motion also? Why?

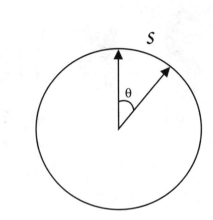

Figure 8.1

▶ Angular Displacement

What quantity can describe motion on this circular trajectory? In between the two positions shown in Figure 8.1, there is a distance, arc length, and an angle (revealed by the two radii). The angle described by an object moving around the circular trajectory will be called *angular displacement*. Also similar to the linear displacement, angular displacement has a positive and negative direction: The positive direction is the counterclockwise rotation, and the negative direction is the clockwise rotation.

When the angular displacement is small, we can determine the angle in *radians* as:

$$\theta = \frac{s}{r}$$

where *s* is the *arc length* and *r* is the *radius*.

The conversion factor between radians and degrees can be found if we think of 2π radians that are equivalent to 360°. Then:

$$2\pi \text{ radians} = 360°$$

$$1 \text{ radian} = 57.3°$$

Example

A rock at the end of a string is spun around in a circle of radius 0.50 m. Between two close instances, the arc length is 10.0 cm. Find the angular displacement in both radians and degrees.

Solution

First, convert the quantities to SI. Next, list the data and solve the problem.

$$r = 0.5 \text{ m}$$

$$s = 10 \text{ cm} = 10 \text{ cm} \cdot 1 \text{ m}/100 \text{ cm} = 0.1 \text{ m}$$

$$\theta = ?$$

$$\theta = \frac{s}{r} = \frac{0.1 \text{ m}}{0.5 \text{ m}} = 0.2 \text{ radians}$$

$$\theta = 0.2 \text{ radians} = 0.2 \text{ rad} \cdot \frac{57.3°}{1 \text{ rad}} = 11.5°$$

Practice

4. The angular displacement of a planet is 0.11 · 10^{-4} degrees per second. Find the angular displacement in one Earth year.

5. For the previous practice problem, find the displacement in a year if the radius is 149,600 km.

6. Figure 8.2 shows two different objects, at two different times, moving in a uniform circular motion. How does the angular displacement of the two objects compare?

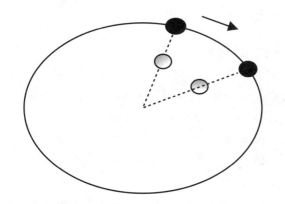

Figure 8.2

▶ Tangential Velocity

Although the uniform circular motion is characterized by constant speed, the direction of motion changes all the time, and therefore, the velocity will have different directions, as is shown in Figures 8.3 and 8.4. At two different times, the object occupies different positions on the circle. This defines the linear displacement, and by dividing it by time, we can determine the linear velocity. In Figure 8.3, we are shown two distant positions on the circle and the corresponding displacement, d, whereas in Figure 8.4, the displacement is very small, $d \to 0$.

As the two dotted lines show, the change in position modifies the direction of the displacement, and for a very small interval of time, $\Delta t \to 0$, displacement becomes tangent to the radius and so does the velocity. So, at every point on the trajectory, the velocity will be tangent to the circle pointing in the direction of motion and defining *tangential velocity*.

The magnitude of the average velocity (for uniform circular motion, this is also the value of the instantaneous speed) is given by:

$$v = s/\Delta t$$

And the direction is tangent to the trajectory at every point. For one revolution, the time is called a *period*, and its symbol is T. T is measured in seconds (s).

$$v = 2 \cdot \pi \cdot r/T$$

The inverse of the period is called the *frequency* and defines the number of rotations per second. Frequency is measured in s^{-1} or hertz (Hz), named

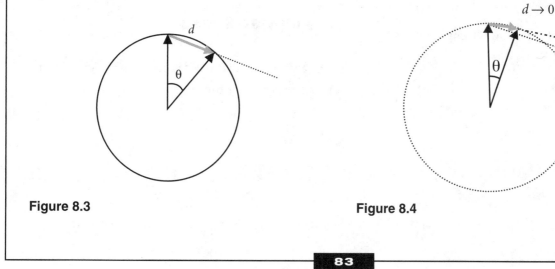

Figure 8.3   **Figure 8.4**

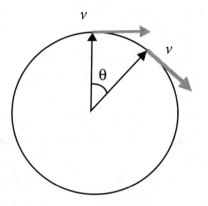

Figure 8.5

for Heinrich Rudolf Hertz (1857–1894), and its symbol is *f*.

Then the expression of the speed becomes:

$$v = 2 \cdot \pi \cdot r \cdot f$$

Example

As in the previous example, a rock at the end of a string is spun around in a circle of radius 0.50 m. Between two close instances, the arc length is 10.0 cm, and the time is 0.2 s. Find the average speed and the period.

Solution

First, convert the quantities to SI, list the data, and solve the problem.

$$r = 0.5 \, \text{m}$$

$$s = 10 \, \text{cm} = 10 \, \text{cm} \cdot 1 \, \text{m}/100 \, \text{cm} = 0.1 \, \text{m}$$

$$\Delta t = 0.2 \, \text{s}$$

$$v = ?$$

$$T = ?$$

First, we find the average speed:

$$v = s/\Delta t = 0.1 \, \text{m}/0.2 \, \text{s} = 0.5 \, \text{m/s}$$

And the period is:

$$v = 2 \cdot \pi \cdot r / T$$

$$T = 2 \cdot \pi \cdot r / v$$

$$T = 2 \cdot \pi \cdot 0.5 \, \text{m}/0.5 \, \text{m/s}$$

$$T = 6.3 \, \text{s}$$

▶ Practice

7. Calculate the period and frequency of the minute indicator on a mechanical clock.

8. Calculate the tangential speed of a merry-go-round of radius 6.0 m that completes a revolution in 50 s.

9. Find the average tangential speed of an object at rest on the surface of Earth (the radius of the earth is $6.4 \cdot 10^3 \, \text{m}$).

10. A turbine engine develops 259 *rotations per minute* (rpm). Find the period of the circular motion.

11. In practice problem 10, find the average speed if the turbine has a radius of 1.2 m.

▶ Angular Speed

The average *angular speed* is given by the angular displacement and the time interval.

$$\overline{\omega} = \frac{\Delta \theta}{\Delta t}$$

The unit of measurement for the angular velocity is *radian per second*.

If we consider an object moving in a uniform circular motion with a speed v, then during one period, the object moves around a circle once and the average angular speed is:

$$\bar{\omega} = \frac{2 \cdot \pi}{\Delta t} = \frac{2 \cdot \pi \cdot r}{r \cdot \Delta t}$$

So if we consider $\Delta t = T$:

$$\bar{\omega} = \frac{v \cdot T}{r \cdot \Delta t} = \frac{v \cdot T}{r \cdot T}$$

$$\bar{\omega} = \frac{v}{r}$$

And because the object describes equal angles in equal times, then the average acceleration and the instantaneous acceleration are equal:

$$\omega = \bar{\omega}$$

$$\omega = \frac{v}{r}$$

Considering the expressions in the previous section:

$$\omega = \frac{v}{r} = \frac{2 \cdot \pi \cdot r / T}{r}$$

$$\omega = \frac{2 \cdot \pi}{T}$$

$$\omega = 2 \cdot \pi \cdot f$$

Example

Consider a couple of pieces of paper on a spinning 45.0 rpm record, one at a distance 10.0 cm from the center, and the other at 5.00 cm. Find the angular speed and tangential speed for each of the pieces.

Solution

The data in the problem requires conversion to SI.

$1 \text{ rpm} = 1 \text{ rotation}/60 \text{ s}$

$45 \text{ rpm} = 45 \text{ rotations}/60 \text{ s} = .75 \text{ rotations/s}$

$T = 1/.75 \text{ s} = 1.33 \text{ s}$

$r_1 = 5.00 \text{ cm} = 0.05 \text{ m}$

$r_2 = 10.0 \text{ cm} = 0.1 \text{ m}$

$\omega = ?$

$v = ?$

For the piece that is closest to the center:

$v_1 = 2 \cdot \pi \cdot r_1 / T$

$v_1 = 0.075\pi \cdot \text{m/s} = 0.24 \text{ m/s}$

$v_2 = 2 \cdot \pi \cdot r_2 / T$

$v_2 = 0.15\,\pi \cdot \text{m/s} = 0.47 \text{ m/s}$

$\omega = 2 \cdot \pi / T = 4.7 \text{ radians/s}$

▶ Practice

12. Consider an object on a rotating platform. When you increase the position of the object relative to the axis of rotation, is the tangential speed or the angular speed of the object changing? Explain briefly.

13. When you increase the angular speed of a rotating object, is the period increasing or decreasing?

14. When you increase the angular speed of a rotating object, is the frequency increasing or decreasing?

▶ Centripetal Force and Acceleration

Let us review the concepts learned: For uniform circular motion, although the speed and angular speed are constant, the velocity is not because the direction of the object constantly changes. In this case, an acceleration associated with the motion can be defined.

Similar to the determination in the previous paragraph regarding the direction of the tangential velocity, we can argue that the change in direction for a finite interval of time results in an acceleration, as shown in Figure 8.6. The acceleration is directed toward the final velocity vector that, although equal in absolute value with the initial vector, is definitely in a different direction.

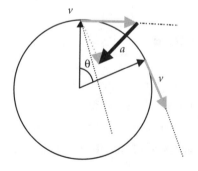

Figure 8.6

For small intervals of time, the displacement is very small and the two vectors—initial and final velocity—are also in proximity. The difference between the two vectors once again determines the vector acceler-

ation, which approaches a direction perpendicular to the initial velocity vector. The acceleration vector points toward the center of the circle, as can be seen in the inset of Figure 8.7.

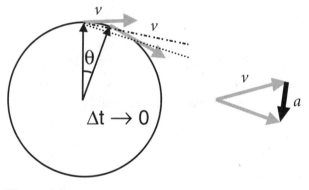

Figure 8.7

The two acceleration vectors look different in these two figures. Their direction is different, as is the size. This last difference is due to the time interval, which is different in the two figures: Larger time has passed between the two positions for the first figure. The acceleration defined by these two figures due to the change in the direction and directed toward the center of the ciruclar motion is called *centripetal acceleration* and is due to the curving of the trajectory and umcompensated forces acting on the object. The corresponding force is called the *centripetal force*.

As a consequence of the change in direction and the variation of the velocity of the object, the centripetal acceleration can be expressed as:

$$a_c = v^2/r$$

And then the centripetal force is:

The centripetal force is the net force required to keep an object moving with speed v on a circular path of radius r. The direction of F_c is along the radius and toward the center of the circle.

$$F_c = m \cdot a_c$$

$$F_c = m \cdot v^2/r$$

And using the relationship established between angular and tangential speeds:

$$F_c = m \cdot a_c = m \cdot (\omega \cdot r)^2/r = m \cdot \omega^2 \cdot r$$

$$F_c = m \cdot \omega^2 \cdot r$$

Example

Find the centripetal acceleration and force exerted on a 1,500 kg car taking a curve at a speed of 60 mi/h if the curvature of the road has a radius of 50 m.

Solution

First, list the data and convert to SI because we have different units for the same quantities. Then, set the equations and solve for the unknown.

$$m = 1,500 \text{ kg}$$

$$v = 60 \text{ mi/h} = 60 \cdot 1,609 \text{ m}/3,600 \text{ s} = 27 \text{ m/s}$$

$$r = 50 \text{ m}$$

$$a_c = ?$$

$$F_c = ?$$

The curve is part of a circle, so at the change of direction, a centripetal acceleration and force will be developed by the change in velocity even if the car keeps running at the same speed.

To determine the first unknown, we have the following expression:

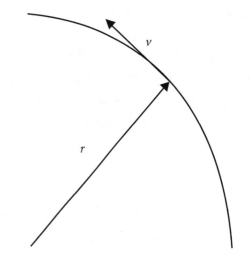

Figure 8.8

$$a_c = v^2/r$$

and replacing the tangential speed and the radius, we get:

$$a_c = (27 \text{ m/s})^2/(50 \text{ m})$$

$$a_c = 15 \text{ m/s}^2$$

And for the second unknown:

$$F_c = m \cdot v^2/r$$

Or:

$$F_c = m \cdot a_c$$

$$F_c = 1{,}500 \text{ kg} \cdot 15 \text{ m/s}^2 = 22{,}500 \text{ N}$$

▶ Practice

15. An Earth satellite rotates with the period of Earth. Find the angular speed and the tangential speed. Consider the distance to the satellite from the center of Earth to be 6,380 km.

16. In practice problem 15, find the centripetal acceleration and the centripetal force on the satellite if the mass is 6,000 kg.

17. Two objects with masses m and $2 \cdot m$ are connected through a string and rotate in a circle together at the same distance from the center. How does the angular speed of the two objects compare, and how does the centripetal force of the two objects compare?

18. An object at the end of a string of length 50 cm is rotated in a uniform circular motion with 80 rpms. Find the frequency, the period of this motion, and the centripetal acceleration.

19. For practice problem 18, find the centripetal force and the tension in the string at the top and the bottom of the trajectory (the object is rotated in a vertical motion). The object has a mass of 1 kg.

Rotational Equilibrium

LESSON SUMMARY

In previous chapters, we have introduced the idea of mechanical equilibrium that refers to objects with zero acceleration and net external force. Now we will approach a more complex system, a rigid object that has constraints that do not permit a linear motion but allow circular motion. We will define *moment of inertia* and *torque inertia*, and we will apply the conditions of equilibrium when rotational motion occurs in different systems.

▶ Rotational Inertia

Similar to the linear motion where we defined inertia, an object rotating around a fixed axis will keep this motion unless acted upon by an external influence. The same will happen with an object at rest: It will keep the state of rest unless acted upon.

An object continues to stay at rest or move in a uniform circular motion as long as there is no external influence to change that motion. This property is called *rotational inertia*.

Whereas mass is a measure of linear inertia, the measure of rotational inertia is the *moment of inertia*, or *I*. This quantity, as inertia, is proportional to the mass of the object but is also related to how the mass is distributed around the axis of rotation. The same object rotating around two different axes will resist rotation differently, and therefore have a different moment of inertia.

Note that the moment of inertia depends on the distribution of mass around an axis. The further the mass is from the axis, the more rotational inertia the object has and the harder it is to change the state of current motion. In this chapter, we will address the behavior of *rigid objects*. These are objects that will keep their shape and form while under external influence.

Example

If you consider a metal rod or a wooden dowel of mass *m* and length *L* rotating in one of the two situations shown by Figure 9.1, you will have different responses to rotation.

Solution

In this figure, the rod rotates around the axis passing through the middle of the rod, halfway between the ends. In this case, the moment of inertia can be calculated as shown to be $I = m \cdot L^2/12$.

If we consider now an axis passing through the end of the rod, as shown in Figure 9.2, the moment of

$$I = m \cdot L^2/12$$

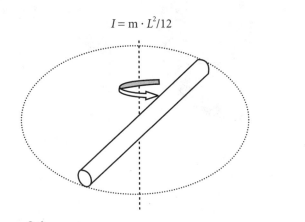

Figure 9.1

inertia can be calculated and the result is larger: $I = m \cdot L^2/3$, hence it is harder to start rotating the object or stop the object if it is in rotation when the axis of rotation is as shown in Figure 9.2.

Other useful expressions for the moment of inertia are shown in Figures 9.3 through 9.6.

$$I = m \cdot L^2/3$$

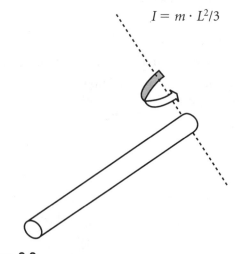

Figure 9.2

diameter of the ball. Does the ball start to spin around its own axis?

Solution

There is no data, so no conversion to SI is necessary.

$$F = -F$$

Net τ = ?

Because the line of action passes through the center of rotation, any thing perpendicular to it from the center would be zero. Hence, there is zero lever arm and zero torque for each of the forces.

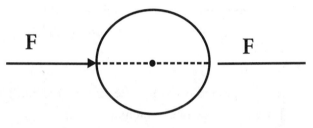

Figure 9.13

Net $F = F + (-F) = 0\,N$

Net $\tau = F \cdot 0 + F \cdot 0 = 0\,N \cdot m$

Example

Consider the seesaw again, now with two children: One is 35 kg and the other 42 kg. Is this system in rotational equilibrium? The two sides of the seesaw are of equal length and the total length is 280 cm. If the seesaw is not in equilibrium, what has to be changed so that it equilibrates (keep masses constant)? Consider the seesaw to be of negligible weight.

Solution

Convert the quantities to SI. Next, draw a diagram and find the equations.

$$m_1 = 35\,kg$$

$$m_2 = 42\,kg$$

$$L = 280\,cm = 2.8\,m$$

Net F = ?

Net τ = ?

The net external force is the sum of the two weights and the normal force. Because the object does not have a linear motion, the three cancel each other out.

Net $F = W_1 + W_2 - N = 0\,N$

Weight W_1 determines a positive torque (CCW), whereas the second weight determines a negative torque.

The weight is perpendicular on the seesaw in both cases, so the lever arm is equal to half of the length of the seesaw.

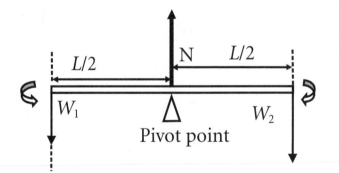

Figure 9.14

$$\tau_1 = F \cdot l = W_1 \cdot l =$$
$$m_1 \cdot g \cdot l = m_1 \cdot g \cdot L/2$$

$$\tau_2 = -F \cdot l = -W_2 \cdot l =$$
$$-m_2 \cdot g \cdot l = -m_2 \cdot g \cdot L/2$$

Net $\tau = \tau_1 + \tau_2 =$

$\quad m_1 \cdot g \cdot L/2 - m_2 \cdot g \cdot L/2 =$

$\quad (m_1 - m_2) \cdot g \cdot L/2 = -96\,\text{N} \cdot m$

Net $\tau = -96\,\text{N} \cdot m$

The minus sign tells us that the seesaw rotates clockwise, hence the system is not in rotational equilibrium.

In order for the seesaw to remain in rotational equilibrium, the net torque has to be zero. Although we cannot change the mass of the two children, we can change their position on the seesaw.

$\tau_1 = F \cdot x = W_1 \cdot x = m_1 \cdot g \cdot x$

$\tau_2 = -F \cdot (L - x) = -W_2 \cdot (L - x) =$

$\quad -m_2 \cdot g \cdot (L - x)$

Net $\tau = \tau_1 + \tau_2 =$

$\quad m_1 \cdot g \cdot x - m_2 \cdot g \cdot (L - x) =$

$\quad [m_1 \cdot x - m_2 \cdot (L - x)] \cdot g = 0\,\text{N} \cdot m$

And we can solve for the unknown, x:

$m_1 \cdot x - m_2 \cdot (L - x) = 0$

$(m_1 + m_2) \cdot x - m_2 \cdot L = 0$

$(m_1 + m_2) \cdot x = m_2 \cdot L$

$x = [m_2/(m_1 + m_2)] \cdot L$

$x = 1.5\,m$

The smaller weight has to have a longer lever arm to equilibrate the torque exerted by the second, larger weight.

$x = [m_2/(m_1 + m_2)] \cdot L = 1.53\,m > L/2$

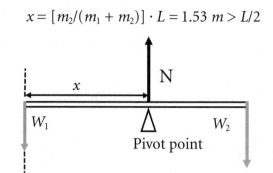

Figure 9.15

▶ Practice

14. Both torque and mechanical work are equal to the product of a force and a distance. Are they different quantities? Why or why not? Explain briefly.

15. Two people on each side of a door push at the same angle and with the same force on the door. Is it possible for one of them to be able to push the door against the other person?

16. A uniform plank of mass $m = 20$ kg is supported as shown in Figure 9.16. Why isn't the weight of the plank and its corresponding normal rotating the plank?

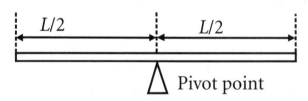

Figure 9.16

17. On a construction site, it is hoped that the plank (shown in Figure 9.17) of mass 8 kg will remain in equilibrium. Based on the diagram and data given, can you determine if a rotational equilibrium can be established? Use $g = 9.8$ m/s².

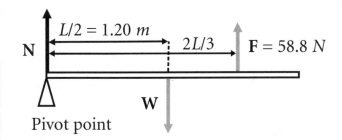

Figure 9.17

18. Is it possible for the system in Figure 9.18 to be in rotational equilibrium? The mass of the object is 2 kg, and its position on the board is fixed. The board is 2.2 m long, and the object is 0.3 m away from the pivot point.

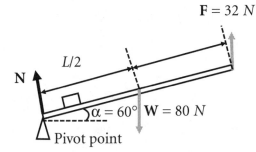

Figure 9.18

10 ▶ Properties of Matter

LESSON SUMMARY

Previous lessons have concentrated on a field of physics that studies the mechanical behavior of rigid objects. The objects of study were found in a solid state, they were rigid (of fixed shape and volume), and they were acted on by forces. In this lesson, we will study different phases: in particular, liquid and gas phases. And we will define basic concepts such as density and pressure. We will also study why some objects float and others don't, and how pressure spreads in a fluid.

▶ Phases of Matter

The previous chapters analyzed one of the states that matter can be found in—the solid phase. At an atomic level, the solid state is defined by a clear structure where atoms and ions occupy rather fixed positions. Solid objects have a clear shape and volume. Although they are characterized by some elastic properties, it takes different strengths to change the shape of a solid object. This strength depends on the internal bonding of the particles.

We will now look at some basic characteristics of two other phases of matter—the liquid phase and gas phase. Liquids and gases together are also known as fluids.

Pressure measures the force exerted perpendicularly per unit area.

$$P = \frac{Force}{Area}$$

If the force is due to the weight of the liquid, then the definition above becomes:

$$P = \frac{Weight}{Area} = \frac{m \cdot g}{Area}$$

▶ Pressure

Analogy is a powerful tool in the world of science. Remember, we defined forces that deal with mechanical interaction and cause static and dynamic effects. We also defined torque as the analog of force, in cases where rotational motion (instead of linear motion) was a possible outcome of interaction. The objects of interaction were solid objects of definite shape. In the case of liquids, the shape is no longer a constraint: Depending on the container, a liquid can change its shape and its effect on the surrounding medium. What do we mean by that? Imagine this case: two liters of water (remember, liter is a unit for volume) divided equally into two containers of shapes as shown in Figure 10.1. Do you think they have the same interaction with the surface of support?

The answer is no because although each liter of water will act with the same weight on the surface of support, but the area is different in the two cases. If a

person wears sneakers and then changes into high heels, the mark left on a soft asphalt will be different. It will be deeper when the person is on heels even though the weight of the person did not change. Although the weight was the same, the surface area of support is smaller with the heels, and therefore, the effect on the support surface area is larger. The quantity measuring the force and the effect on the surface on which it acts is called *pressure.*

There are many units for pressure, but the SI unit is N/m². Different fields of application deal with different ranges of pressure and with different measuring instruments. Therefore, applications have imposed different scales. Some of the most used scales are the pascal (Pa), the milibar (mb), the inch of mercury or milimeter of mercury (mmHg), and the pound per square inch (PSI).

Example

At sea level, the average atmospheric pressure is 760 mmHg. Find the SI value of this pressure and in inch Hg.

Solution

This problem requires us to convert pressure to SI units.

$$P = 760.0 \text{ mm Hg}$$

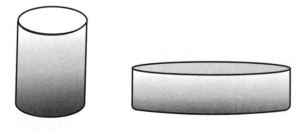

Figure 10.1

$$1 \text{ atm} = 101{,}325 \text{ } N/m^2$$

$$1 \text{ mb} = 1 \text{ hPa (hecto pascal)} = 100 \text{ } Pa$$

$$1 \text{ } in \text{ } Hg = 33.8639 \text{ } mb = 3{,}386.39 \text{ } Pa$$

$$1 \text{ } mmHg = 133.32 \text{ } Pa$$

$$1 \text{ } PSI = 6.895 \text{ } kPa$$

$$P = 760 \text{ mmHg} \cdot \frac{133.32 \text{ Pa}}{1 \text{ mmHg}} =$$

$$101{,}323 \text{ Pa} = 101{,}323 \text{ N}/m^2$$

$$P = 760 \text{ mmHg} \cdot \frac{133.32 \text{ Pa}}{1 \text{ mmHg}} \cdot$$

$$\frac{1 \text{ in Hg}}{3{,}386.39 \text{ Pa}} = 29.92 \text{ in Hg}$$

▶ Practice

1. Consider two glass cylinders with diameters d and $\frac{3}{4} d$ and the same quantity of liquid in each. How does the pressure at the bottom of the cylinders compare? Show calculations.

2. Consider a bathroom scale. If you step up on the scale, you are able to measure your weight converted to mass. If you lift a foot, is that going to change the final reading?

3. A high-vacuum pump can pump down to 10^{-3} mb. Express the value of this low pressure in mmHg and in SI.

4. A one-leg table has a mass of 25 kg, and the surface of support is a rectangle 32 cm by 24 cm. If you set the table for dinner, the mass of the table will be increased by $\frac{3}{4}$. Find the pressure on the floor exerted by the table set for dinner.

5. A hydraulic press operates at 1,500 PSI. Convert this pressure to SI units.

▶ Density

As pressure takes the place of the simple forces acting on an area, what is similar to mass in the case of fluids? Mass is a quantity associated with matter, but at the same amount of mass, some objects occupy a lot of space. In fact, they will take all that you give them in the case of gases; some other objects will take very little space. The quantity that measures the amount of mass relative to the space occupied is called *density*.

As with pressure, density can be measured in many different units. The SI unit is kg/m³. Other units for density are l/cm³, g/m³, lb/ft³, oz/in³, and lb/gal. The device used to measure density is a specific gravity bottle, called a *pyknometer*. The most commonly known density is for water at standard atmospheric pressure and temperature of 4° C: 1,000 kg/m³, or 1 kilogram of water occupying a volume of 1 liter.

Atomically, the explanation of different densities associated with different materials and phases is the arrangement of atoms in the structure of the material. Solids are more compact, presenting a clear structure, and their atoms and ions are closer to each other amounting to a larger mass in a given volume. This structure is mostly missing in liquids and is not existent in gases, where particles are freely moving, hence, they can occupy large volumes.

Example

The Malibu Maxx's cargo space, according to GM data from 2003, is about 50% larger than other midsize sedans, and it is calculated to be 22.8 cubic feet. If the air density is 1.2 kg/m^3, what is the quantity of air occupying that space?

Solution

The first step is to convert all data into SI.

$V = 22.8 \text{ ft}^3 = 22.8 \text{ ft}^3 \cdot$
$\quad 0.0283168 \text{ m}^3/1 \text{ ft}^3 = 0.65 \text{ m}^3$

$\rho = 1.2 \text{ kg/m}^3$

$m = ?$

$\rho = m/V$

$1.2 \text{ kg/m}^3 = m/0.65 \text{ m}^3$

$m = 1.2 \text{ kg/m}^3 \cdot 0.65 \text{ m}^3 = 0.78 \text{ kg}$

$m = 0.78 \text{ kg}$

▶ Practice

6. A copper kitchen container has a circumference diameter of 9 inches and a height of 5 inches. Find the mass of the container if it were filled with water ($\rho = 1,000$ kg/m^3). We will assume that the walls are so thin, the empty container has a negligible mass.

7. Two objects have the same mass, but the volume of the first object is $2\frac{3}{4}$ larger than that of the second object. They both are cylindrical in shape and have the same size circumference. Find the ratio of the densities.

8. For practice problem 7, find the ratio of the pressures that the two objects exert on the support surface if they are both cylinders of equal height.

▶ Pressure and Depth

Let's begin with the definition of *pressure* and then isolate a cylindrical volume inside a container filled with a liquid as shown in Figure 10.2. The liquid is at rest and is occupying a space between levels h_1 and h_2 inside the water. The volume considered has a certain

The pressure exerted by a fluid at rest is proportional to the height or depth of the fluid column and the density of the liquid.

$$P = \rho \cdot (h_2 - h_1) \cdot g$$

mass, and the pressure at the bottom of the column is due to the weight of the liquid. Hence, we can calculate the pressure of this volume of liquid.

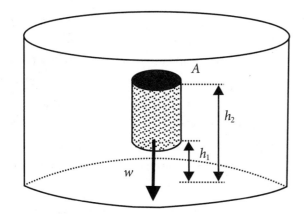

Figure 10.2

$$P = \frac{Weight}{Area} = \frac{m \cdot g}{A}$$

$$P = \frac{(\rho \cdot V) \cdot g}{A}$$

$$V = \left[\rho \cdot (h_2 - h_1) \cdot A\right]$$

$$P = \frac{\left[\rho \cdot (h_2 - h_1) \cdot A\right] \cdot g}{A} = \rho \cdot (h_2 - h_1) \cdot g$$

If we consider a pressure exerted upon a fluid (air pressure at the surface of a lake for instance), then the variation of the pressure with depth is:

$$P = P_0 + \rho \cdot (h_2 - h_1) \cdot g$$

Where P_0 is the pressure of the air and the second term, $\rho \cdot (h_2 - h_1) \cdot g$, is the contribution of the liquid.

In addition to this depth dependence, we have to add that at the same level in a fluid, the pressure is the same in all directions as shown in Figure 10.3. For example, an object floating in a liquid will be exerted with a pressure P in all directions.

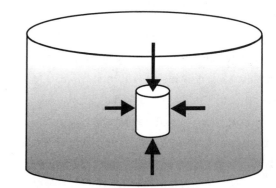

Figure 10.3

Example

Lake Baikal in Russia has a depth of 5,371 ft. Find the pressure exerted on the bottom of the lake by the water layer.

Solution

Convert first into SI units and then solve for the unknown: pressure.

$$h = 5,371 \text{ ft}$$

$$\rho = 1,000 \text{ kg/m}^3$$

The upward force exerted by a fluid on an object immersed in the fluid is equal to the weight of the displaced fluid.

$P = ?$

$h = 5,371 \text{ ft} =$
    $5,371 \text{ ft} \cdot 0.3048 \text{ m}/1 \text{ ft} = 1,637 \text{ m}$

$P = \rho \cdot h \cdot g = 1,000 \text{ kg/m}^3 \cdot 1,637 \text{ m} \cdot$
    $9.8 \text{ m/s}^2 = 16,040 \text{ N/m}^2 = 1.604 \cdot 10^4 \text{ N/m}^2$

$P = 1.604 \cdot 10^7 \text{ N/m}^2$

▶ Practice

9. Calculate the pressure at the bottom of the Pacific Ocean's Marianas Trench (35,810 feet depth and 1,000 kg/m³). What can you say when you compare this with atmospheric pressure?

10. A swimmer plunges deeper and deeper into the water. Is the pressure he or she experiences constant or not? Explain briefly.

11. The *CRC Handbook of Chemistry and Physics* says the density of cooking oil is 0.918 g/cm³. If you have a glass filled half with water and half with oil, what is the liquid(s) pressure at the bottom of the glass? The glass is 220 mm tall.

12. For the information in practice problem 11, what is the total pressure at the top of the water layer? Consider atmospheric pressure at the top of the oil.

▶ Archimedes's Principle

Recall that in mechanics, we defined the condition of equilibrium as referring to the net force on the object being zero. For an object to be at rest on a table, gravity has to be counteracted by another force, an equal and opposite force, and we call that *reaction force*. In a similar way, you can relate to the new concept we will discuss here: *buoyancy*. When an object is immersed in a fluid and floats at some level, the weight will act as if weighted down and there is no other force to be noted, or is there? Well, a piece of wood will not sink. And that is because the wood is pushed up by a force. We call this phenomena buoyancy. How large is the force of buoyancy? This is the subject of *Archimedes's principle*.

The force of buoyancy is usually symbolized by B and according to the principle, the expression is:

$$B = \rho_{fluid} \cdot V_{fluid} \cdot g$$

Because in some cases, the object floats inside the liquid, the volume displaced is equal to the object's volume: $V_{liquid} = V_{object}$. In other cases, the object floats at the surface of the liquid, and only part of the volume of the object will have to be taken into account.

Example

A totally submerged object floats in water as shown in Figure 10.4. Find the ratio of the object's density to the density of water.

Pascal's Principle

Any pressure applied to a static fluid is transmitted equally in all directions through the liquid.

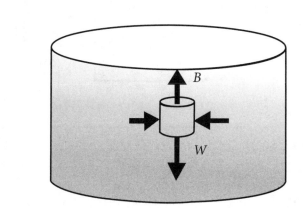

Figure 10.4

Solution

First, let's show the forces acting on this object. The horizontal forces determined by the surrounding pressure will cancel each other out because at equal levels, the pressure is the same, and therefore, the forces will be the same. The object floats inside the liquid, so the weight and the buoyancy force are also equal. Using Archimedes's principle, we can write the equation for the vertical forces.

$$W - B = 0$$

$$W - B = m \cdot g - \rho_{liquid} \cdot V_{liquid} \cdot g = 0$$

$$m = \rho_{object} \cdot V_{object}$$

$$0 = \rho_{object} \cdot V_{obejct} \cdot g - \rho_{liquid} \cdot V_{liquid} \cdot g$$

$$V_{object} = V_{liquid}$$

$$0 = (\rho_{object} - \rho_{liquid}) \cdot V_{liquid} \cdot g$$

$$0 = (\rho_{object} - \rho_{liquid})$$

$$\frac{\rho_{object}}{\rho_{liquid}} = 1$$

▶ Practice

13. Helium gas has a density of 0.18 g/l. Based on Archimedes's principle, can you determine what a helium balloon will do in air? Make sure you draw a diagram showing the forces acting on the balloon.

14. A wooden board has a density of 600.0 kg/m³, and it floats in water such that only part of the board is submerged. Find the depth to which the board is submerged if it has a rectangular shape of 2.00 × 3.00 × 1.00 meters.

15. In a shallow pond, an aluminum fountain is placed such that $\frac{3}{4}$ of its height is immersed in water. What is the resultant force per volume acting on the fountain? Density is 2,700 kg/m³.

▶ Pascal's Principle

As we mentioned at the beginning of this lesson, pressure is exerted in all directions in the same manner. Therefore, when the pressure changes, it will change in all directions and is also transmitted through the liquid. The manner of transmission constitutes the subject of *Pascal's principle*.

This phenomenon is very important in the way hydraulic presses function: A liquid transmits pressure between two mobile pistons reducing, the forces necessary to counteract a weight (see the following example).

Example

The diagram in Figure 10.5 shows a hydraulic press used in a car shop to lift cars. An automobile is placed on the large area of the press. The automobile has a mass of 1,540 kg, and the two sides of the press have a diameter of 25 and 15 cm, respectively. Find how much force will need to be applied on the right piston to counteract the weight of the car.

Solution

First, we convert the data into SI units. Next, complete the diagram with the forces and pressure acting on the liquid, and then solve the problem.

$$25 \text{ cm} = 25 \text{ cm} \cdot 1 \text{ m}/100 \text{ cm} = 0.25 \text{ m}$$

$$15 \text{ cm} = 15 \text{ cm} \cdot 1 \text{ m}/100 \text{ cm} = 0.15 \text{ cm}$$

$$m = 1,540 \text{ kg}$$

$$F = ?$$

According to Pascal's principle, the pressure exerted by the automobile spreads equally in the liquid, and it will reach the piston on the left-hand side of the press.

$$P_1 = P_2$$

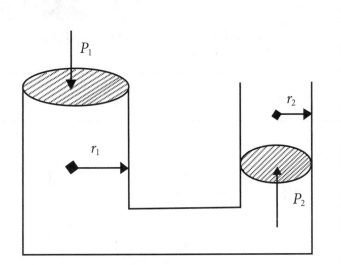

Figure 10.5

The pressure exerted by the car is:

$$P_1 = \frac{Weight}{Area} = \frac{m \cdot g}{A}$$

$$P_1 = \frac{1,540 \text{ kg} \cdot 9.8 \text{ m/s}^2}{A}$$

The platform on which the car rests pushes down on a cylindrical piston of radius 0.25 m:

$$A_1 = \pi \cdot r^2 = \pi \cdot (0.25 \text{ m})^2 = 0.196 \text{ m}^2$$

The piston on which the counteraction is applied is also a cylindrical piston of radius 0.15 m:

$$A_2 = \pi \cdot r^2 = \pi \cdot (0.15 \text{ m})^2 = 0.071 \text{ m}^2$$

The pressures exerted on the pistons are:

$$P_1 = \frac{1,540 \text{ kg} \cdot 9.8 \text{ m/s}^2}{0.196 \text{ m}^2}$$

$$P_2 = \frac{F}{0.071 \text{ m}^2}$$

And now we can solve for the unknown force.

$$\frac{1,540 \text{ kg} \cdot 9.8 \text{ m/s}^2}{0.196 \text{ m}^2} = \frac{F}{0.071 \text{ m}^2}$$

$$F = \frac{1,540 \text{ kg} \cdot 9.8 \text{ m/s}^2 \cdot 0.071 \text{ m}^2}{0.196 \text{ m}^2} = 5,467 \text{ N}$$

Compare this force with the weight of the car:

$$W = 1,540 \text{ kg} \cdot 9.8 \text{ m/s}^2 = 15,092 \text{ N}$$

$$W = 1,540 \text{ kg} \cdot 9.8 \text{ m/s}^2 = 15,092 \text{ N}$$

▶ Practice

16. In a hydraulic press, a ratio of the radii of the pistons of $r_1/r_2 = 3$ will decrease by how much the force that counteracts the weight on the larger piston? Show calculations.

17. The diagram in Figure 10.6 shows a hydraulic press used in a car shop to lift cars. An automobile is placed on the large area of the press. The automobile has a mass of 1,540 kg and the two sides of the press have a diameter of 25 and 15 cm, respectively. In the process of raising the car, the left piston lifts 1.85 m. Find how much the right piston has dropped.

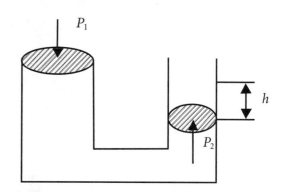

Figure 10.6

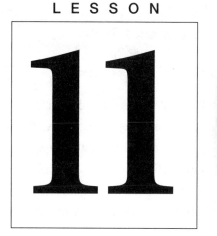

11 ▶ Temperature and Heat

LESSON SUMMARY

In this lesson, we will shift our attention from forces to energy, and we will learn about heat as a form of energy, characterized by temperature. We will also discuss the various types of heat transfer between objects, and the effect of heat transfer on solids, that is, *thermal expansion*.

▶ Temperature and Temperature Scales

Compared to simpler quantities such as distance and mass, temperature is more difficult to explain because it is more abstract. It's not as visible or tangible a measurement as is mass. All things constant, the larger the object, the more the mass, or volume; that is, the larger the size of the cube, the greater the volume. Temperature, on the other hand, characterizes a state of the matter, and a thermometer placed in contact with an object at different times can show different values although the object itself remains the same. Temperature measures the motion of the particles in the matter, and we will learn about this dependence later in the book. An increase in the speed of motion produces an increase in the temperature.

Historically, only a few temperature scales have been defined and adopted, the most common ones being the Celsius, or centigrade scale, and the Fahrenheit scale. Both of these scales depend on some reference points. The Celsius scale defines 0° C as the temperature where water freezes at normal atmospheric pressure, and defines 100° C as the boiling point of water. One one-hundredth of this interval is called a *Celsius degree*. As you can see, the scale was defined taking into consideration a specific substance—water and its properties at two standard points (0 and 100).

The Fahrenheit scale considers the same specific substance, but the standard points were assigned at the values of 32 (freezing) and 212 (boiling). So, not only does the Fahrenheit scale have an offset with respect to Celsius, it's not a centigrade (or 100-grade) scale (212 − 32 = 180). Therefore, the conversion between the two is not through a conversion factor but is a linear dependence.

If we call the Celsius temperature $t(°C)$ and the Fahrenheit temperature $t(°F)$, then, as we said, there is an offset between the two and a difference in the degrees. The Celsius degree is larger than the Fahrenheit degree, for example, 100 degrees Celsius equals 180 degrees Fahrenheit.

$$t(°F) = \frac{9}{5}t(°C) + 32$$

In order to eliminate the dependence on the specific substance and standard points, a more universal scale is needed. The result of that search is the absolute Kelvin scale, and its definition is based on empirical observation of the temperature dependence of the pressure of a gas at a constant volume. By lowering the temperature of a gas, the pressure is shown to decrease linearly. The pressure cannot be measured for very low temperatures where the gas liquefies, but if we extrapolate the data, we can obtain the point where the pressure becomes zero.

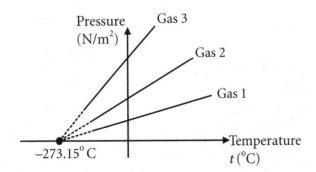

Figure 11.1

This point is called the *zero absolute temperature*, and the scale defined is Kelvin temperature scale. We can think about the Kelvin scale as an offset of the Celsius scale by −273.15 degrees; hence, the conversion between the two scales is stated simply as:

$$T(K) = t(°C) + 273.15$$

When we talk about the state of an object, we say the temperature is so many degrees Celsius (°C) or Fahrenheit (°F). When we talk about a process, a process whereby temperature increases or decreases by a value, then one says the temperature changed by so many Celsius or Fahrenheit degrees.

Example

Find the conversion from Fahrenheit to Kelvin scale. Find the value of 32° F in Kelvin degrees and check your work.

Solution

We have already determined that the conversion between Fahrenheit and Celsius is:

$$t(°F) = \frac{9}{5}t(°C) + 32$$

We can use this equation to solve for $t(°C)$ as a function of $t(°F)$ and then use the result in $T(K)$.

$$t(°F) - 32 = \frac{9}{5}t(°C)$$

$$\frac{5}{9} \cdot [t(°F) - 32] = t(°C)$$

With this expression, we go back to $T(K)$ as a function of $t(°C)$.

$$T(K) = \frac{5}{9} \cdot [t(°F) - 32] + 273.15$$

$$t(°F) = 32° F$$

Heat will flow freely from a high-temperature object to a low-temperature object because of the difference in temperature.

$$T(K) = \frac{5}{9} \cdot [32 - 32] + 273.15$$

$$T(K) = 273.15 \text{ K}$$

or

$$t(°C) = 0° C$$

The result agrees with our initial discussion about the Kelvin scale and its direct connection with the Celsius scale.

▶ Practice

1. A child has a viral infection and his body temperature is 101.5° F. Find the corresponding temperature in °C.

2. For the information given in practice problem 1, find the corresponding Kelvin temperature.

3. If the temperature-pressure drop was not linear, would scientists be able to determine the zero absolute by a linear extrapolation? Explain briefly.

4. The outside temperature changes from morning to noon by about 20° F. Find the corresponding change in temperature in Celsius degrees.

5. For the information given in practice problem 4, find the corresponding change in temperature in Kelvin. What do you observe about the two answers?

6. Determine the relationship between Celsius scale and a made-up scale, call it FAKE, that considers 55 degrees the freezing point of water and 135 degrees the boiling point of water? Show the equation.

▶ Heat

For a system to change its temperature, the object exchanges energy with its surroundings. We call this energy *heat*, and we measure heat in *joules* (from James Joule, 1818–1889).

We have seen previously that temperature is specific to a certain state. Therefore, we call temperature a *quantity of state*. In contrast, heat is an energy flow established when there is a thermal contact between two different temperature states. We call heat a *quantity of process*.

Heat is related to a measure of the change in the motion and interaction of the particles, which is called *internal energy*. Internal energy is equal to the kinetic energy and the potential energy of the particles. Kinetic energy measures the translational, rotational, and vibrational motion of the atoms and molecules in the object, whereas potential energy measures the interaction between the particles. When the temperature increases, the kinetic energy increases. One way to accomplish this process is by exchanging heat with the object.

▶ Practice

7. Give examples of other quantities you learned about in previous lessons that represent quantities of state.

8. Give examples of other quantities you learned about in previous lessons that represent quantities of process.

9. An object is cooling off. Are particles slowing down or speeding up in this process? Explain briefly.

10. If you raise an object from the floor, does the internal energy of the object increase, decrease, or stay the same? Explain briefly.

▶ Heat Transfer

We have seen why heat flows; let's learn now about the means of this flow. On an atomic scale, materials in different states are built differently: Solids have an internal structure, and the atoms and molecules are bound through strong bonds. Disturbing the bonds in one place will create a disturbance in the lattice, and so we end up with a propagation of the initial effect. Liquids and gases are different in the sense that the structure is not isotropic (the same in all directions, or completely absent as in the case of gases). Hence, a disturbance in one side of the container with fluid will spread differently than it does in a solid.

There are three types of heat transfer: *conduction*, *convection*, and *radiation*.

In the case of *conduction*, the heat is transferred through the material itself, and a difference in temperature between different sides of the object is required. On an atomic scale, the particles on the side of the object where the temperature is larger are characterized by a greater kinetic energy. While moving, they will collide with slower particles and, in the

process, lose some of their kinetic energy to the slower moving particles that now accelerate.

Metals are good thermal conductors because of the free electrons that move through the lattice. Other materials such as glass, plastic, and paper are poor conductors due to the light interaction between constituent particles. Still other materials, such as gases, are isolators due to the large distance between particles.

The situation is different in *convection*, where the transfer of heat happens due to movement of the substance through space. Consider forcing warm air into a room through floor-level inlets. What happens in time? The warm air rises, and the cold air sinks. Warm air has atoms and molecules that move faster, and they are farther apart; therefore, the density is less than the density of cold air. And, as we have seen in the last lesson, a lower density material will be buoyed up.

A different process that does not require contact is called *radiation*. With this transfer, heating is accomplished by electromagnetic radiation. Every object with a temperature more than zero absolute Kelvin radiates infrared radiation, which in turn is absorbed by other objects and increases their temperature.

▶ Practice

11. A copper-based pot filled with water sits on a heating device. Explain the process of warming up the water.

12. With the information given in practice problem 11, where is the water hotter? Why?

▶ Heat and Temperature Change

An object that is warmed up will experience an increase in temperature. The variation of temperature is different depending on the nature of the object. To characterize this dependence, we define two coefficients: the *heat capacity* and the *specific heat*. The coefficients of heat capacity and specific heat for different materials are tabulated.

If a quantity of heat Q is transferred to a substance thereby increasing its temperature by $\Delta T = T_2 - T_1$, the heat capacity is defined to be:

$$c = \frac{Q}{\Delta T} = \frac{Q}{T_2 - T_1}$$

This coefficient *is not* dependent on the mass of the specific object and *is* measured in J/K or J/C°.

If a quantity of heat Q is transferred to a substance of mass m and is increasing its temperature by $\Delta T = T_2 - T_1$, the specific heat is defined to be:

$$c = \frac{Q}{m \cdot \Delta T} = \frac{Q}{m \cdot (T_2 - T_1)}$$

We can also rewrite the equation as:

$$Q = m \cdot c \cdot (T_2 - T_1)$$

Using this equation, we define a new unit for heat called the *calorie*. One calorie (1 cal) is the heat necessary to be transferred to 1 g of water to increase its temperature by one Celsius degree (from 14.5 to 15.5° C). The conversion from calories to joules is:

$$1 \text{ cal} = 4.186 \text{ J}$$

The nutritional calorie that you see on food labels is actually 1,000 calories and is symbolized by C.

$$1 \text{ } C = 1,000 \text{ } cal$$

Another usual unit is one *British thermal unit* (BTU), which is the heat necessary to be transferred to 1 pound of water to raise its temperature from 63 to 64° F.

Some containers are built such that they make good isolators. The heat transferred to a fluid is completely exchanged with the fluid and none lost to its surroundings. Such containers are called *calorimeters*, and the study of the heat exchange in these systems is called *calorimetry*. In this case, the heat coming from a hot reservoir is completely transferred to the cold reservoir:

$$Q_{hot} = -Q_{cold}$$

The minus sign indicates that the system that cools down looses energy (heat is coming out), and therefore, the heat transfer is negative. This is called the *calorimetric equation*.

Some of the most usual materials encountered and their specific heats are shown in Table 11.1.

Table 11.1

SPECIFIC HEAT OF COMMON MATERIALS

SUBSTANCE	C (J/KG · °C)
Aluminum	900
Copper	387
Glass	837
Gold	129
Ice	2,090
Iron	448
Silver	234
Steam	2,010
Water	4,186

Example

An aluminum piece of 400 g is placed in a container that holds 100 g water at 80° C. The water cools down to 20° C. In the process, the aluminum piece gets warmer and reaches a temperature of 45° C. What was the initial temperature of the aluminum piece? Consider the only heat exchange to be between the aluminum and the water.

Solution

First, convert all quantities to SI units. Next, set the equations and solve for the initial temperature.

$$m_{al} = 400 \text{ g} = 400 \text{ g} \cdot 1 \text{ kg}/1,000 \text{ g} = 0.4 \text{ kg}$$

$$m_{water} = 100 \text{ g} = 100 \text{ g} \cdot 1 \text{ kg}/1,000 \text{ g} = 0.1 \text{ kg}$$

$$t_{water\ initial} = 80° \text{ C}$$

$$t_{water\ final} = 20° \text{ C}$$

$$t_{Al\ final} = 45° \text{ C}$$

$$t_{Al\ initial} = ?$$

Because the system is thermally isolated, the heat released by the water is absorbed by the aluminum.

$$Q_{water} = -Q_{aluminum}$$

$$Q_{water} = m_{water} \cdot c_{water} \cdot (t_{water\ final} - t_{water\ initial})$$

$$Q_{water} =$$

$$0.1 \text{ kg} \cdot 4,186 \text{ J/kg} \cdot °\text{C} \cdot (80° \text{ C} - 20° \text{ C})$$

$$Q_{water} = 0.1 \cdot 4,186 \text{ J} \cdot 60$$

$$Q_{water} = 2.5 \cdot 10^4 \text{ J}$$

$$-Q_{aluminum} =$$

$$-m_{Al} \cdot c_{Al} \cdot (t_{Al\ final} - t_{Al\ initial})$$

$$-Q_{aluminum} =$$

$$-0.4 \text{ kg} \cdot 900 \text{ J/kg} °\text{C} \cdot (45 - t_{Al\ initial})$$

$$2.5 \cdot 10^4 \text{ J} = 0.4 \cdot 900 \text{ J/°C} \cdot (45 - t_{Al\ initial})$$

$$2.5 \cdot 10^4 \text{ J}/(0.4 \cdot 900 \text{ J/°C}) = (45 - t_{Al\ initial})$$

$$2.5 \cdot 10^{4°} \text{ C}/(0.4 \cdot 900) = (45 - t_{Al\ initial})$$

$$70° \text{ C} = (45 - t_{Al\ initial})$$

$$t_{Al\ initial} = (45 - 70)° \text{ C} = -25° \text{ C}$$

$$t_{Al\ initial} = -25° \text{ C}$$

▶ Practice

13. Two objects of equal mass are exchanging heat with two heat reservoirs at the same rate. One object has a specific heat twice as large as the heat of the second object. How do the temperature variations for each object compare? Show your calculations.

14. Water has a very large specific heat. Is it easy to change the temperature of a body of water: lake, sea, or ocean?

15. What difference would it make in the calorimetric equation if the system is not isolated? Explain briefly.

16. An iron rod receives an amount of heat of 2,380 J from a heat reservoir. The rod has a mass of 0.500 kg. Find the temperature change.

17. With the information given in practice problem 16, find the initial and final temperatures if the final temperature is 2¾ larger than the initial temperature.

▶ Heat and Phase Change

Is the heat absorbed or released by an object always changing its temperature? The answer is no. Think, for example, about boiling water: Once the water boils,

If a quantity of heat Q is transferred to a substance of mass m and the substance has a phase change, then the coefficient of latent heat L is given as follows:

$$L = \frac{Q}{m}$$

This coefficient depends on the nature of the substance and on the type of phase change occurring.

there is another phenomenon taking place called *vaporization*. So, in this example, the heat absorbed is used first to increase the water temperature and then to change the phase from liquid to gas. This transformation is called a *phase change*, and in our example, the pressure is considered to be constant because the transformation takes place in open space. The heat exchanged when the liquid is experiencing a phase change is called *latent heat*. Measurements show that in a phase change, the *temperature is constant* until the transformation to another phase happens in the bulk of the substance.

There are a few processes regarding phase changes: from solid to liquid and the inverse. These are called *melting* and *freezing*. Together, they are called *fusion*; specifically, they are *vaporization* at evaporation or condensation, and *sublimation* at the phase change from solid to gas or gas to solid.

The heat exchanged in a phase change has the same value regardless of the direction of change: The coefficient of latent heat of melting is equal to the coefficient of latent heat of freezing.

In many books, these processes are summarized in a graph (see Figure 11.2) of the temperature dependence of the absorbed energy (heat).

If you interpret the graph, you will see that the slopes of the graphs for ice and for steam are almost the same. All things being equal, this translates to the ratio of heat and temperature change, which gives us

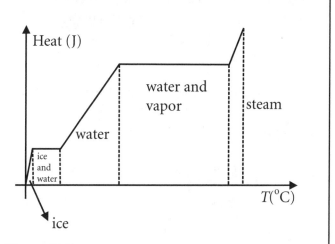

Figure 11.2

the specific heat. If you check with the table, you will see the two coefficients close in value. How about the water phase? The slope is smoother in this case, as shown also by the numbers in the coefficients of specific heat.

In a calorimetry measurement, the hot reservoir or/and the cold reservoir heat might contain terms similar to $m \cdot c \cdot \Delta T$ as we have already seen before. However, there are new terms involving a process with no temperature change, a process called *phase transition*. Let's try to define a measure of the transition from the point of view of heat transfer.

Example

An aluminum piece of 400 g is placed in a container that holds 100 g of ice at $-10°$ C. The water warms up to 5° C. In the process, the aluminum piece gets colder and reaches a temperature of 45° C. What was the initial temperature of the aluminum piece? The experiment takes place in a calorimeter.

Solution

First, convert all quantities to SI units. Next, set the equations and solve for the initial temperature.

According to the problem, the exchange happens in a calorimeter. Therefore, the only heat exchange happens between the aluminum and the ice.

$$m_{al} = 400 \text{ g} = 400 \text{ g} \cdot 1 \text{ kg}/1{,}000 \text{ g} = 0.4 \text{ kg}$$

$$m_{ice} = 100 \text{ g} = 100 \text{ g} \cdot 1 \text{ kg}/1{,}000 \text{ g} = 0.1 \text{ kg}$$

$$t_{ice\ initial} = -10° \text{ C}$$

$$t_{water\ final} = 5° \text{ C}$$

$$t_{Al\ final} = 45° \text{ C}$$

$$t_{Al\ initial} = ?$$

Because the system is thermally isolated, the heat released by the aluminum is absorbed by the ice and then the water.

$$Q_{ice} = -Q_{aluminum}$$

The process of heating of water goes through three different steps: First, the ice absorbs heat and the temperature increases from -10 to $0°$ C; second, the ice melts and there is no change in temperature; and last, the water warms up from 0 to 5° C. So we will have three terms referring to the ice to water heat absorption.

$$Q_{ice} =$$

$$Q_{-10\ to\ 0°\ C} + \text{Latent heat of melting} + Q_{0\ to\ 5°\ C}$$

$$Q_{ice} = m_{ice} \cdot c_{ice} \cdot (0°\text{ C} - t_{ice\ initial}) +$$

$$m \cdot L + m_{ice} \cdot c_{water} \cdot (t_{water\ final} - 0°\text{ C})$$

$$(L = 3.33 \times 10^5 \text{ J/kg})$$

$$Q_{ice} = m_{ice} \cdot c_{ice} \cdot (0 - (-10)) +$$

$$m_{ice} \cdot L + m_{ice} \cdot c_{water} \cdot (5 - 0)$$

$$Q_{ice} = 3.74 \cdot 10^4 \text{ J}$$

$$Q_{aluminum} = m_{Al} \cdot c_{Al} \cdot (t_{Al\ final} - t_{Al\ initial})$$

$$Q_{aluminum} = 0.4 \text{ kg} \cdot 900 \text{ J/kg} \cdot °\text{C} \cdot (45 - t_{Al\ initial})$$

$$3.74 \cdot 10^4 \text{ J} = -0.4 \cdot 900 \text{ J/°C} \cdot (45 - t_{Al\ initial})$$

$$3.74 \cdot 10^4 \text{ J}/(0.4 \cdot 900 \text{ J/°C}) = -(45 - t_{Al\ initial})$$

$$3.74 \cdot 10^{4°} \text{ C}/(0.4 \cdot 900) = -(45 - t_{Al\ initial})$$

$$104° \text{ C} = (45 - t_{Al\ initial})$$

$$t_{Al\ initial} = (45 + 104)° \text{ C} = 149° \text{ C}$$

$$t_{Al\ initial} = 149° \text{ C}$$

▶ Practice

18. During the boiling process, what happens to the temperature of the liquid?

19. Consider your answer to practice problem 18. Now, if you exchange more heat with the liquid, is that going to change its temperature?

20. An object is placed in a steamy location, and condensation occurs on its surface. Does that change the temperature of the object? If yes, in what way?

21. Ethyl alcohol has a latent heat of vaporization of 200 cal/g. Find out what quantity would be necessary to condense to create enough heat to bring to boil 200 g of water from 98° C.

▶ Thermal Expansion

We have now discussed the effect of heat exchange on a solid, and we learned that in the process, the particles inside a solid will move apart from each other as they acquire kinetic energy (due to an increase of average speed). The effect is easily observed if you make a careful measurement of the length of a rod that is subjected to increased temperature. This process of *expansion* is dependent not only on the amount of energy exchanged but also on the nature of the material.

In order to have a quantitative explanation of how substances expand, a few characteristics should be defined and measured: $\Delta L = L - L_0 =$ change in length; $\alpha =$ coefficient of thermal expansion (1/°C); $L_0 =$ initial length; $\Delta T =$ change in temperature.

The expansion along one direction is called *linear thermal expansion* and can be related to these coefficients and parameters through the following expression:

$$\Delta L = \alpha \cdot L_0 \cdot \Delta T$$

But the structure of a solid is three dimensional so we cannot assume that the process of thermal expansion happens linearly. All x, y, and z directions will be affected by the expansion. A simple way to correlate 3-D expansion with linear expansion is to imagine a cube of initial side L_0 that is heated up to a temperature $T_0 + \Delta T$. All the sides of the cube will expand, and the change in volume can be found by subtracting the initial and final volumes. The *volume thermal expansion* then is characterized by the following equation:

$$\Delta V = \beta \cdot V_0 \, \Delta T$$

where $\Delta V =$ change in volume; $\beta =$ coefficient of volume thermal expansion; $V_0 =$ initial volume; $\Delta T =$ change in temperature. If we consider that:

$$\Delta V = V - V_0 = L^3 - L_0^3$$

and we write an expression for L as a function of L_0 as given by

$$\Delta L = L - L_0 = \alpha \cdot L_0 \cdot \Delta T$$

then we can show that by neglecting higher order terms in α (measurement shows this coefficient being very small; therefore, the higher orders will be even smaller. They can be neglected):

$$\beta = 3 \cdot \alpha$$

And:

$$\Delta V = 3 \cdot \alpha \cdot V_0 \, \Delta T$$

Example

A copper cube of size 25 cm has a coefficient of linear expansion of $17 \cdot 10^{-6°} \, C^{-1}$. Find the change in length and volume if the temperature changes 12° C from morning to noon.

Solution

First, convert the units to SI. Next, build our equations to determine the unknown.

$$\alpha = 17 \cdot 10^{-6°} \, C^{-1}$$

$$\Delta T = 12° \, C$$

$$L_0 = 25 \, cm = 0.25 \, m$$

$\Delta L = ?$

$\Delta V = ?$

We can determine first the change in length:

$\Delta L = \alpha \cdot L_0 \cdot \Delta T =$

$17 \cdot 10^{-6°} C^{-1} \cdot 0.25 \, m \cdot 12° \, C = 5.1 \cdot 10^{-5} \, m$

$\Delta L = 5.1 \cdot 10^{-5} \, m$

$\Delta V = 3 \cdot \alpha \cdot V_0 \cdot \Delta T$

$V_0 = L_0^3$

$\Delta V = 3 \cdot \alpha \cdot L_0^3 \cdot \Delta T =$

$3 \cdot 17 \cdot 10^{-6°} C^{-1} \cdot (0.25 \, m)^3 \cdot 12° \, C =$
$9.6 \cdot 10^{-6} \, m^3$

$\Delta V = 9.6 \cdot 10^{-6} \, m^3$

You can see that the change is small in both cases but is definitely something measurable.

▶ Practice

22. Consider two aluminum rods: Rod 1 has a length three times smaller than Rod 2 but the same size diameter. How do the rods change their length if they are subjected to the same change in temperature? Show your calculations.

23. For the information given in practice problem 22, how does the change in volume for the two rods compare? Show your calculations.

24. When is it easier to measure thermal expansion? When the object has a large initial length? A small initial length? Or it does not matter what the initial length is?

25. A silver teaspoon is placed in a hot cup of tea. The room temperature is 24.0° C and the tea is at 82.0° C. Silver has a coefficient of thermal expansion of $1.90 \cdot 10^{-5°} C^{-1}$. In the process of thermal expansion, the change in length is measured to be 165 μm. Find the initial and final lengths of the teaspoon.

Thermo-dynamics

LESSON SUMMARY

The previous lessons introduced a different form of energy—heat—and quantities that relate directly to it: temperature and internal energy. The purpose of this lesson is to take this knowledge one step forward and put into law some of the "natural" behaviors of fluids when they exchange heat with their surroundings—the law of thermodynamics. *Thermodynamics* is a compound word meaning change of heat, in Greek. We will relate heat, work, and internal energy, and then study the laws of thermodynamics. We will exemplify these laws through simple processes that are the foundation of applications such as engines and refrigerators.

▶ Thermodynamic Work

From a microscopic point of view, we have learned that particles—atoms, molecules, and ions—are in a continuous motion. They also interact with their neighbors. These facts are measured by two types of energies that can characterize the atomic components of each object, be it in a solid, a liquid, or a gas phase. The two types of energies are called *kinetic* and *potential energies*. *Kinetic energy* measures the translational, rotational, and vibrational motion, whereas the *potential energy* deals with the interaction between particles. The two energies together constitute the *internal energy* of the system regardless of its phase (solid, liquid, or gas).

The work performed by a thermodynamic system on its surroundings is considered negative (as in the case of an exploding pop bottle). The work performed by the surroundings on the system is considered positive (as in the previous example where the gas is compressed from outside).

The question we will be asking now is how to change this state of motion and interaction? The answer is through *energy exchange*. Then, the next step is to realize what forms of energy are appropriate for this goal. One evident answer, from the past lesson, is *heat*. Heat transferred to or from an object will change the state of the object, its temperature, and its internal energy. Particles will move faster or slower with the input or release of heat (respectively).

But is heat the only way to accomplish the change in internal energy? The answer: With objects, you can always use mechanical interaction, or *work*. The mechanical parameters characterizing the object are the pressure, P, and the volume, V. Both of them will affect the internal state of the system.

The mechanical parameters depend on each other through an equation called the *equation of state*. In the special case of the ideal gas, where particles are considered identical and independent of each other, these two parameters are connected through the expression called the ideal gas law:

$$P \cdot V = n \cdot R \cdot T$$

Where T is the temperature in Kelvin, n is the number of moles of substance studied, and R is the universal gas constant and is equal to:

$$R = 8.314472[15] \, J \cdot K^1 \cdot mol^{-1}$$

Consider now a thermodynamic system on which we apply mechanical work (for instance, the pis-

ton in a car), and assume that there is a gas in the piston. Next, assume that we compress the volume by applying an external force. What we are doing is performing work on the gas; so the gas receives energy, this time in the form of mechanical work. We can use the definition of work we studied a few lessons back and calculate this work by replacing the force with the corresponding constant pressure (force exerted on an area A, as shown in Figure 12.1).

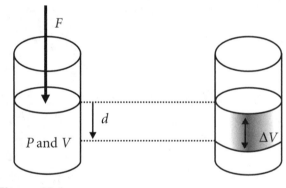

Figure 12.1

$$W = F \cdot d = (P \cdot A) \cdot d$$

But $A \cdot d = \Delta V$ is the change of volume for the gas. You can see that because the piston is pushed in, the volume decreases, and then the change in volume is negative. In order to maintain a positive work performed on the system, the previous work equation has to be modified by including a minus sign.

$$W = -P \cdot \Delta V$$

The work done on a gas at constant pressure is equal to the product of pressure and the change in volume.

As we can see from the above definition, work is dependent on a mechanical change. Therefore, a certain state has no characteristic work; rather the change in state can be triggered by work being exerted on the system or by the system exerting work on its surroundings.

Example

Consider a piston like the ones discussed previously with a radius of 8 cm. The pressure inside the pistons is about equal to the atmospheric pressure, and, due to some internal reactions, the system expands by about 5 cm. Find the volume change and the work done by the system on the surrounding.

Solution

Start by converting to SI. Next, set up your equation to solve the problem.

$$r = 8\,\text{cm} = 0.08\,\text{m}$$

$$\Delta L = 5\,\text{cm} = 0.05\,\text{m}$$

$$P = 1.013 \cdot 10^5\,\text{N/m}^2$$

$$\Delta V = ?$$

$$W = ?$$

The change in volume, for a cylinder, is the area of the section, a circle, multiplied by the height.

$$\Delta V = A \cdot \Delta L$$

$$A = \pi \cdot r^2$$

$$\Delta V = \pi \cdot r^2 \cdot \Delta L = \pi \cdot (0.08\,\text{m})^2 \cdot 0.05\,\text{m}$$

$$\Delta V = 1 \cdot 10^{-3}\,\text{m}^3$$

$$W = -P \cdot \Delta V =$$

$$-1.013 \cdot 10^5\,\text{N/m}^2 \cdot 1 \cdot 10^{-3}\,\text{m}^3$$

$$W = -1.013 \cdot 10^2\,\text{N} \cdot \text{m}$$

or with one number of significant figures, as the problem gives us: $W = -1 \cdot 10^2\,\text{J}$.

The work is negative because the system makes work on its surrounding, or, in other words, is losing some of its energy.

A geometric approach to interpreting the formula for work offers a second method to measure work performed in a thermodynamic process. Because work is proportional to pressure and volume, we can represent the two parameters and graph their dependence. In the previous case where volume is increasing, the graph will look like the one in Figure 12.2.

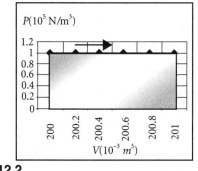

Figure 12.2

The arrow shows us the direction of the process (the volume is increasing; there is work done by the system on its surroundings to push the air out and make room for itself). The definition of work also considers the product of the pressure and the change in volume. According to the geometry of the graph, this is exactly the area darkened between the initial and final volumes and the constant pressure.

The graph is called a *PV-diagram*, and the work can be calculated by finding the area under the graph in the PV-diagram.

Example

Consider the graph in Figure 12.2. Reading the measurements from the graph, calculate the amount of work performed by the system on the surroundings.

Solution

To our advantage, all data is already in SI. The area is a simple geometrical shape: a rectangle. The area under the graph will be:

$width \cdot height =$

$(201 \cdot 10^{-3} \, m^3 - 200 \cdot 10^{-3} \, m^3) \cdot$

$1 \cdot 10^5 \, N/m^2 = 1 \cdot 10^2 \cdot J$

The decision regarding the sign will have to come from interpreting the graph according to the convention: Expanding objects yield a negative value of work. So, our final result is:

$W = -1 \cdot 10^2 \, J$

This is exactly the same as the previous answer, with one error. The error stems from the fact that the graph does not give enough detail on the pressure measurements.

▶ Practice

1. What do you think: Is work a quantity of state or of process?
2. If the temperature and number of moles remain constant and the volume of an ideal gas increases, what does the pressure do? Explain briefly.
3. A piston is slowly acted on by a force of 20.0 N such that the pressure inside the piston remains constant at all times. The section of the piston is 201 cm², and its final volume is 20% of the initial volume. If the piston's final volume is

$4.02 \cdot 10^{-3} \, m^3$, find out the work performed by the force.

4. For the information given in practice problem 3, what is the sign of the work and what is its meaning?
5. Find the piston's initial height, final height, and change in height for the process described in practice problem 3.
6. Consider the PV-diagram in Figure 12.3, and find the work performed. The arrows indicate the direction of the process.

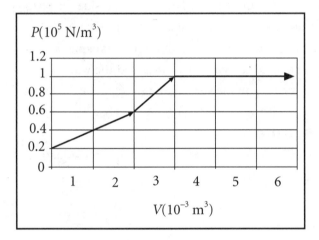

Figure 12.3

7. Can you apply the $W = -P \cdot \Delta V$ formula to all parts of the graph? Why or why not? Explain briefly.

▶ Zeroth Law of Thermodynamics

We have seen that pressure and volume are mechanical parameters. There are also other properties of a system that are dependent on the motion of the constituent atoms and molecules. Characterizing this motion is not an easy job though, because the number of particles in any one material is astronomic. In one

Two systems, each in thermal equilibrium with a third system (1 with 2, and 2 with 3), are in thermal equilibrium with each other (1 with 3).

mole of every substance, you can count a certain number of particles; that number is called *Avogadro's number*, or $N_A = 6.022 \cdot 10^{23}$ particles/mol. Given the number of particles in a substance, N, one can find the number of moles from:

$$n = N/N_A$$

Also, the mass of the substance can be determined based on the number of particles and the mass per particle:

$$m = m_{particle} \cdot N$$

With this, we can define the parameters necessary to completely characterize a thermodynamic state: pressure, P, volume, V, number of moles, n, and mass, m.

A first law that summarizes one of these parameters, temperature, is the *zeroth law of thermodynamics*. In all natural phenomena, two or more systems are in thermal contact. They can exchange energy through heat and, after a period of time, will have the same temperature: The colder object warms up and the warmer object cools down. In other words, they will ultimately be in *thermal equilibrium*. To generalize this behavior, the zeroth law states: Two systems, each in thermal equilibrium with a third system (1 with 2, and 2 with 3), are in thermal equilibrium with each other (1 with 3).

Hence, each part of this system has the same temeprature. The idea of equilibrium is so important that it was determined that it was necessary for this statement to preceede the first and second laws of ther-

Thermometers

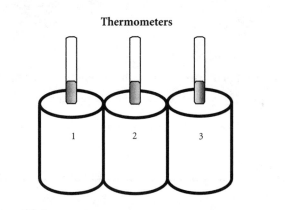

Figure 12.4

modynamics, thus the name *zeroth*. The contact between two or more objects when they exchange heat but no mass is called *thermal contact*.

▶ Practice

8. On a cold winter morning, you cool off a cup of coffee by leaving it outside. Is it reasonable to say that the change in temperature when thermal equilibrium is reached is drastic for the coffee but not for the surrounding air? Explain your answer.

9. Consider room-temperature air in a closed container. The container is in thermal contact with a heat source. Consider the air behaving as an ideal gas. At thermal equilibrium, is the pressure of the air in the container larger or smaller than it was initially?

The first law of thermodynamics, also called *conservation of energy*, says that the internal energy of a system changes from an initial value U_i to a final value U_f due to heat exchange Q and work performed on or by the system, W.

$$\Delta U = U_f - U_i = Q + W$$

Convention for Work
- Work is a positive quantity when work is performed on the system.
- Work is a negative quantity when work is performed by the system.

Convention for Heat
- Heat is a positive quantity when heat is absorbed by the system.
- Heat is a negative quantity when heat is lost by the system.

▶ First Law of Thermodynamics

As one defines the parameters in mechanics that characterize the mechanical state, position, and speed, then the interactions (force and torque) and the energies, we will similarly define parameters for the next concept. We have introduced the thermodynamic parameters previously (pressure, volume, temperature, and moles). We have talked about heat and internal energy exchange between systems. Now it is time to apply the principle of *conservation of energy* to this subject. The statement of the *first law of thermodynamics* does exactly this.

Any change in the system is due to exchange of energy with its surroundings. Energy is not a vector quantity, and therefore, we need a convention to establish the sign of these energies because of the different consequences of exchanging energy. For confirmation of this need, read ahead to the next example. At the beginning of this lesson, we talked about the convention for work; now it is time to define a convention for heat.

Example

You have two completely identical containers, and the same quantity of liquid is in both of them. You put one of them in contact with a colder object and it loses 100 J of heat. The other one you put in contact with a warm source and it gains 100 J. The energy is the same. Is the final state of the two containers the same?

Solution

The state is not similar because the system absorbing heat will have atoms and molecules moving faster: It has larger temperature, while the system that cools down will have slower particles and smaller temperature. Because the thermodynamic state is characterized by P, V, T, and m, even if the rest of the parameters are the same, the temperature is different, so the states are different.

▶ Practice

10. Consider a process in which the internal energy of a system increases by 125 J and the heat

Second Law of Thermodynamics

Heat flows from a substance at a higher temperature to a substance at a lower temperature and does not flow spontaneously in the reverse direction.

exchange is $Q = -32$ J. Find out what the work is and if it is performed by or on the system.

11. In practice problem 10, is the heat absorbed or released by the system? Explain.

▶ Second Law of Thermodynamics

The second and final law of thermodynamics refers to a "natural" process—the flow of heat. Numerous circumstances in your life have allowed you to experience the essence of this law.

There are other ways to express the meaning of this law. These other expressions require the introduction of machines, such as engines and refrigerators, or concepts, such as entropy. The formulation of these expressions varies with the field of study. So don't be surprised if you open a book geared toward engineering professionals and find the law expressed with engines or if you open a more advanced textbook and find a discussion about entropy. Each and every field of study introduces the law based on previous knowledge of that field of study.

▶ Simple Thermodynamic Processes

In nature, rarely is there complete and self-sustained thermal isolation of a system. That means that in most cases, the states of a system have at least one variable parameter, if not more. We will consider simple thermodynamic processes where all but one parameter vary.

Isobar process: This is a process in which pressure is constant (P = constant). In the section on thermodynamic work, we studied an isobar process and its PV-diagram, and we were able to find a simple way to calculate work from a geometrical interpretation. The work in such a process is the area under the PV-diagram.

Isochoric process or isovolumic process: This is a process in which the volume is constant while the pressure varies, as in Figure 12.5.

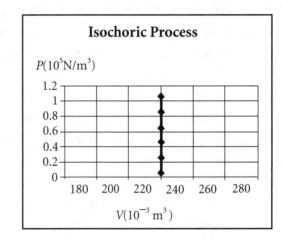

Figure 12.5

At a constant volume:

$$\Delta V = 0$$

$$W = -P \cdot \Delta V = 0 \text{ J}$$

$$\Delta U = Q + W = Q$$

The internal energy increases ($\Delta U > 0$) if the system absorbs heat, and it decreases ($\Delta U < 0$) if the system loses heat. As you can see in the figure, there is no area under the PV-curve, so there is no work.

Isothermal process: This is the process in which the temperature is constant. For an ideal gas, internal energy can be shown to be proportional with the temperature, hence in this process:

$T = $ constant

$\Delta U = 0$ J

$\Delta U = Q + W = 0$

$Q = -W$

We interpret this expression as follows: If a system evolves without changing its internal energy, work will be done by the system only if it receives heat, and heat will be released by the system only if work will be done on it.

Adiabatic process: This is a process where no exchange of heat happens. When there is no heat exchange with the surroundings (thermal isolated system), the work can be done only at the expense of the changing internal energy.

If you compare the PV-diagram of the adiabatic and isothermal processes, you might mistakenly consider them identical. Although both of them are curves, in a PV-diagram, the slope of the adiabatic transformation is steeper than the slope of the isotherm at the same volume, as shown in Figure 12.6.

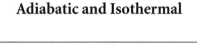

Adiabatic and Isothermal

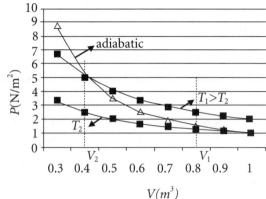

Figure 12.6

The two isothermals, shown by the ■ symbol in the graph, intersect the adiabatic curve (△) evolving between T_1 and T_2 temperatures and the same volumes V_1 and V_2.

Let's study the first law:

$Q = 0$ J

$\Delta U = W = -P \cdot \Delta V$

If the system expands, then the work is negative and the change in internal energy is negative also. This means the energy of the constituent particles and the temperature of the system decreases.

Based on these processes, machines such as heat engines and refrigerators have been constructed. A *heat engine* is a device that converts internal energy into work by heat flow from a high temperature source to a low temperature source. Because these machines have to go through multiple repetitions of the same process, we call the sequence of process a *thermodynamic cycle*. A *refrigerator* uses mechanical work to take heat from a cold source and release it to a hot source, effectively lowering the temperature of a system.

▶ Practice

12. If a system is thermal isolated (no heat exchange) and no work is performed by or on the system, how does the temperature of this system vary? Explain.

13. A container of dimensions $12 \times 16 \times 6$ cm holds a fluid at a temperature $T = 300$ K. The fluid is heated through an isothermal process ($\Delta U = 0$ J) and an energy of 150 J is absorbed. Find the work produced in the process. Is the system expanding or contracting? Explain.

14. In practice problem 13, consider an ideal gas inside the container, and the initial pressure of the gas is $\frac{2}{3}$ of the final pressure. Find the final volume.

15. You are constructing a machine that works on a cycle similar to the one in Figure 12.7. Is any work being done by the system or on the system through the entire process? If yes, calculate the work. The arrows show the evolution of the parameters for this system.

16. In practice problem 15, what is the amount of heat exchanged by the fluid?

17. Is the heat absorbed or released by the system?

$P(10^5 \text{ N/m}^3)$

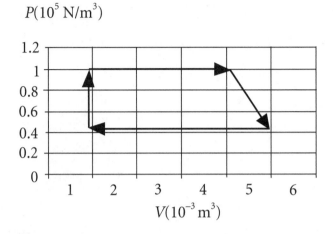

Figure 12.7

13 ▶ Electrostatics

LESSON SUMMARY

Analogy is a powerful tool, and we use it often in physics. Remember, we started this journey with the static of mechanical objects. Now we move further from macroscopic to microscopic and analyze interaction between charges and the effect on the surrounding medium.

▶ Electric Charge and Charge Conservation

A basic description of substances leads us to the concepts of electrical charges and the fundamental particle—the electron. Empirically, it has been found that a piece of amber gemstone, rubbed with a piece of animal fur, will create a new type of interaction; it will be able to attract to its surface small pieces of material and dust particles. The material is said to be *electrically charged*, and the smallest particle of charge is called the *electron*. The electron was assigned a negative charge of $1.6 \cdot 10^{-19}$ Coulombs. These electrons are considered one of the elementary subatomic particles. Electrons (negatively charged) are constituents of atoms, which are electrically neutral (zero net charge). The atom also contains positive charges, or *protons*, which are positioned in the central part of the atom, the *nucleus*. The nucleus is also composed of neutral particles, called *neutrons*.

Contrary to the previous example where the amber was charged up with electrons, other materials tend to charge positively (with protons). This has been summarized in the *electrostatic series*. Materials such as amber, rubber, and polyethylene charge negatively, whereas paper, cat's fur, and nylon charge positively. The difference between the types of charge can be easily shown by letting two of these materials interact. Materials from the same group repel each other, and materials from the opposite group attract each other. This defines the *electrical interaction*.

Materials are considered to be conductors, semiconductors, or insulators. The nomenclature is revealing. *Conductors* will let charge spread in the volume. *Semiconductors* will vary their electrical properties and sometimes behave as conductors while at other times behaving as insulators. *Insulators* will localize the charge acquired; their electrons bond strongly to the atoms and make it hard for electrical charge to flow through the material.

A last observation. Charging an object can be achieved by different means: friction, conduction, or induction. Charging by *friction* involves rubbing two materials against each other and in the process electrons are transferred from one object to the other. *Conduction* involves a conductive material in which electrons are free to move in the volume. *Induction* is established between two materials that do not touch, but where the material that is charged interacts with particles in the uncharged material, creating a distribution of charge on the surface close to it.

In the neutral state, the atom has an equal number of electrons and protons, and the net charge is zero.

$$n = p$$

where n is the number of electrons and p is the number of protons. If an electron is given sufficient energy to be able to break the bond with the atom and leave it, then the atom becomes charged, as it now has one

more proton than electrons. The atom becomes positively charged, and we call this new particle a *positive ion* ($n < p$). If by friction between two objects, one of the objects is charging positively (losing electrons), we typically retrieve the electrons on the second object. Then the second object, initially neutral, becomes negatively charged. This ion is called a *negative ion* ($n > p$). If the two objects are isolated from the exterior (that is, isolated from other objects), then the charges are moving from one to the other, and the total number of electrons and protons will stay the same; the ions simply rearrange between the two objects. We can define this as a new law of conservation, similar to the conservation of energy and conservation of momentum in mechanics and to the conservation of thermal energy in thermodynamics. This new law is the *conservation of charge*.

After the charge is rearranged between the objects in contact, the state remains unchanged as long as there is no other interaction. This defines a situation of equilibrium similar to previous cases of mechanical and thermal equilibrium where the charge, whether positive or negative, is measured in Coulombs (1 C), and its usual symbol is q. As mentioned previously, an electron has negative charge:

$$q_e = -1.6 \cdot 10^{-19} \, C$$

The proton is equal in charge but has more mass:

$$q_p = +1.6 \cdot 10^{-19} \, C$$

Example

Consider two objects, one made of rubber and the other of nylon that is electrically neutral. You rub the two objects together and the rubber becomes charged with $-2.88 \cdot 10^{-16}$ Coulombs. What is the nylon's charge, and how many electrons have been shifted to the rubber from the nylon in the process?

Solution

Initially, both objects have a zero net charge, and, because the system will be considered to be isolated, the same amount of charge will be retrieved in the final state.

$$q_{rubber} = -2.88 \cdot 10^{-16}\,C$$

$$q_{nylon} = ?$$

$$N = ?$$

$$q_{rubber} + q_{nylon} = 0\,C$$

$$-2.88 \cdot 10^{-16}\,C + q_{nylon} = 0\,C$$

$$q_{nylon} = -(-2.88 \cdot 10^{-16}\,C)$$

$$q_{nylon} = +2.88 \cdot 10^{-16}\,C$$

The number of electrons that make up the charge of the rubber is:

$$N = q_{rubber}/q_e$$

$$N = (-2.88 \cdot 10^{-16}\,C)/$$
$$(-1.6 \cdot 10^{-19}\,C) =$$

1,800 electrons pass from nylon to rubber

▶ Practice

1. Two strings are hooked to the ceiling and form two close pendulums that have two identical small metal objects hanging on one end and touching as shown in Figure 13.1. The objects are initially electrically neutral. One will be isolated from the second and charged. The charged object is then placed in contact with the other object. What will happen to the charge of the two pendulums after contact? Explain.

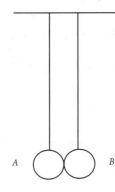

Figure 13.1

2. For the information given in practice problem 1, 120 electrons are initially charging one metal object. After contact, what is the charge on each object?

3. After equilibrium is established, an insulator is brought in close proximity with one of the objects in the system but not touching either *A* or *B* objects. Explain what happens in the new situation of equilibrium.

▶ Electric Forces and Coulomb's Law

We have talked about interaction between materials in the electrostatic series. We can summarize that there are two types of electrical interactions: attraction and repulsion. *Attraction forces* are established between particles of different charge sign (positive and negative charges). *Repulsion forces* act between charges of the same kind.

The quantitative expression of the electrical force is known as *Coulomb's law* (from Charles de Coulomb, 1736–1806). If one considers the charges to be point-like (that is, all charges gather in one point), then the law says: The magnitude of the electrical force exerted by a point-like charge q_1 on a charge q_2 is proportional to the product of the charges and inversely

The magnitude of the electrical force exerted by a point-like charge q_1 on a charge q_2 is proportional to the product of the charges and inversely proportional to the square of the distance between the charges.

proportional to the square of the distance between the charges.

$$F = k \cdot \frac{q_1 \cdot q_2}{r^2}$$

Where the *proportionality constant* is:

$$k = 9 \cdot 10^9 \, N \cdot m^2/C^2$$

The electric force, as are all other forces, is a vector. The direction is given by the type of particles interacting, as shown in Figures 13.2 and 13.3 and defined previously.

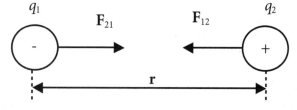

q_1 $\mathbf{F}_{21}$ $\mathbf{F}_{12}$ q_2

r

Figure 13.2

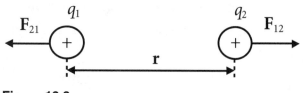

$\mathbf{F}_{21}$ q_1 q_2 $\mathbf{F}_{12}$

r

Figure 13.3

Although the names given to the forces are different to show the action charge and the test-charge (for example, F_{21} indicates that charge 2 is acting on charge 1), the absolute value is the same.

$$\mathbf{F}_{21} = \mathbf{F}_{12}$$

Also shown in the figures is the opposite direction of interaction.

In a vector form, the law is expressed as:

$$\mathbf{F} = k \cdot \frac{q_1 \cdot q_2}{r^3} \cdot \mathbf{r}$$

One can see that the new formula shows that the direction of the electric force is the same as the direction between the two charges.

Example

Two amber beads are brought in proximity after being charged with 10 and 50 electrons. They are placed at a distance of 20 cm from each other. Find the force acting on each bead.

Solution

First, convert to the units necessary to work with Coulomb's law and then find the charges. Then, calculate the forces on each object.

$$R = 20 \, cm = 0.2 \, m$$

$$q_1 = 10 \cdot (-1.6 \cdot 10^{-19} \, C) = -1.6 \cdot 10^{-18} \, C$$

$$q_2 = 50 \cdot (-1.6 \cdot 10^{-19} \, C) = -8.0 \cdot 10^{-18} \, C$$

$$F_{21} = F_{12} = ?$$

$$F_{21} = k \cdot \frac{q_1 \cdot q_2}{r^2} =$$

$$9 \cdot 10^9 \, \text{N} \cdot \text{m}^2/\text{C}^2 \cdot \frac{q_1 \cdot q_2}{r^2}$$

$$F_{21} = 9 \cdot 10^9 \, \text{N} \cdot \text{m}^2/\text{C}^2 \cdot$$

$$\frac{(-1.6 \cdot 10^{-18} \, \text{C}) \cdot (-8.0 \cdot 10^{-18} \, \text{C})}{(0.2 \, \text{m})^2}$$

$$F_{21} = 28.8 \cdot 10^{-23} \, \text{N}$$

$$F_{21} = F_{12} = 28.8 \cdot 10^{-23} \, \text{N}$$

The charges are the same sign, and therefore, the force is of repulsion.

If there are three or more objects charged and interacting, you will have to find the force that one charge is acted upon by all the other neighboring charges, and then find the net force. Remember that the force will be a vector, so the net force is the sum of vectors (value and direction).

Example

Consider three equal charges placed on the *x*-axis such that the distances between are 100 cm and 300 cm between charge 1 and charge 2 and between charge 1 and charge 3, respectively. Find whether the charge in the middle is at rest or not.

Solution

In order to find our answer, we start by converting all values to SI. Then, we will find the net force on the middle charge and see if it is zero or nonzero. In the case the force is zero, the charge is at rest (Newton's second law). If the net force is nonzero, the charge will be accelerated in the direction of the net force.

$$r_{12} = 100 \, \text{cm} = 1 \, \text{m}$$

$$r_{13} = 300 \, \text{cm} = 3 \, \text{m}$$

$$r_{23} = 300 \, \text{cm} - 100 \, \text{cm} = 2 \, \text{m} = 2 \cdot r_{12}$$

$$q_1 = q_2 = q_3 = q$$

$$F_{net} = ?$$

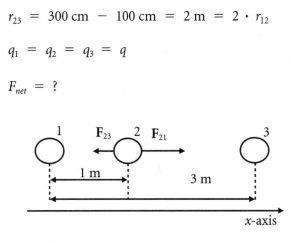

Figure 13.4

Charge 2 is acted upon by two forces because of repulsion with the charges 1 and 3. The forces are F_{23} exerted by charge 3 on charge 2 and F_{21} exerted by charge 1 on charge 2. As you can see from the figure, they are in opposite directions.

If we consider the positive direction as in the figure, then F_{21} is positive and F_{23} is negative.

$$F_{21} = k \cdot \frac{q_2 \cdot q_1}{r_2} = k \cdot \frac{q \cdot q}{r_{23}^2} = k \cdot \frac{q^2}{r_{21}^2}$$

$$F_{23} = k \cdot \frac{q_2 \cdot q_3}{r_2} = k \cdot \frac{q \cdot q}{r_{23}^2} = k \cdot \frac{q^2}{r_{23}^2}$$

As mentioned in the problem statement:

$$r_{23} = 2 \cdot r_{12} = 2 \cdot r_{21}$$

The last term in the equality is possible to write because we are interested in the absolute value and not the direction (which was considered in drawing the figure).

$$F_{21} = k \cdot \frac{q^2}{r_{21}^2}$$

$$F_{23} = k \cdot \frac{q^2}{r_{23}^2} = k \cdot \frac{q^2}{(2 \cdot r_{21})^2} =$$

$$\frac{1}{4} \cdot k \cdot \frac{q^2}{r_{21}^2} = \frac{1}{4} \cdot F_{21}$$

Fnet = **F**$_{23}$ + **F**$_{21}$

$Fnet = -F_{23} + F_{21}$

$Fnet = -\dfrac{1}{4} \cdot F_{21} + F_{21} = \dfrac{3}{4} \cdot F_{21}$

This result tells us that the charge is acted upon by a net force and subsequently will be accelerated by an acceleration that can be calculated based on Newton's second law if the mass of the charge is known:

$Fnet = m \cdot a$

$a = \dfrac{Fnet}{m}$

The force is in the direction of F_{21}, meaning the object is accelerated toward the positive x direction.

▶ Practice

4. Two amber beads are brought in proximity after being charged with 10 and 50 electrons. They are placed at a distance of 20 cm from each other. The force acting between the two charges was calculated in the example before. If the second object is charged with a charge that is three times larger, find the force acting between the new charges.

5. In practice problem 4, the distance between the charges is increased to 2 m. What is the new force and what is the ratio between this force and the force you calculated in practice problem 4?

6. Three amber beads are brought in proximity after being charged with 10.0 and 20.0 and 30.0 electrons, respectively. They are placed, as shown in Figure 13.5. Find the total force acting on charge A.

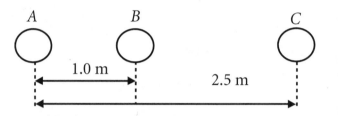

Figure 13.5

7. In practice problem 6, the 30-electron charge is replaced by a charge of 30 protons. Find the new force on charge A.

8. Consider the setup of charges in Figure 13.6. Find the net force on charge A on the x direction, on the y direction and the net force.

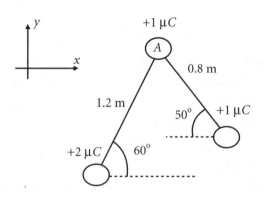

Figure 13.6

9. In practice problem 8, is the net force the same on the other two charges? Explain.

The electric field at a location around a charge q is defined to be proportional to the force at the specified location and inversely proportional to the charge by the field.

$$E = \frac{F}{q}$$

▶ Electric Field and Potential

As we discovered previously, there is no need for contact in order to have electrical interaction, and this is not the only case we learned about so far. Gravitational force is carried out by the gravitational field, which changes the properties of the space around an object: The more massive the object, the larger the gravitational field and the greater the interaction with other objects found in proximity. Heating though radiation is another noncontact interaction we discussed. In the case of radiation, electromagnetic waves produced by a far-away source, such as the sun, can heat up an object, effectively increasing its temperature.

The space around an electrically charged object carries special properties, and we call this an *electrical field*. Any other charge in this region will interact with the electrical field, and we call this charge a *test-charge*. Hence, we have both a field-producing charge and a test-charge(s) that will be affected by the electrical field.

The electric field that propagates electrical interaction has vector properties because a positive charge will affect the charges around it in a different way than a negative charge will. The direction of the electric field and of the electric force is the same at any point around the charge.

The vectors starting or finishing on the charges are called *electrical field lines*, and they represent the direction of the electric field and electric force, as seen

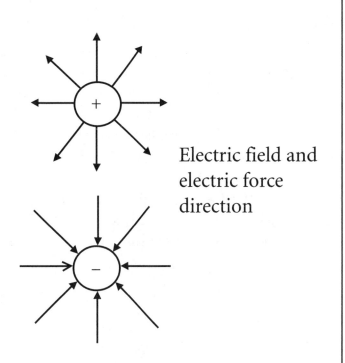

Electric field and electric force direction

Figure 13.7

in Figure 13.7. The density of electrical field lines in a region represents the strength of the field in that area.

Depending on the position of the test-charge, there are many arrangements of the field lines encountered in applications. One is shown in the following example and figure.

Example

Consider positive and negative spherical charges in proximity. Draw the field lines.

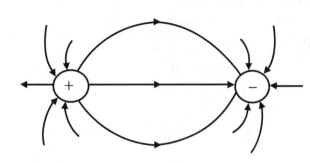

Figure 13.8

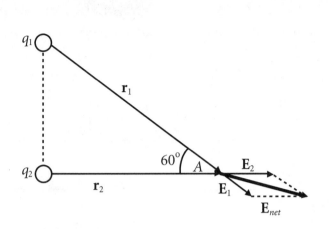

Figure 13.9

Solution

The field lines are similar to the ones we have shown previously, but because the two particles interact, the field created by each will affect the other particle. The final arrangement looks like that in Figure 13.8.

According to the definition for electric field, the unit for the electric field will be the Newton/Coulomb (N/C). Because force was previously defined by Coulomb's law, if we consider the charge q_1 creating a field E and a test-charge q_2 to be present in the field, then the field at point $\mathbf{r}$ with respect to charge q_1 is:

$$\mathbf{E} = \frac{F_{21}}{q_2} = k \cdot \frac{q_2 \cdot q_1}{r^3} \cdot \mathbf{r} \cdot \frac{1}{q_2} = k \cdot \frac{q_1}{r^3} \cdot \mathbf{r}$$

$$\mathbf{E} = k \cdot \frac{q_1}{r^3} \cdot \mathbf{r}$$

where F_{21} is the force that charge q_2 feels due to the field created by charge q_1. In the last expression, the field created by the charge q_1 is seen to be in the same direction as the vector position $\mathbf{r}$ if the charge is positive and opposite to $\mathbf{r}$ if the charge is negative, relative to the field lines drawn at the beginning of this section.

If we are interested in the value of the field created by charge q_1 then:

$$E = k \cdot \frac{q_1}{r^3} \cdot r = k \cdot \frac{q_1}{r^2}$$

If the field is created by two or more electrical charges, the vector expression is helpful in finding the net electric field at one location as we will see in the following example.

Example

Consider two charges, as shown in Figure 13.9, creating a net electric field. Find the direction and the value of the net field at point A. The charges are $q_1 = +1.6 \cdot 10^{-19}$ C and $q_2 = -1.6 \cdot 10^{-19}$ C, and the distance to the point is $r_1 = 22$ cm and $r_2 = 12$ cm.

Solution

First, convert the data into SI units. Then, find the field determined by each charge respectively at point A, and next find the net field.

$$r_1 = 22 \text{ cm} = 0.22 \text{ m}$$

$$r_2 = 12 \text{ cm} = 0.12 \text{ m}$$

$$q_1 = +1.6 \cdot 10^{-19} \text{ C}$$

$$q_2 = -1.6 \cdot 10^{-19} \text{ C}$$

$$\mathbf{E}_{net} = ?$$

$$\mathbf{E}_1 = k \cdot \frac{q_1}{r_1^3} \cdot \mathbf{r}_1$$

The vector position has both a horizontal and a vertical component, and they can be represented as:

Electric Potential Energy

The *electric potential energy* (EPE) per unit of charge defines the electric potential.

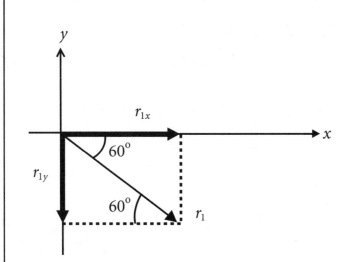

Figure 13.10

$$\mathbf{r}_1 = (r_{1x}, r_{1y}) = (r_1 \cdot \cos\alpha; r_1 \cdot \sin\alpha)$$

where α is the angle the vector makes with the positive x-axis. In the case of the vector r_1, the angle is $360° - 60° = 300°$.

$$\mathbf{r}_1 = (r_{1x}, r_{1y}) = (r_1 \cdot \cos 300°; r_1 \cdot \sin 300°)$$

$$\mathbf{r}_1 = (r_{1x}, r_{1y}) = (0.22 \cdot \cos 300°; 0.22 \cdot \sin 300°)$$

$$\mathbf{r}_1 = (r_{1x}, r_{1y}) = (0.11; -0.19)\,\text{m}$$

$$\mathbf{E}_1 = k \cdot \frac{q_1}{r_1^3} \cdot \mathbf{r}_1$$

$$\mathbf{E}_1 = 9 \cdot 10^9 \cdot \frac{1.6 \cdot 10^{-19}}{(0.22)^3} \cdot \mathbf{r}_1$$

$$\mathbf{E}_1 = 1.4 \cdot 10^{-7} \cdot (0.11; -0.19)\,\text{N/C}$$

$$\mathbf{E}_1 = (0.15; -0.27) \cdot 10^{-7}\,\text{N/C}$$

A similar calculation can be made for the components of the second charge distance and electric field, and it can be said that:

$$\mathbf{r}_2 = (r_{2x}, r_{2y}) = (r_2 \cdot \cos 0°; r_2 \cdot \sin 0°)$$

$$\mathbf{r}_2 = (r_{2x}, r_{2y}) = (0.12 \cdot \cos 0°; 0.12 \cdot \sin 0°)$$

$$\mathbf{r}_2 = (r_{2x}, r_{2y}) = (0.12; 0)\,\text{m}$$

$$\mathbf{E}_2 = k \cdot \frac{q_2}{r_2^3} \cdot \mathbf{r}_2$$

$$\mathbf{E}_2 = 9 \cdot 10^9 \cdot \frac{1.6 \cdot 10^{-19}}{(0.12)^3} \cdot \mathbf{r}_2$$

$$\mathbf{E}_2 = 9 \cdot 10^9 \cdot \frac{1.6 \cdot 10^{-19}}{(0.12)^3} \cdot (0.12; 0)$$

$$\mathbf{E}_2 = (1; 0) \cdot 10^{-7}\,\text{N/C}$$

The net electric field is the vector sum of the two fields:

$$E_{net} =$$

$$E_1 + E_2 = [(0.15; -0.27) + (1; 0)] \cdot 10^{-7}\,\text{N/C}$$

$$E_{net} = E_1 + E_2 = (1.15; -0.27) \cdot 10^{-7}\,\text{N/C}$$

And the direction of the field can be found from the E_x and E_y components of the field:

$$\tan\theta = \frac{E_y}{E_x} = \frac{-0.27 \cdot 10^{-7}\,\text{N/C}}{1.15 \cdot 10^{-7}\,\text{N/C}}$$

$$\tan\theta = \frac{-0.27}{1.15} = -0.23$$

$$\theta = -13°$$

Similar to the situation of a moving object in a gravitational field (where a potential energy is associated with the position of the object in the field), an electric potential energy can be defined for a charge placed in an electric field. As a greater mass needs more energy to be moved in a gravitational field, so does a larger charge need more energy to be moved through an electric field.

Electric potential, known as V, is "measured" in joule/coulombs and is called a *volt* (from Alessandro Volta, 1745–1827). Due to the unit for electric potential, this quantity is also called *voltage*. The voltage is seen previously to depend on energy, which is a scalar quantity; therefore, voltage is also a scalar. Voltage will still be positive or negative depending on the type of charge. The quotation marks in the first sentence of this paragraph are intended to emphasize the fact that voltage based on electric potential energy is a relative quantity. Potential energy, if you remember from mechanics, is proportional to the position of an object but with respect to an origin. A more measurable quantity is the difference in potential energy, hence the difference of voltage between two positions.

If a charge q is moving in an electric field E between positions A and B, then the field does work on the charge that is equal to the variation of the electric potential energy (analogous to the work done by gravity: $W = -\Delta PE$).

In this case, the work to move the charge from point A to B is:

$$W = -\Delta EPE = -(EPE_B - EPE_A)$$

Dividing both sides by the charge q:

$$\frac{W}{q} = -\frac{EPE_B - EPE_A}{q}$$

$$\frac{W}{q} = \frac{EPE_A}{q} - \frac{EPE_B}{q}$$

And considering the previous definition of voltage:

$$\frac{EPE_A}{q} = V_A$$

$$\frac{EPE_B}{q} = V_B$$

The work can be related to the voltage difference by:

$$\frac{W}{q} = V_A - V_B$$

$$\frac{W}{q} = -\Delta V$$

Example

Consider a test-charge $q = -1.6$ pC move in an electric field E from point A to point B. The work done by the field to move the charge is 2.8 fJ. Find the potential difference between the two points.

Solution

First, convert the units and then proceed in formulating the solution.

$$W = 2.8 \text{ fJ} = 2.8 \cdot 10^{-15} \text{ J}$$

$$q = -1.6 \cdot 10^{-12} \text{ C}$$

$$\Delta V = ?$$

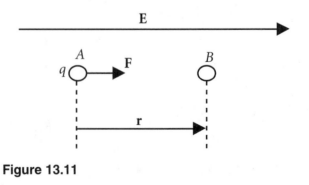

Figure 13.11

$$\frac{W}{q} = -\Delta V$$

$$\frac{2.8 \cdot 10^{-15} \text{ J}}{-1.6 \cdot 10^{-12} \text{ C}} = -\Delta V$$

$$\Delta V = 1.7 \cdot 10^{-3} \text{ V}$$

► Practice

10. If a charge q produces a field E at a distance r, what is the electric field at a distance twice as large? Explain.

11. If the distance is kept constant, $2 \cdot r$, but the charge is replaced by a charge $\frac{1}{3}$ of the initial one, what happens to the value of the electric field?

12. What is the electric field created by a point-like charge very close to the charge? Explain.

13. What is the electric field created by a point-like charge far away from the position where the charge is located? Explain.

14. Three point-like charges arranged as in Figure 13.12 create an electric field. Determine the net field at position A. Charges are, from left to right: 1.0, 2.0, and 3.0 pC.

15. Can three electric charges create a zero electric field? Explain.

16. An electron is moving between two positions in a constant electric field such that the potential difference is -25 V. Find the work done by the field to move the electron between the two points.

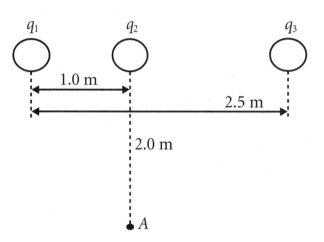

Figure 13.12

14 ▶ Electrical Current

LESSON SUMMARY

We have learned about charges in a static state. We now shift our attention to moving charges and the effects they produce on their surroundings. We will define electrical current, electrical resistance and capacitance, Ohm's law and Kirchoff's law, resistor series, and parallel circuits.

▶ Electrical Current

A new equilibrium situation arises in electricity. In thermal phenomena, as particles move around and collide with each other, we say they reach thermal equilibrium when the temperature becomes the same across all parts of the system. In the case of electrical phenomena, the charges are the ones determining a situation of equilibrium. Charges move between two points when a potential difference (electrical potential energy per charge) exists between the two ends of a conductor. If the ends are at the same potential, there is no flow of charge through the conductor. The flow of charge rapidly stops if we do not insure that the potential difference is maintained between the ends of the conductor by supplying energy to the conductor through a battery or an electrical generator such as a Van der Graaff generator. The maximum potential difference given out by a battery is called *electromotive force (emf)*, is symbolized by $\mathcal{E}$, and is measured in volts by an instrument called a *voltmeter*. A device that can measure more than one electrical property (such as resistance, voltage, and current) is called a *multimeter*.

The electrical current is the amount of charge that passes through the cross-sectional area of the conductor per unit time.

$$I = \frac{\Delta q}{\Delta t}$$

where Δq is the total charge that passes through the area and Δt is the time considered. Electrical current is measured in coulombs per second, or *amperes*, *A*, named after Andrè-Marie Ampère (1775–1836).

A battery is usually symbolized by a diagram such as that shown in Figure 14.1, where the two electrodes are charged with positive and negative charges, and the current, as the convention we agreed upon tells us, travels from the positive electrode out in the circuit toward the negative electrode.

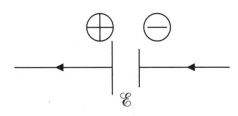

Figure 14.1

The charges moving through the conductor are, in a majority of cases, the free electrons in the conductor; for this reason, they are also called *conduction electrons*. Positive charges moving through the conductor are usually positive ions because the protons are strongly bonded to the nucleus.

The flow of charge can be continuous and at a constant rate, and the current is called *direct current*, or *dc*. Or it can flow in alternating directions, and then the current is called *alternative current*, or *ac*.

Example

In a conducting wire, electrons move as shown in Figure 14.2. Determine the electric current if 10^8 electrons move through the cross-sectional area A in 1 ms.

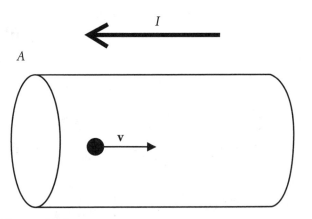

Figure 14.2

Solution

First, convert all quantities to SI and then set your formulas to determine I.

The electron charge is:

$$q_e = -1.6 \cdot 10^{-19}\, C$$

And because we have a number of 10^8 electrons, the total charge is:

$$\Delta q = 10^8 \cdot q_e =$$

$$10^8 \cdot (-1.6 \cdot 10^{-19}C) = -1.6 \cdot 10^{-11}C$$

History Note

Historically, it is considered that the flow of electrons is opposite to the electrical current, because in the beginning, it was believed that positive charges—and not electrons—determine the electrical current through a conductor.

$\Delta t = 1 \text{ ms} = 10^{-3} \text{s}$

$I = ?$

By the definition of the electrical current:

$$I = \frac{\Delta q}{\Delta t} = \frac{-1.6 \cdot 10^{-11}}{10^{-3}} = -1.6 \cdot 10^{-8} A$$

Because the current is created by electrons moving through the conductor, and considering the previous note, the current is taken to be opposite to the velocity v.

▶ Practice

1. Consider the previous example. If the same number of electrons speed up and pass through the same cross-sectional area in a nanosecond (nano = 10^{-9}), what happens to the electrical current? Show calculations.
2. What happens to the current if the particles moving through the conductor are positive ions with the same absolute value of the charge as electrons?

▶ Electrical Resistance and Ohm's Law

Mechanical motion or heat transfer are sometimes associated with loss of energy (as, for example, with friction). The same situation is encountered in electricity. The same battery hooked up to different wires will establish currents of different values. Therefore, we can introduce the concept of resistance: electrical resistance.

Electrical resistances are measured in volts per ampere, and the unit is called an *ohm* (Ω) after Georg Ohm (1789–1854).

The electrical resistance varies with some factors, but for most materials, the ratio stays the same for a large range of currents and voltages. In these cases, the resistance is a constant, and this observation is known as *Ohm's law*:

$$R = \frac{V}{I} = \text{constant}$$

Electrical resistance R varies with physical properties of the wires (length and cross-sectional area) and with the nature of the material (coefficient known as resistivity, ρ). The value of the resistivity helps classify materials into conductors, semiconductors, and insulators. Electrical conductors have small resistivities and conduct electrical current well (examples include: copper and silver), whereas insulators hinder the flow of charges (examples include: wood and Teflon). Semiconductors have a varying resistivity, and in certain conditions, they can behave as conductors and in other conditions as insulators. These are intrinsic properties of the materials and are highly dependent on the type of bonding between subatomic particles.

With this new insight, we can also define the electrical resistance in the following way. Electrical

Electrical resistance is the ratio of the voltage V applied across the ends of a material to the current I established through the material.

$$R = \frac{V}{I}$$

resistance R is proportional to the electrical resistivity, ρ, of the material and the length and it is inversely proportional to the cross-sectional area A.

$$R = \rho \cdot \frac{L}{A}$$

Example

Determine the unit for the electrical resistivity.

Solution

We start with the definition and solve for resistivity by multiplying each side with A/L:

$$R = \rho \cdot \frac{L}{A}$$

$$R \cdot \frac{A}{L} = \rho \cdot \frac{L}{A} \cdot \frac{A}{L}$$

$$R \cdot \frac{A}{L} = \rho$$

So, the emerging unit is

$$\frac{\Omega \cdot m^2}{m} = \Omega \cdot m$$

A few examples of the most encountered conductor materials and their resistivity are listed in Table 14.1.

Table 14.1

RESISTIVITY OF COMMON CONDUCTOR MATERIALS

MATERIAL	P · (Ω · m)
Aluminum	$2.8 \cdot 10^{-8}$
Copper	$1.7 \cdot 10^{-8}$
Gold	$2.4 \cdot 10^{-8}$
Iron	$9.7 \cdot 10^{-8}$
Nichrome	$100 \cdot 10^{-8}$
Silver	$1.6 \cdot 10^{-8}$

Most diagrams containing a resistor are going to represent it in a manner similar to that shown in Figure 14.3.

R

Figure 14.3

▶ Practice

3. Two wires are made of the same material and both have a cross-sectional area A. One has a length L, and the other is three times longer.

Electrical Resistance

Electrical resistance R is proportional to the electrical resistivity, ρ, of the material and the length and is inversely proportional to the cross-sectional area A.

How do the resistances of the wires compare? Show calculations.

4. Two wires are made of the same material and both have a length L and circular cross-sectional areas. One has a diameter 2.5 times larger than the other. How do the resistances of the wires compare? Show calculations.

5. One 1.5-volt battery is connected to an aluminum (Al) wire and another to an iron (Fe) wire. The two wires have the same length but the Al has a cross-sectional area $\frac{1}{10}$ of the Fe wire. Calculate the ratio of the currents through the two wires.

▶ Electrical Capacitance

Wires are not the only electrical devices that perform a function when a potential difference is applied. Another important category of devices is *capacitors*.

Capacitors are systems composed of two conductors placed in proximity but not in contact. The space between the conductors is filled with insulating materials called *dielectrics*. The plates of the capacitor are charged with equal and opposite charges. An electrical field is established as shown in Figure 14.4.

The amount of charge that a capacitor can store on each plate is proportional to the voltage V applied and the capacitance C.

$$q = C \cdot V$$

Figure 14.4

If we solve for the capacitance:

$$C = \frac{q}{v}$$

The capacitance is measured in SI, in coulombs per volt in a unit called a *farad* (F), named after Michael Faraday (1791–1867). Usual capacitances are in the range of microfaradds to picofarads.

Dielectrics placed in between the plates increase the capacitance and therefore the charge of the capacitor. They decrease the field established between the plates. A measure of this property is the *dielectric constant κ* that represents the ratio of the field without and with dielectric. Therefore, this coefficient is unitless.

Similar to the dependence noted previously for electrical resistance, the electrical capacitance is dependent upon intrinsic properties of the dielectric and on the geometry of the plates. For a parallel plate

The electrical capacitance is proportional to the dielectric constant • κ and the area of the plates A and inversely proportional to the distance between the plates d.

capacitor, such as the one shown previously in Figure 14.4, the dependence is summarized in the expression:

$$C = \frac{\kappa \cdot \varepsilon_0 \cdot A}{d}$$

The other constant is called *permittivity of vacuum* and is expressed by:

$$\varepsilon_0 = 8.8 \cdot 10^{-12} C^2/(N \cdot m^2)$$

Example

How does the increase in the distance between the two parallel plates of a capacitor affect capacitance?

Solution

If the distance between the plates increases two times, then we have an initial distance d_0 and a final distance $2 \cdot d_0$, and then we can compare the two capacitances:

$$C_0 = \frac{\kappa \cdot \varepsilon_0 \cdot A}{d_0}$$

$$C = \frac{\kappa \cdot \varepsilon_0 \cdot A}{d} = \frac{\kappa \cdot \varepsilon_0 \cdot A}{2 \cdot d_0} = \frac{1}{2} \cdot \frac{\kappa \cdot \varepsilon_0 \cdot A}{d_0} = \frac{1}{2} \cdot C_0$$

Hence, the capacitance decreases by 2.

Table 14.2 lists some of most common insulators and shows the value of their dielectric constant.

Considering the definition of the capacitance and the few examples in the table, you can say that the capacitance will increase when a dielectric other than a vacuum is placed between the plates, and it increases by the value of the dielectric constant.

Table 14.2

DIALECTRIC CONSTANTS OF COMMON INSULATORS

MATERIAL	DIELECTRIC CONSTANT κ
Vacuum	1
Air	1.00054
Teflon	2.1
Paper	3
Water	80

▶ Practice

6. The capacitance of a capacitor free of dielectric is 1.2 pF, and the capacitor is connected to a 9-volt battery. Find the charge on the capacitor's plates.
7. The space between the plates of the capacitor is filled with paper. Find the new capacitance as well as the new charge the plates can store if the battery voltage is kept the same.

▶ Kirchoff's Laws

Conservation of charge is expressed in the Kirchoff's laws. In order to introduce these laws, we must define an electrical circuit. An *electrical circuit* is a set of electrical consumers and electrical sources that form a closed path in which an electrical current can be established. A closed electrical circuit will have batteries or other electrical sources, resistors and capacitors, switches, and conductors. The point where two or more conductors meet is called a *junction*, and a closed path is called a *loop*.

The *junction law* expresses the fact that the total current entering a junction has to be equal to the current leaving the junction. In other words, the charge arriving at the junction should be the same as the amount of charge leaving the junction. In a closed circuit, the voltage difference at the ends of the circuit provides the energy for charge circulation through the circuit.

In a *closed circuit,* the total potential drop on the consumers is equal to the potential supplied from the sources. And again we have a rule very similar to the conservation of energy we worked with in mechanics and heat. The closed circuit is the analog of the previous mechanical and thermal isolated systems.

The two laws provide us with sufficient equations to be able to solve different characteristics of a circuit.

Example

In a simple circuit, we have two identical light bulbs and two identical batteries connected to each other as in Figure 14.5. Considering the electrical resistance is 100 Ω, find out the emf of the batteries and the currents through all the branches of the circuit. The current through the top resistor is 2 *mA*.

Solutions

First, determine the given quantities and then set up the equation to solve for the unknowns. The currents are:

$R = 100 \, \Omega$

$I_1 = 2 \, mA$

$\mathcal{E} = ?$

$I_2 \text{ and } I_3 = ?$

According to the convention of positive-charge motion determining the direction of the current, we will choose a convenient direction for the three currents in this circuit. When we analyze the results regarding the currents, we are able to see if our choice was valid for this circuit by looking at the sign. If the result for a current is negative, the current flows in the opposite direction to the one considered. As an example: If the result in the current below will be $I_1 = -2A$, then the direction of the real current is toward the left, not the right as we considered.

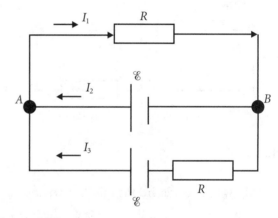

Figure 14.5

Using Kirchoff's laws, we consider first the junctions *A* and *B*. They are equivalent in this case, as they connect the same branches of the circuit. Let's look at the currents entering junction *A*: I_2 and I_3. And exiting junction *A*: I_1. Then the first law is:

$$(1) \, I_2 \, + \, I_3 \, = \, I_1$$

And it is the same for the junction *B*.

Now we can see there are three loops in the circuit, and we will consider a direction for looping (which is completely arbitrary, and therefore, I have decided to use clockwise). First, one will be considering the upper half of the circuit:

(A)

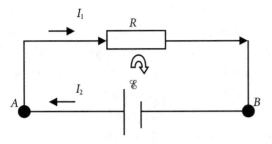

Figure 14.6

The second loop is the lower part of the circuit:

(B)

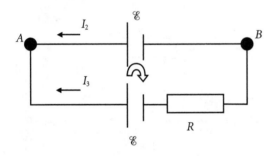

Figure 14.7

And lastly, we can disregard the middle part and have a circuit composed only of the outside conductors and electrical components.

(C)

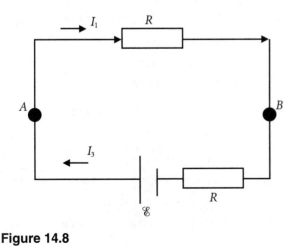

Figure 14.8

Out of the total number of loops N, only $N - 1$ are independent (as a condition, we need to be able to write independent equations), in this case 3 loops $- 1$ = 2 loops.

We will look at Figure 14.6 and 14.7.

For Figure 14.6, there is only a resistor (batteries have no resistance considered in this example, and they run at maximum energy, emf).

$$(2) \quad I_1 \cdot R + I_3 \cdot 0 = E$$

For Figure 14.7, there is again one resistor but two batteries. Around the circuit, the two batteries are supplying opposite voltages to the loop.

$$(3) \quad I_2 \cdot 0 + I_3 \cdot R = E - E$$

And so, we have three equations and three unknowns, and we can solve for each of the unknowns. From the third of these equations (Equation 3), we can solve for I_3.

$$I_2 \cdot 0 + I_3 \cdot R = E - E = 0$$

$$I_3 \cdot R = 0$$

Because R is a nonzero resistor, the only possibility is for the current to be zero:

$$I_3 = 0 \, A$$

Next, we use Equation 2, and solve for E:

$$I_1 \cdot R + I_3 \cdot 0 = E$$

$$I_1 \cdot R + 0 = E$$

$$I_1 \cdot R = E$$

$$2 \, mA \cdot 100 \, \Omega = E$$

$$E = 200 \, mV$$

And lastly, we can use the junction law to figure the current through the middle branch of the circuit.

$$I_2 + I_3 = I_1$$

$$I_2 + 0 = 2 \ mA$$

$$I_2 = 2 \ mA$$

All currents are positive, so the direction considered in the diagram was correct. As you can see, no current runs through the lower branch of the battery.

▶ Practice

8. Consider the diagram in Figure 14.9 of part of a complex circuit. Find the value of the missing current.

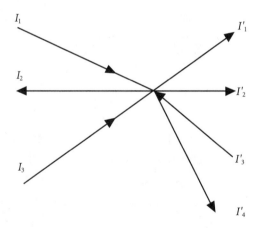

Figure 14.9

$$I_1 = 2.25 \ mA \quad I_2 = 8.32 \ mA \quad I_3 = 5.53 \ mA$$

$$I'_1 = 3.30 \ mA \quad I'_2 = 0.58 \ mA \quad I'_4 = 6.50 \ mA$$

9. In providing current for a few electrical devices, the battery and the resistors are connected as shown in Figure 14.10. Find the voltage of the

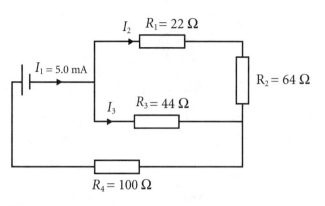

Figure 14.10

battery so that the currents can be supplied as noted in the diagram. Find results to three significant figures.

10. In the previous practice problem, find the current passing through each of the four electrical conductors. Find results to three significant figures.

11. In the previous practice problem, find the voltage drop on each of the four conductors. Find results to three significant figures.

▶ Series and Parallel Resistor Circuits

The previous examples show, as practice does, that circuits usually have more than one component. The question is, can we find a way to simplify calculations using Kirchoff's laws? The answer is yes, and the elements can be coupled together into two types of connections: series and parallel connections. We will now investigate the series and parallel connections for electrical resistances.

A *series connection* has all resistors connected in a line and the same amount of current passes through each resistor as shown in Figure 14.11.

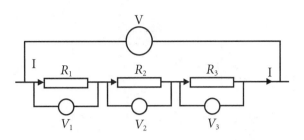

Figure 14.11

If the three resistors are of different resistances, the voltage drop on each of them is different (they oppose differently charge motion). According to Ohm's law, the voltage is:

$$V_1 = R_1 \cdot I, \ V_2 = R_2 \cdot I, \ V_3 = R_3 \cdot I$$

The voltage drop on the entire line of resistors has to be the same as the sum of all the voltages in the previous equation:

$$V = V_1 + V_2 + V_3$$

$$V = R_1 \cdot I + R_2 \cdot I + R_3 \cdot I$$

$$V = (R_1 + R_2 + R_3) \cdot I$$

If we imagine the entire circuit represented by just one resistor that has the same effect on the current as do the three, we can consider the previous equation to be written as:

$$V = R_S \cdot I$$

If we put together the last equations, we have:

$$(R_1 + R_2 + R_3) \cdot I = R_S \cdot I$$

$$R_1 + R_2 + R_3 = R_S$$

The resistance of an equivalent circuit of resistors connected in series is equal to the sum of the resistances. More generally, the previous equation can be written as:

$$\sum_i R_i = R_S$$

where *i* is the number of resistors connected in series.

A *parallel connection* has multiple resistors hooked to the same junction (see Figure 14.12), and the current splits, taking the *path of least resistance*, literally! The same equations of currents and voltages in junctions and loops can be set to determine the equivalent parallel connection resistance.

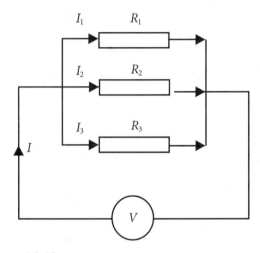

Figure 14.12

The current in the resistors is different and dependent on the value of the resistors, but the voltage drop between the ends of each resistance is the same, as the voltage on the parallel connection, *V*.

The resistance of an equivalent circuit of resistors connected in parallel is equal to the sum of the inverse of the resistances. More generally, the previous equation can be written as:

$$\sum_i {}^1\!/_{R_i} = {}^1\!/_{R_p}$$

where *i* is the number of resistors connected in parallel.

Example

Two resistors, $R_1 = 100$ mΩ and $R_2 = 50$ mΩ are connected first in series and then in parallel to the same battery. When is the equivalent resistance larger: in the series or in the parallel connection?

Solution

To answer this problem, set up the equations for each of the series and parallel connections for the two resistors.

$$\sum_i R_i = R_S$$

$$R_1 + R_2 = R_S$$

$$100 + 50 = R_S$$

$$R_S = 150 \text{ m}\Omega$$

$$\sum_i \frac{1}{R_i} = \frac{1}{R_p}$$

$$\frac{1}{R_1} + \frac{1}{R_2} = \frac{1}{R_p}$$

$$\frac{R_1 + R_2}{R_1 \cdot R_2} = \frac{1}{R_p}$$

$$\frac{R_S}{R_1 \cdot R_2} = \frac{1}{R_p}$$

$$R_p = \frac{R_1 \cdot R_2}{R_S} = \frac{100 \text{ m}\Omega \cdot 50 \text{ m}\Omega}{150 \text{ m}\Omega}$$

$$R_p = 33 \text{ m}\Omega$$

$$R_S > R_p$$

Actually, the above result is true for all resistors, and the parallel connection will always yield a smaller value of the equivalent resistance than does a series

connection made up of the same resistors as in the parallel one.

▶ Practice

12. Show that for three resistors connected in series and then in parallel, the equation $R_S > R_P$ stands true. The resistors are 20, 30, and 50 ohms.

13. In the circuit shown in Figure 14.13, find the equivalent resistance of the circuit if the resistors are $R_1 = R_5 = 20\ \Omega$, $R_2 = R_4 = 30\ \Omega$, and $R_3 = 50\ \Omega$.

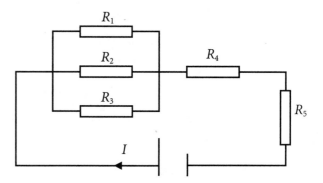

Figure 14.3

14. In the previous practice problem, find the current I if the battery supplies maximum voltage of 12 V.

15. In practice problem 13, find the currents I_1, I_2, and I_3.

16. In practice problem 13, find the voltage drop on each resistor.

LESSON

15 ▶ Magnetism

LESSON SUMMARY

There is a strong connection between the electric and magnetic fields, which will allow us to build on the previous lessons and move into the concept of magnetic field interactions. We will discuss magnetic materials, magnetic forces, motion of a charge in magnetic field, and magnetic field created by an electrical current.

▶ Magnetic Materials, Magnetic Field, and Magnetic Forces

What properties do refrigerator magnets have in common with Earth? First, the medium around each of them is characterized by a certain property called a *magnetic field*. A magnetic field manifests itself by the interaction between the magnet producing the field and other magnets or iron-based objects that might be in the vicinity. Any magnet, regardless of shape, has two poles: a *north* pole and a *south* pole. If you divide the magnet into two pieces, each of the pieces will also display the properties of north and south poles. Further reducing the size of the magnet does not separate the poles but keeps a north and a south pole in each of the pieces.

Some materials are naturally magnetic (for example, *magnetite* discovered to be magnetic for the first time about 2,000 years ago), and others can be magnetized (for example, iron-based objects), and still others will never display any magnetic properties. The existence of these categories is determined, as before with electrical charges, by the structure of the substance and the specific bonds between the atoms and molecules that are connected with each other.

The magnetic force is proportional to the strength of the magnetic field, to the velocity of the moving charge, and to the value of the charge.

$$F = q \cdot v \otimes B$$

Around a magnetic field, the magnetic properties can be described by the *magnetic field lines*, which are similar to the electric field lines. The direction of the magnetic field lines is from the N to the S pole outside the magnet and the other way inside the magnet (as shown in Figure 15.1 for a bar magnet).

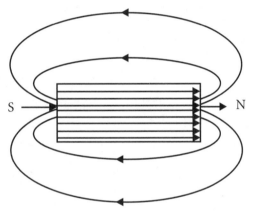

Figure 15.1

The magnetic interaction, like that in the case of electrical charge interaction, is of two kinds: attraction and repulsion. The *attraction* force is established between two magnets facing each other with the different poles (N and S). The *repulsion* force is established between two poles of the same kind (N and N, or S and S).

▶ Motion of a Point Charge in a Magnetic Field

Consider a point-like charge in a magnetic field. If the charge is in motion in the field, it can be shown that a force is acting on the charge that will curve the straight trajectory of the charge in the absence of any other interaction.

B is the value of the magnetic field at a point. This quantity is a vector because the magnetic field, similar to the electric field, has a definite direction. The unit for the magnetic field can be determined from the equation for magnetic force if we take only the scalar part of the magnetic force. Then you can see that magnetic field is measured in

$$\frac{N}{C \cdot m/s}$$

This is a unit called a *tesla* (1 T) for Nicola Tesla (1856–1943). A field of 1 T is a very large field (compare to the field of Earth, which is less than 10^{-4} T). Therefore, the usual unit for magnetic fields is *gauss* (1 G).

$$1 \, G = 10^{-4} \, T$$

The cross-product between the velocity and the magnetic field **B** can be interpreted in the following manner. To determine the magnetic force, you should consider only the speed perpendicular to the magnetic field, hence the magnetic force value is:

$$F = q \cdot v \cdot B \cdot \sin \alpha$$

Right-Hand Rule

Using the right hand, palm up, point the fingers in the direction of the vector magnetic field **B** and the thumb in the direction of the vector velocity **v**. The force will be perpendicular to the palm, and, if the charge is positive, the force will point upward. The force will be pointing downward if the charge is negative.

where α is the angle between the velocity **v** and magnetic field **B**.

If you construct a plane that contains both the velocity and the magnetic field, the resultant magnetic force is perpendicular to the field, whereas the direction (up or down) is given to the sign of the charge. See Figure 15.2.

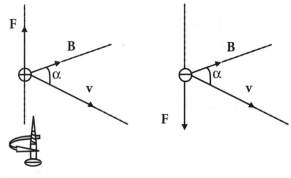

Figure 15.2

The rule to determine the direction of the force is called the *right-hand rule* or the *corkscrew* rule.

In the case of the corkscrew for a positive charge, as shown in Figure 15.2, if you rotate the screw so that the velocity vector becomes superimposed on the magnetic field, the direction of advance of the screw is the direction of the force.

If the magnetic force is the net force on the particle, then the charge will be accelerated in the direction of the net force and the trajectory will be curved.

Example

In a particle accelerator, an electron is accelerated in a field of 5,000 gauss. If the speed of the electron is 3 · 10^6 m/s, find the magnetic force on the electron if the electron enters the field at an angle of 30° with respect to the magnetic field.

Solution

Set the quantities we are given and the unknown in the equation of the magnetic field.

$$B = 5,000\,G = 5,000\,G \cdot 1\,T/10^4\,G = 0.5\,T$$

$$v = 3 \cdot 10^6\,m/s$$

$$\alpha = 30°$$

$$F = ?$$

$$F = q \cdot v \cdot B \cdot \sin \alpha$$

$$F = -1.6 \cdot 10^{-19}\,C \cdot 3 \cdot 10^6\,m/s \cdot 0.5\,T \cdot \sin 30°$$

$$F = -120 \cdot 10^{-15}\,N$$

$$F = -1.2 \cdot 10^{-13}\,N$$

▶ Practice

1. In Figure 15.3, find the direction of the magnetic force acting on the negative charge.

2. Under what conditions can the force on a charge in a magnetic field be zero?

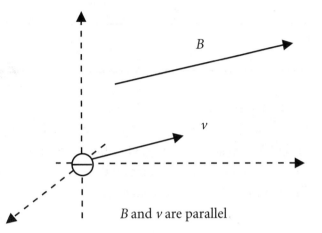

B and v are parallel

Figure 15.3

3. A laboratory superconductive magnet can achieve a field of 9 T. How does the force on an electron moving at the same speed in a superconductive magnet compare to the one in a permanent magnet (field of 10 gauss)?

4. In a laboratory experiment, a proton accelerates linearly (on the x-axis direction) and then passes a magnetic field oriented along z direction. Neglecting all other forces, in what direction is the net force acting, and what effect will it have on the initial direction of motion of the proton?

5. At what angle will a $3 \cdot 10^6$ m/s moving proton enter an accelerating magnetic field of 8,000 gauss if the net force is required to be $3 \cdot 10^{-13}$ N? Consider only the magnetic force to be acting on the charge.

6. Two electrons enter a magnetic field of 0.5 T with speeds $3 \cdot 10^6$ m/s and $6 \cdot 10^6$ m/s. The first electron is oriented perpendicular to the field, but the second one is not. What is the angle between the velocity of the second electron and the field if they both experience the same force?

▶ The Magnetic Force on an Electrical Current in a Magnetic Field

As we have seen, a charge is acted upon by a magnetic field. But a charge in motion creates an electrical current, so some interaction must take place between a wire carrying current and an applied magnetic field.

We will consider a long wire of length L carrying a current I. If the free electrons are conducting electricity through the wire then once we have a magnetic field, each electron will sense the field and interact with it.

In a time Δt, N electrons will be passing through the cross-sectional area with a charge of $N \cdot q_e$. Let's consider a wire with a circular cross-sectional area and electrons moving with an average velocity $\mathbf{v}$ (this is also called *drift velocity*). See Figure 15.4.

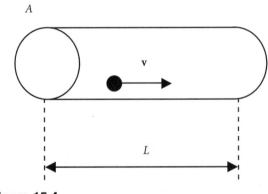

Figure 15.4

Then, by the definition of the electrical current:

$$I = N \cdot q_e / \Delta t$$

where N is the density of charges moving through the conductor.

Solving for the total charge:

$$I \cdot \Delta t = N \cdot q_e$$

Also, the volume that the N charges occupy:

$$V = A \cdot L = A \cdot (v \cdot \Delta t)$$

And then the time can be found to be:

$$\Delta t = V/A \cdot v$$

Introducing this is the current formula:

$$I \cdot V/A \cdot v = N \cdot q_e$$

We also know that for a charge, the magnetic force is:

$$F = q \cdot v \cdot B \cdot \sin \alpha$$

Then for N charges, the magnetic force will be calculated the same, but the charge is $N \cdot q_e$. Replacing the charge and simplifying, we get:

$$F = \frac{I \cdot V}{A \cdot v} \cdot v \cdot B \cdot \sin \alpha$$

$$F = \frac{I \cdot V}{A \cdot v} \cdot v \cdot B \cdot \sin \alpha$$

$$F = \frac{I \cdot V}{A} \cdot B \cdot \sin \alpha$$

$$F = I \cdot L \cdot B \cdot \sin \alpha$$

In this formula, the angle α is the angle between the electrical current and the applied magnetic field.

This result is very similar to the magnetic force on a moving charge that we worked with at the beginning of this lesson, although the place of the $q \cdot v$ product is taken by the $I \cdot L$. The same rules, the right-hand rule or the corkscrew rule, can be employed to find the direction of the resultant force, and you can probably already draw the conclusion that the force will be perpendicular to the plane formed by the current and magnetic field directions, similar to the conclusion of the first part. However, determination of the magnetic force direction is made easier by the fact that we work directly with current and not charge: The right-hand thumb will take the direction of the electric current, the

fingers point in the direction of the magnetic field, and the magnetic force will exit the palm perpendicularly.

Example

In Figure 15.5, the same wire is conducting the same current, but the direction of the field and of the magnetic field are different in the two images. Determine the direction of the magnetic force.

Solution

As shown by the figure below, the right hand rule is applied for each of the drawings:

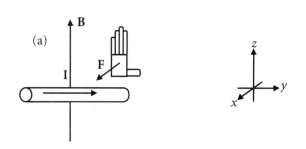

Figure 15.5

(a) The current is in the direction of the y-axis, magnetic field is in the direction of the z-axis. The resultant magnetic force vector is in the direction of the direction of the x-axis.

(b) Both the current and the magnetic field are in the direction of the z-axis, and so the angle between them is $\alpha = 0°$. The product is zero. So, no magnetic force is acting on the conductor in Figure 15.6.

(c) In Figure 15.7, the current is in the $-x$-axis direction, and the magnetic field is on z-axis direction. If you use the right-hand rule or the corkscrew rule, you determine a y direction for the magnetic force.

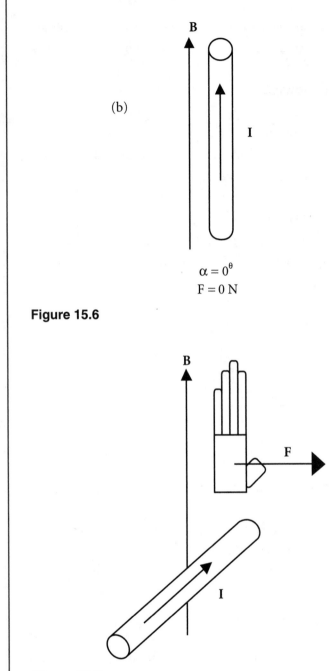

(b)

$\alpha = 0^{\theta}$
$F = 0\,N$

Figure 15.6

Figure 15.7

7. Consider a wire conducting a current I in a magnetic field. What is the relative orientation of the current with respect to the field so that the magnetic force on the wire is maximum?

8. Consider a wire conducting a current I in a magnetic field. What is the relative orientation of the current with respect to the field so that the magnetic force on the wire is zero?

► Magnetic Field Created by an Electric Current

As we learned in the previous section, an electric current is acted upon by a magnetic force. Our question now is: Does an electric current influence or create a magnetic field? The answer to this can be demonstrated with a battery, a wire, and a compass. In the presence of current through the wire, the compass is deflected from its normal position showing the magnetic field of Earth.

If we consider a long, current-carrying wire, the compass around the wire will show magnetic field lines of a circular pattern with direction influenced by the direction of the current through the wire. Again, the right-hand rule can be used to determine the magnetic field direction this time.

Experimentally, one can find the value of the magnetic field, its dependence on the current strength, and the distance relative to the wire.

In Figure 15.8, we show the magnetic field vector drawn as a vector tangent to the magnetic field line, and the size of the vector decreases with increased distance from the wire.

The magnetic field generated by a long, straight wire transporting an electrical current I at a point around the wire is proportional to the value of the

To determine the direction, the extended thumb of the right hand points in the direction of the current, and the fingers are wrapped around the wire. The fingers will point in the direction of the magnetic field.

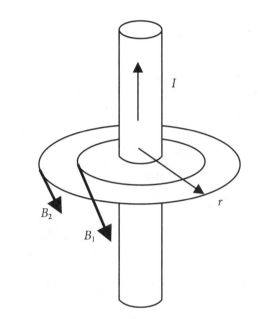

Figure 15.8

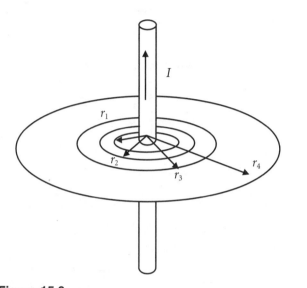

Figure 15.9

current and inversely proportional to the relative distance to the wire.

$$B = \frac{\mu_0 \cdot I}{2 \cdot \pi \cdot r}$$

The constant μ_0 is called *permeability of the vacuum*, and its universal value is:

$$\mu_0 = 4 \cdot \pi \cdot 10^{-7}\, T \cdot m/A$$

Magnetic field around the wire decreases as the larger the distance as shown in the equation. The pictorial interpretation in Figure 15.9 shows magnetic field lines at different distances from the current (concentric circles).

$$r_2 - r_1 < r_3 - r_2 < r_4 - r_3$$

In the presence of a current passing through a wire, a charge moving in proximity will be affected by the magnetic field produced by the wire, in the same manner as it would be affected by the same field created by a magnet.

Example

Consider a positive charge moving in an upward direction and in close proximity to a magnetic field, such as the one in Figure 15.10. Find the direction of the magnetic force on the charge.

Solution

As seen in the figure, the current I is creating a magnetic field. The magnetic field line shows the direction of the field according to the application of the right-hand rule. The vector describes a counterclockwise direction.

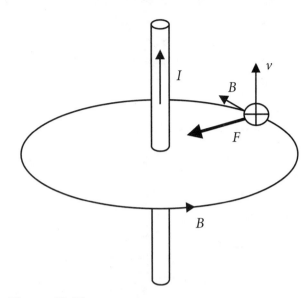

Figure 15.10

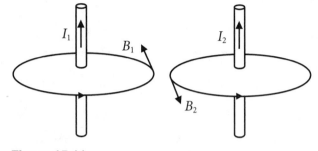

learned about the interaction between magnets, figure the type of interaction in this example.

Figure 15.11

The magnetic force is seen to be oriented perpendicular to the plane of the velocity and the magnetic field and (for this case) toward the center of the circle. This means that the linear trajectory of the particle is going to be affected and curved as a result of the magnetic interaction.

If the wire in the previous figure affects a moving charge, then it could affect a number of charges, thus forming a current. So, the logical conclusion is that two currents in proximity to each other will affect each other. Because both currents determine a magnetic field around them, their interaction can be of attraction or of repulsion depending on the field, hence of the current.

Example

Find the type of interaction between two parallel wires in which electrical currents flow in the same direction.

Solution

Start by drawing the parallel wires and their corresponding flow (see Figure 15.11). Then figure the direction of the magnetic field, and, based on what we

The significance of the diagram is that the two wires behave as two magnets with opposite poles close to each other, and, as you may remember, this means that the two wires will attract each other.

There will also be a magnetic force acting on each of these wires because the magnetic field created by a current will interact with the electric current passing through the second wire as shown in Figure 15.12.

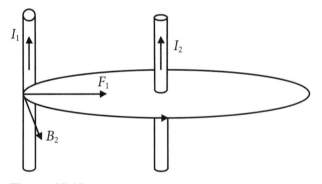

Figure 15.12

The general expression we learned in the previous sections was:

$$F = I \cdot L \cdot B \cdot \sin \alpha$$

The angle between the current and the magnetic field is 90°; therefore, the sin of 90° = 1.

$$F = I \cdot L \cdot B$$

The force on wire 1 then is:

$$F_1 = I_1 \cdot L \cdot B_2$$

Whereas the force on the second wire, considering the same length, is:

$$F_2 = I_2 \cdot L \cdot B_1$$

If we also consider the expression of the magnetic field:

$$B = \frac{\mu_0 \cdot I}{2 \cdot \pi \cdot r}$$

For each of the currents, the magnetic field is:

$$B_1 = \frac{\mu_0 \cdot I_1}{2 \cdot \pi \cdot r}$$

$$B_2 = \frac{\mu_0 \cdot I_2}{2 \cdot \pi \cdot r}$$

The distance between the two wires is the same. Then the forces become:

$$F_1 = I_1 \cdot L \cdot \frac{\mu_0 \cdot I_2}{2 \cdot \pi \cdot r} = \frac{\mu_0 \cdot L \cdot I_1 \cdot I_2}{2 \cdot \pi \cdot r}$$

And on the second current:

$$F_2 = I_2 \cdot L \cdot \frac{\mu_0 \cdot I_1}{2 \cdot \pi \cdot r} = \frac{\mu_0 \cdot L \cdot I_1 \cdot I_2}{2 \cdot \pi \cdot r}$$

The two expressions are identical, which means that each current will influence the other current with the same strength.

$$F = \frac{\mu_0 \cdot L \cdot I_1 \cdot I_2}{2 \cdot \pi \cdot r}$$

▶ Practice

9. The magnetic field of Earth is about 10 gauss. Convert that into tesla.

10. Consider a negative charge moving in a downward direction and in close proximity to an electric current passing through a wire such as the one in Figure 15.13. Find the direction of the magnetic force on the charge.

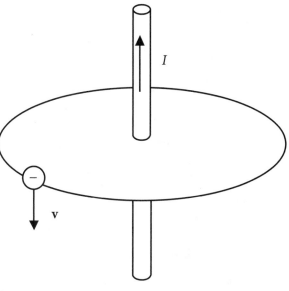

Figure 15.13

11. Show in a diagram the interaction between two parallel wires in which electrical currents flow in opposite direction.

12. If two parallel current-carrying wires move apart to twice the initial distance, what happens to the initial magnetic force between the two currents.

13. Find the maximum magnetic force per unit of length on a wire conducting a current of 10 A in the presence of a field of 300 G.

14. A number of 10^{20} electrons pass through the area of a conductor during a time period of 1 μs. Find the magnetic field at a distance of 30 cm from the wire.

15. If a straight wire was to create a magnetic field of 1 T at a distance of 10 cm, what would the current through the wire have to be?

Simple Harmonic Motion

LESSON SUMMARY
This chapter builds on Lesson 8 and is an application of the uniform rotational motion on the study of the simple pendulum. We will define period, frequency, and elastic force for the simple pendulum. We will discuss the time dependence of the position, speed, and acceleration. We will also study the mechanical energy of the simple oscillator.

▶ Simple Harmonic Motion and Elastic Force in a Simple Pendulum

You are already familiar with basic quantities such as *frequency*, *period*, and *angular speed*. We will now see how these quantities fit with a simple harmonic motion.

Simple harmonic motion is the repetitive motion of an object with respect to an origin. If an object is hanging by a spring, it will, under its own weight, come to an *equilibrium position* and in the meantime extend the spring. The equilibrium position happens due to two forces that are equal and opposite: the *gravity* on the object and the *elastic force* (equivalent to the tension in the spring).

The elastic force acting in an ideal spring is proportional to the spring elastic constant k and to the elongation or displacement of the spring from its initial length Δx. The elastic force is opposite to the displacement of the spring (shown by the minus sign). This is also known as Hooke's law.

$$W = F_{elastic}$$

The elastic force is always opposing the change in the size of the spring: So if you pull the spring, the elastic force acts to keep the length small, and if you compress the spring, the elastic force will try to bring the spring back to the initial length.

Mathematically, the expression of the elastic force is summarized as:

$$F_{elastic} = -k \cdot \Delta x$$

where Δx is the extension of the spring due to the hanging mass also known as *elongation* or *displacement* (see Figure 16.1).

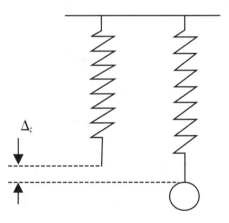

Figure 16.1

If the spring in the previous example is further extended and the object is allowed to move, the object will oscillate (symmetrical motion) around the equilibrium position creating a *simple pendulum*. In the absence of any frictional forces, the object will continue to oscillate at the same distance with respect to the equilibrium position, and the same interval will be measured every time the object reaches maximum extension. This spring is considered an *ideal spring* and the motion *simple harmonic motion*.

The elastic spring constant is dependent on the material and the strength of the chemical bonds. The unit for the elastic constant can be easily found from the definition of the force:

$$k = -F_{elastic}/\Delta x$$

The SI unit is N/m.

In reality, frictional forces spend the kinetic energy of the object. In addition, the spring itself has a mass that needs to be accelerated, so another amount of energy goes into the spring itself. The harmonic motion will become *dampened*, and the extension of the string, Δx, will decrease with each oscillation until the pendulum comes to a complete stop.

In this lesson, we will be involved with a spring of negligible mass and frictionless motion.

▶ Practice

1. The elastic constant of a spring holding an object in equilibrium is 600 N/m. Find the extension of the spring with respect to its initial length if the object has a mass of 480 g.

2. Draw a free-body diagram for an object hanging in equilibrium from a spring. Compare the magnitude of the forces you draw.

▶ Period, Frequency, and Speed of Oscillatory Motion

In order to have a visual representation of the quantities involved in the simple harmonic motion, let's look at Figure 16.2. Imagine the object oscillating around the equilibrium position and finally touching and making an impression on a screen that is moving horizontally. What is the final trajectory of the object on the screen? If we analyze Figure 16.2, we will see that the elongation or displacement varies with time in a repetitive way. We say we have an *oscillation*. One complete oscillation takes us from one point on the graph to another completely identical point further along. One example is shown in the figure: Points A and B are 1 oscillation apart. This is called a *cycle*.

This is similar to the uniform rotational motion and the related quantities we defined. Imagine a platform rotating uniformly and a side light shining on an object on the platform. The shadow of the object is

projected on a moving screen in order to obtain a trajectory for this motion. See Figure 16.3.

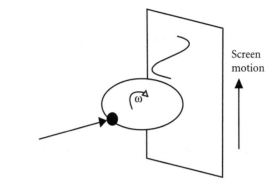

Figure 16.3

The image obtained on the screen is very similar to the one we had shown previously for the moving spring, and it describes the oscillation of the object.

In the representation in Figure 16.4, the maximum displacement is achieved when the object passes through points A and −A away from the origin, called also *amplitude*. Note that at $t = 0$ seconds, displacement is zero.

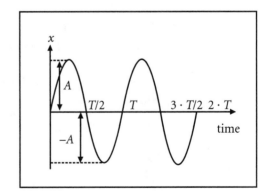

Figure 16.4

The shape of the graph is also similar to the angle dependence of the simple trigonometric functions: sin θ will start at 0 for zero angle, and will reach +1 when the angle is 90° and −1 when the angle is 270°. Therefore, the displacement can be written in terms of

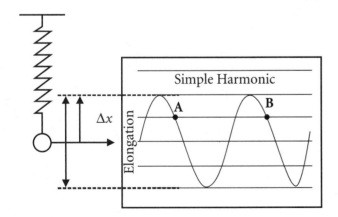

Figure 16.2

the amplitude A and as a function of the sine if we can determine the angle characterizing the oscillatory motion.

$x \sim A$ (you would read: Displacement is proportional to amplitude)
and

$x \sim \sin(\text{angle})$

For this proportionality, the last representation of the uniform circular motion is very useful. If we consider starting at time $t = 0$ seconds and consider the angular displacement of the object on the platform is $0°$, then after a time equal with one period of rotation, T, the angular displacement is 2π. Hence, the angular speed is:

$$\omega = \frac{2 \cdot \pi}{T}$$

as defined previously for uniform circular motion. The angular displacement after a time t will be:

$$\theta = \omega \cdot t$$

And the desired trigonometric function to relate the uniform circular motion to the projection on the screen is:

$$\sin(\omega \cdot t)$$

Hence the time dependence of the displacement can be written as:

$$x(t) = A \cdot \sin(\omega \cdot t)$$

One can see that at the initial time when $t = 0$ seconds, angular displacement is zero and x is zero. At $90°$, angle displacement is $+A$, and at $270°$, displacement is $-A$.

Example

Determine the amplitude A of an oscillatory motion if the displacement is 20.0 cm between times $t_0 = 0$ seconds and time $t = T/3$, where T is the period of oscillations.

Solution

Convert units to SI and set the equations to determine the unknown.

$$\Delta x = x - x_0 = 20 \text{ cm} = 0.20 \text{ m}$$

$$t_0 = 0$$

$$t = T/3$$

$$A = ?$$

$$0.2 \text{ m} = A \cdot \sin(\omega \cdot t) - A \cdot \sin(\omega \cdot t_0)$$

$$0.2 \text{ m} = A \cdot [\sin(\omega \cdot t) - \sin(\omega \cdot t_0)]$$

$$0.2 \text{ m} = A \cdot [\sin(\omega \cdot T/3) - \sin(\omega \cdot 0)]$$

$$0.2 \text{ m} = A \cdot [\sin(\omega \cdot T/3) - 0]$$

$$0.2 \text{ m} = A \cdot \sin(\omega \cdot T/3)$$

We can replace the angular speed with its previous definition

$$\omega = \frac{2 \cdot \pi}{T}$$

and:

$$0.2 \text{ m} = A \cdot \sin[(2 \cdot \pi/T) \cdot T/3]$$

$$0.2 \text{ m} = A \cdot \sin(2 \cdot \pi/3)$$

$$0.2 \text{ m} = A \cdot 0.87$$

$$A = 0.2 \text{ m}/0.87 = 0.23 \text{ m}$$

Hence, the amplitude of oscillation is:

$$A = 0.23 \text{ m}$$

The inverse of the period is *frequency*, and it represents the number of oscillations completed in a unit of time (1 second).

$$f = \frac{1}{T}$$

Therefore, the angular speed, also called *angular frequency*, can be expressed as:

$$\omega = \frac{2 \cdot \pi}{T} = 2 \cdot \pi \cdot f$$

The unit for the angular speed is radian/second (rad/s), whereas frequency is measured in hertz (Hz = 1/s), and period is in seconds.

Example

For the previous example, find the period and frequency if the angular speed is 2 degrees per second. Find the angular speed in SI.

Solution

First, set your units in SI and then solve for the unknowns according to the definitions.

$$\omega \cdot = 2° = 2° \cdot \pi/180° = \pi/90 \text{ rad/s}$$

$$\omega \cdot = 3.5 \cdot 10^{-2} \text{ rad/s}$$

$$T = ?$$

$$f = ?$$

$$T = 2\pi/\omega$$

$$T = 2 \cdot \pi/3 \cdot 5 \cdot 10^{-2} \text{ rad/s}$$

$$T = 180 \text{ s}$$

Then, frequency is nothing other than the inverse of the period:

$$f = 1/T = 1/180 \text{ s}$$

$$f = 5.5 \cdot 10^{-3} \text{ Hz}$$

Tangential speed of the uniformly rotating object can be used to determine the speed for the simple harmonic oscillator. In the uniform circular motion, the tangential speed and the angular speed are related as:

$$v_T = \omega \cdot r$$

where r is the radius of the circular motion.

The diagram in Figure 16.5 shows the speed of the oscillator to be the vertical component of the tangential speed (the projection on the screen). For the far left point, that is exactly the tangential speed (the projection of v_T is the speed itself). While moving away from the equilibrium position, the speed decreases (projection is smaller), and when the object is at maximum displacement, the speed becomes zero only to increase when the object returns to the equilibrium position (although it now has a negative sign because this time, it is approaching the origin contrary to before when it was moving away).

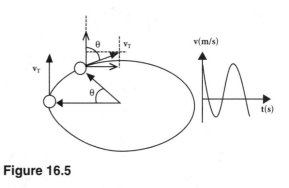

Figure 16.5

The vertical component of the speed is seen to be:

$$v = v_T \cdot \cos(\theta)$$

But because the object experiences a uniform circular motion, the angular displacement is given by the angular speed:

$$v(t) = v_T \cdot \cos(\omega \cdot t)$$

Or:

$$v(t) = \omega \cdot r \cdot \cos(\theta) = \omega \cdot r \cdot \cos(\omega \cdot t)$$

If you also compare the circular motion to the shadow the object leaves on the screen, one can determine the radius to be the amplitude of the oscillatory motion A.

$$r = A$$

And then the final formula for the speed is:

$$v(t) = \omega \cdot A \cdot \cos(\theta) = \omega \cdot A \cdot \cos(\omega \cdot t)$$

Even more interesting is to see that we start with a uniform rotational motion (speed constant) and end up with a time-dependent speed for the oscillatory motion that will involve acceleration also.

If we study the time dependence in the previous equation, we can determine the acceleration to be:

$$a(t) = -\omega^2 \cdot A \cdot \sin(\theta) = -\omega^2 \cdot A \cdot \sin(\omega \cdot t)$$

But we already have defined the elastic force, so how does this acceleration translate into the force? Imagine we extend the spring and then release it. The oscillations will occur due to the elastic force that tries to restore equilibrium. So in the absence of other forces, the elastic force is the net force:

$$F = m \cdot a = F_{\text{elastic}}$$

$$m \cdot a = -k \cdot \Delta x$$

$$m \cdot [-\omega^2 \cdot A \cdot \sin(\omega \cdot t)] = -k \cdot \Delta x$$

If we consider that at equilibrium, the displacement is zero, then:

$$\Delta x = x - x_0 = x - 0 = x$$

And plugging this back into the forces equation, we have:

$$m \cdot [-\omega^2 \cdot A \cdot \sin(\omega \cdot t)] = -k \cdot x$$

Or:

$$m \cdot [-\omega^2 \cdot A \cdot \sin(\omega \cdot t)] = -k \cdot A \cdot \sin(\omega \cdot t)$$

Eliminating the similar factors from the left- and right-hand sides, we get:

$$k = m \cdot \omega^2$$

And the elastic force is:

$$F_{\text{elastic}} = -m \cdot \omega^2 \cdot A \cdot \sin(\omega \cdot t)$$

$$F_{\text{elastic}} = -k \cdot A \cdot \sin(\omega \cdot t)$$

Because the sine function varies between -1 and $+1$, the elastic force is seen to be variable with time. Its extremes are:

$$F_{\text{elastic MAX}} = +k \cdot A$$

$$F_{\text{elastic MIN}} = -k \cdot A$$

Example

Following the example of finding the extreme values of the elastic force, find the minimum acceleration and explain what the position is and what the speed of the object is when this happens.

Solution

So, we are to find a_{MIN} and the position at the time. For this, we start with the general expression of the acceleration:

$$a(t) = -\omega^2 \cdot A \cdot \sin(\theta) = -\omega^2 \cdot A \cdot \sin(\omega \cdot t)$$

Because this expression is also dependent on the sine of the angular displacement at the time t, and because sine takes values between $+1$ and -1, we have the following situation. When

$$\sin(\omega \cdot t) = +1$$

$$a = -\omega^2 \cdot A \cdot \sin(\omega \cdot t)$$

$$a = -\omega^2 \cdot A = -k \cdot A/m$$

and acceleration is minimum. In the same time, we know that force is minimum and this makes sense because the two, acceleration and force, are directly proportional.

If $\sin\theta = 1$, then according to the relationship between the sine and cosine of an angle:

$$\sin\theta^2 + \cos\theta^2 = 1$$

the cosine will be zero, which means that speed is zero:

$$v(t) = A \cdot \omega \cdot \cos \cdot \theta$$

$$v = A \cdot \omega \cdot 0 = 0 \, m/s$$

and the displacement is maximum:

$$x(t) = A \cdot \sin\theta$$

$$x = A$$

Interpreting these results, starting with the displacement, we can argue that the object is at the "top of the crest" and on the verge of changing its motion away from the origin to a motion of coming back. At that point, the force and acceleration are maximum in absolute value but negative (which makes them minimum), the speed is zero (the object is changing direction of motion), and the displacement is maximum and positive.

▶ Practice

3. If the period of an oscillatory motion is 2.4 seconds, what is the angular speed in rad/s and in degrees/s?

4. For the information given in practice problem 3, calculate the frequency and the angular displacement after $T/4$, $T/3$, $T/2$, and T.

5. Find the maximum acceleration and explain what the position is and what the speed of the object is when this happens.

6. An object of mass 250 g oscillates by a spring and its motion is described by the following time dependence:

$$x(t) = 1.2 \, m \cdot \sin(5 \cdot t + 30°)$$

Determine the equations for the speed, acceleration, and force acting on the object as functions of time.

7. For the information given in practice problem 6, determine the initial angular displacement at time $t = 0$ s, the initial displacement, and speed.

► Energy of a Simple Harmonic Oscillator

As with all our mechanical concepts, we will define a mechanical energy for the simple harmonic oscillator. This energy will be composed of the energy of motion and the energy of position—that is, kinetic and potential energies.

Kinetic energy (KE) is proportional, as before, with the mass of the oscillating object (not of the spring, which is considered massless) and the square of the speed.

$$KE = \frac{m \cdot v^2}{2}$$

Replacing the speed by its time dependence:

$$KE = \frac{m \cdot (A \cdot \omega \cdot \cos\theta)^2}{2} = m \cdot A^2 \cdot \omega^2 \cdot \frac{\cos^2\theta}{2}$$

One can see that *KE* is maximum at times when $\cos\theta = +1$, and $\theta = \omega \cdot t = n \cdot \pi$, where n is any integer number. But we already have a definition of the angular speed:

$$\omega = \frac{2 \cdot \pi}{T}$$

and with this:

$$\theta = \frac{2 \cdot \pi}{T} \cdot t = n \cdot \pi$$

$$t = \frac{n \cdot \pi}{2 \cdot \pi} \cdot T = \frac{n}{2} \cdot T$$

So, for every half a period: $T/2, T, 3 \cdot T/2, 2 \cdot T$, and so on, the *KE* is maximum. But that is the time when speed also reaches its limits, and displacement and acceleration are zero.

KE is zero when $\cos\theta = 0$, and $\theta = n \cdot \pi/2$, where n is an integer. In this case, the speed is zero and the acceleration and displacement are at a maximum (top and bottom of the crest).

So what happens with all that energy at that position? All of it will be converted into potential energy. What is potential energy? When the spring is extended, the particles inside are at different positions with respect to each other and compared to the equilibrium position, and this relative position is summed by the potential energy, *PE*.

$$PE = \frac{k \cdot x^2}{2}$$

and replacing displacement into this equation:

$$PE = \frac{k \cdot (A \cdot \sin\theta)^2}{2} = k \cdot A^2 \cdot \frac{\sin^2\theta}{2}$$

Or using the expression for elastic constant:

$$k = m \cdot \omega^2$$

$$PE = m \cdot \omega^2 \cdot A^2 \cdot \frac{\sin^2\theta}{2}$$

Remember, we work in a conservative case (no loss through friction), and the mechanical energy is conserved. Let's check and see if it is true that:

$$E = KE + PE = \text{constant}$$

If we imagine the oscillatory motion through the angular displacement θ and at two moments of time the angular displacement to be θ_1 and θ_2, then the mechanical energy at these two times is:

$$E_1 = KE_1 + PE_1 = m \cdot A^2 \cdot \omega^2 \cdot \frac{\cos^2\theta_1}{2} +$$

$$m \cdot A^2 \cdot \omega^2 \cdot \frac{\sin^2\theta_1}{2}$$

$$E_1 = m \cdot A^2 \cdot \omega^2 \cdot \frac{1}{2}(\cos^2\theta_1 + \sin^2\theta_1)$$

And the trigonometric equality

$$\cos^2\theta_1 + \sin^2\theta_1 = 1$$

then:

$$E_1 = \frac{1}{2} \cdot m \cdot A^2 \cdot \omega^2$$

Evidently, the same result will be obtained for E_2 because this result is in no way dependent on the value of the angular displacement or on any value that is not constant for the motion.

$$E_2 = \frac{1}{2} \cdot m \cdot A^2 \cdot \omega^2$$

Hence $E_1 = E_2$ and E = constant as shown in Figure 16.6. The total mechanical energy is represented by the thick line (— symbol forming a line at the top of the two oscillatory functions), and it is seen to be a horizontal line running along the graph.

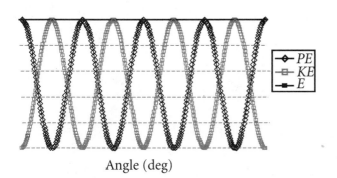

Angle (deg)

Figure 16.6

▶ **Practice**

8. At maximum displacement, an object in simple harmonic oscillation motion reaches the amplitude of 3.20 cm. The object is 1,250 g, and the mechanical energy of the object is measured to be 30 J. Find the maximum speed of the object.

9. For the previous practice problem, find the angular frequency of the motion.

10. Based on the information given in the graph in Figure 16.7, find the period, frequency, and angular frequency.

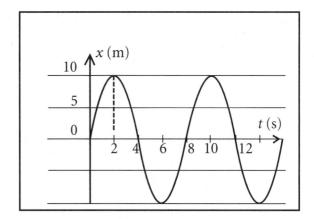

Figure 16.7

11. Based on the information given in Figure 16.7, find the maximum potential energy and kinetic energy and the total energy of an object of mass 1 kg that describes an oscillatory motion as the one shown.

12. Considering that between two consecutive positions the potential energy of an oscillator increases three times, what happens to the kinetic energy of the oscillator? Explain.

13. Two completely identical oscillators are put in motion such that the amplitude of one is four times larger than the amplitude of the other, with all other parameters of motion being identical. Compare the total energies of the oscillators.

17 ▶ Waves

LESSON SUMMARY

This lesson studies the general characteristics of waves such as frequency, speed, and wavelength; sound waves and propagation in a medium; and electromagnetic waves and electromagnetic spectrum.

▶ Characteristics of a Wave

The physical appearance of a water wave or of a string that's fixed at one end but pulsed vertically at the other is very similar to the time dependence of the displacement we have studied in the previous lesson. The quantities we have defined there will be reused in the case of waves.

Waves are disturbances produced in matter by the interaction with a source that supplies an energy. This energy comes from the wind in the case of the ocean waves, from an earthquake in the case of tsunami waves, or from your finger in the case of guitar strings.

Also, a wave has the disturbance propagated through the material with no bulk flow of matter; therefore, a wave is not the motion of masses of water but simply the propagation of the energy from one position to another. The motion of a particle of water in a wave is actually circular, as shown in Figure 17.1.

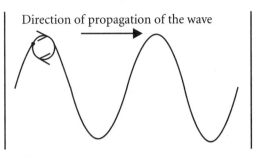

Figure 17.1

The water particle is seen to move up and down and not in the direction of propagation of the wave. In conclusion, waves have some characteristics that are worth summarizing: They represent a disturbance in the matter, they carry energy through the matter, and they do not involve bulk flow of matter.

The way the water particles travel while acted on by a wave is the more complex part of the idea of a wave. We can break the behavior down into two more simple types of propagation. According to the relative direction of the disturbance with respect to the propagation of the wave, there are *longitudinal* and *transversal* waves.

Longitudinal waves have the disturbance and the wave propagation parallel to each other, such as in the case of a slinky set on a table and pushed back and forth. Regions along the slinky will be compressed, and others will be stretched. See Figure 17.2.

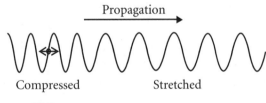

Figure 17.2

Transversal waves have the disturbance and the wave propagation perpendicular to each other, such as in the case of a slinky set on a table and pulsed up and down.

If you now take a string and fix it at one end and leave the other one free as seen in Figure 17.3, and at the free end, you start applying an up and down pulse, the string will be disturbed in a vertical direction while the wave will propagate to the right as in Figure 17.4.

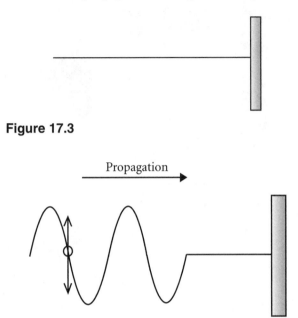

Figure 17.3

Figure 17.4

As one can see, the waves discussed here have the same cyclic behavior as encountered previously in the simple harmonic motion. We will call these waves *periodic* waves, and we will define their period, frequency, amplitude, and speed, as we did for harmonic motion. See Figures 17.5 and 17.6 for graphic representations of these quantities.

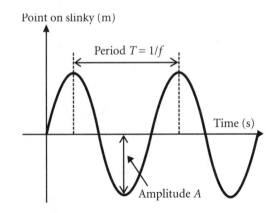

Figure 17.5

The *period* will be the time it takes a point acted on by the disturbance to repeat motion, and it is the inverse of the *frequency* (which represents the number of complete cyclic motions that a point describes in a second). The *wavelength* is the distance between two identical positions that the wave has reached. And the *amplitude* is the maximum displacement of the particle relative to the equilibrium position.

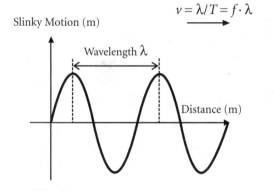

$$v = \lambda / T = f \cdot \lambda$$

Slinky Motion (m)

Wavelength λ

Distance (m)

Figure 17.6

The speed of the wave is defined as the ratio of the wavelength to the period:

$$v = \frac{\lambda}{T}$$

But because the period and frequency are inversely proportional, we have also:

$$v = f \cdot \lambda$$

Example

A microwave oven works based on microwaves that have a wavelength between 30 cm and 10^{-3} m. Find the range of frequencies if the speed is $3 \cdot 10^8$ m/s.

Solution

We need the frequencies, so the previous definition of speed will be needed, and then we can solve for frequency in two cases:

$$\lambda_1 = 30 \, \text{cm} = 3 \cdot 10^{-1} \, \text{m}$$

$$\lambda_2 = 10^{-3} \, \text{m}$$

$$v = 3 \cdot 10^8 \, \text{m/s}$$

$$f_1 = ?$$

$$f_2 = ?$$

$$v = f \cdot \lambda$$

$$f = \frac{v}{\lambda}$$

$$f_1 = \frac{v}{\lambda_1} = \frac{3 \cdot 10^8 \, \text{m/s}}{0.3 \, \text{m}} = 1 \cdot 10^9 \, \text{Hz}$$

and

$$f_2 = \frac{v}{\lambda_2} = \frac{3 \cdot 10^8 \, \text{m/s}}{10^{-3} \, \text{m}} = 3 \cdot 10^{11} \, \text{Hz}$$

So, the range of frequencies is between 10^9 and $3 \cdot 10^{11}$ Hz.

Mechanical waves in the examples before need a medium in which to propagate: for example, water, string, a spring, and so on. The speed of propagation though is different according to the intrinsic properties of the material. The same interaction, or force, can produce different frequency waves depending on the characteristics of the string. An expression of the speed in a string shows speed to be:

$$v = \sqrt{\frac{T}{m/L}}$$

In this expression, T is the tension created in the material through interaction, and m/L is called *linear density* and refers to the mass per unit of length.

Example

Consider a string acted upon by a tension of 152 N and having a length of 52 cm and a mass of 134 g. Find the speed of the wave propagating through the cord.

Solution

First, look for known data and SI units. Then, set your equation for wave propagation and solve for the unknown.

$T = 152\,\text{N}$

$L = 52\,\text{m} = 0.52\,\text{m}$

$m = 134\,\text{g} = 0.134\,\text{kg}$

$v = ?$

$$v = \sqrt{\frac{T}{m/L}} = \sqrt{\frac{152\,\text{N}}{0.134\,\text{kg}/0.52\,\text{m}}}$$

$v = \sqrt{590\,\text{s}^2/\text{m}^2}$

$v = 24\,\text{m/s}$

▶ Practice

1. The speed of a radio wave is $3 \cdot 10^5$ km/s and the frequency is 10^4 Hz. Find the wavelength and the period of the wave.
2. A particle on the surface of a string acted on by a transversal wave repeats 10 cycles in 6 seconds. The wave propagates at a rate of 10 cm/s. Find the frequency and speed of the wave.
3. If two musical cords are acted on by the same force, but at the same length, one is two times heavier than the other, how do the speeds of the waves in the two cords compare?

▶ Sound Waves

One special type of wave that can be created mechanically and propagates through matter is called *sound*. Although the frequency range for sound is rather large, human beings can hear sounds only between about 12 and 20 Hz and between 14 and 20 KHz. Below the 20 Hz extreme, frequencies are called *infrasonic*, whereas above 20 KHz, they are called *ultrasonic*.

We hear sounds not only with different frequencies but also with different intensities. The loudness of the sound is given (measured) by the amplitude of the wave. And the amplitude of the wave is given (measured) by the pressure change with the wave.

As mentioned previously, in order for sound to propagate, a medium is needed—be it a gas, a liquid, or a solid. Sound will not propagate in a vacuum. The reason for this is that sound waves propagate by creating regions of *compression* (or *condensation*) and *rarefaction* in the medium where the sounds acts. Once propagation has started, the *change of pressure* due to the sound waves has a pattern similar to the other waves we studied previously (see Figure 17.7).

As with the case of waves in strings, the speed of sound is affected by the intrinsic properties of the material. We will define three different speed expressions—one for gas, one for liquids, and one for solids.

When a disturbance is produced, particles collide with each other forming a region of high concentration in the direction of propagation (condensation or compression area) and leaving behind a region of low density (rarefaction). Hence, the disturbance and the

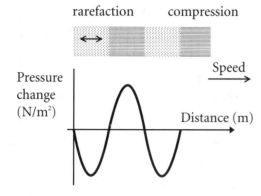

Figure 17.7

wave are in the same direction, and we conclude that sound waves are *longitudinal waves*.

Experimental work shows that the speed of sound in gases (ideal gases) is:

$$v = \sqrt{\frac{\gamma \cdot k \cdot T}{m}}$$

In this expression, the γ is the *adiabatic factor* and depends on the material, T is the temperature in Kelvin, m is the mass of a molecule of substance in the specific medium, and k is Boltzmann's constant and is equal to $1.38 \cdot 10^{-23}$ J/K.

Example

The laboratory motion sensors used in mechanics experiments are ultrasonic sensors that send a wave out and measure the amount of time to its return. By knowing the time and the speed of the sound, you can measure the position of different objects relative to the position of the sensor. Considering the speed of sound to be 343 m/s in a room where the temperature is 20° C, find the mass of a molecule of the gas present in the room. (γ is 1.2.)

Solution

First, inventory your known data and then set the equation necessary to find the mass.

$v = 343$ m/s

$T = t + 273.15$ K $=$

$20°$ C $+ 273.15$ K $= 293.15$ K

$\gamma = 1.2$

$m = ?$

$$v = \sqrt{\frac{\gamma \cdot k \cdot T}{m}} =$$

$$\sqrt{\frac{1.2 \cdot 1.38 \cdot 10^{-23} \text{ J/K} \cdot 293.15 \text{ K}}{m}}$$

$$v = \sqrt{\frac{485 \cdot 10^{-23} \text{ J}}{m}}$$

$$v^2 = \frac{485 \cdot 10^{-23} \text{ J}}{m}$$

$$m = \frac{485 \cdot 10^{-23} \text{ J}}{v^2}$$

$$m = \frac{485 \cdot 10^{-23} \text{ J}}{(343 \text{ m/s})^2}$$

$$m = 1.41 \cdot 10^{-23} \text{ kg}$$

In the case of a liquid, the speed of sound is:

$$v = \sqrt{\frac{K}{\rho}}$$

where K is a coefficient that depends on the pressure change with volume and ρ is the density of the liquid. Both factors are material dependent.

And lastly, the speed of sound is also affected by the nature of the solid in which it travels. The expression is:

$$v = \sqrt{\frac{E}{\rho}}$$

where E is Young's modulus that measures the elastic properties of an object subject to a force, and ρ is the density of the solid.

▶ Practice

4. Sound travels with a speed of 343 m/s in air. Find the speed of sound in steel where $K = 200$ GPa and $\rho = 7{,}870$ kg/m³, and in water where $E = 2{,}200$ GPa and $\rho = 1{,}000$ kg/m³. Compare to the speed in air.

5. The same source is used to propagate sound between two points. Two different materials are tested to find one that can achieve greater speed. At the same modulus of elasticity, which material will perform better: the lower density or the higher density one? Explain

6. Based on the answer in practice problem 4, what is your expectation for the speed of sound in ice, water, and steam: increase, decrease, stay the same? Explain.

7. When sound travels in between two different media, the frequency remains the same. What happens to the wavelength of a sound that travels from air to water?

▶ Electromagnetic Waves

Mechanical sources produce mechanical waves that require a medium in which to propagate, but there are other sources that produce waves that can travel through a vacuum. The fluctuation of a magnetic and electric field can produce a propagating wave called an *electromagnetic wave.*

How is it possible to have propagation without mass? Remember a few lessons ago, we learned that a current can induce a magnetic field and a magnetic field can induce a current. The two factors together can propagate through space with no requirement of matter. The magnetic and electric field fluctuation was studied by James Maxwell (1831–1879), and the diagram of the effect is shown in Figure 17.8.

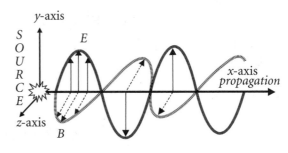

Figure 17.8

Although electromagnetic waves propagate through media, the maximum speed is achieved in a vacuum. And for the purpose of this lesson, we will work with a value of:

$$c = 3.0 \cdot 10^8 \, \text{m/s}$$

The electromagnetic spectrum contains the visible spectrum, or *light* as we call it. But this is only a small part of the range of electromagnetic frequencies, which vary from $4.05 \cdot 10^{14}$ to $7.9 \cdot 10^{14}$ Hz. Other components of the *electromagnetic spectrum* are listed in Table 17.1.

The wavelength for the ranges of frequency can be easily found by using the definition of the speed of the wave:

$$v = f \cdot \lambda$$

$$\lambda = \frac{v}{f}$$

For a vacuum, the speed of an electromagnetic wave is c:

$$\lambda = \frac{c}{f}$$

Table 17.1

COMPONENTS OF THE ELECTROMAGNETIC SPECTRUM

WAVE TYPE	FREQUENCY
Gamma rays	10^{18} to 10^{23} Hz
X-rays	10^{16} to 10^{20} Hz
Ultra-violet	10^{15} to 10^{17} Hz
Visible	10^{14} to 10^{15} Hz
Infrared	10^{12} to 10^{14} Hz
Microwaves	10^{9} to 10^{11} Hz
Radio waves FM	around 10^{8} Hz
Radio waves AM	around 10^{6} Hz

Example

Find the range of wavelength for visible light if the light spectrum corresponds to the range from $4.05 \cdot 10^{14}$ to $7.9 \cdot 10^{14}$ Hz.

Solution

Set up the previous equation with the proper data and solve for the frequency.

$$\lambda = \frac{c}{f} = \frac{3 \cdot 10^{8}\,\text{m/s}}{4.05 \cdot 10^{14}\,1/\text{s}} = 740.7 \cdot 10^{-9}\,\text{m}$$

A unit very often used in optics is the nanometer: $1\,\text{nm} = 10^{-9}\,\text{m}$.

$$\lambda = \frac{c}{f} = \frac{3 \cdot 10^{8}\,\text{m/s}}{7.9 \cdot 10^{14}\,1/\text{s}} = 379.7 \cdot 10^{-9}\,\text{m}$$

Hence, we have a range of 380 nm to 741 nm.

The *energy* carried by the electromagnetic wave is dependent on the properties of the two propagating fields, and its expression is:

$$u = \frac{1}{2} \cdot \varepsilon_0 \cdot E^2 + \frac{1}{2 \cdot \mu_0} \cdot B^2$$

where E and B are the electric and magnetic fields, and ε_0 and μ_0 are the permittivity and permeability of vacuum.

$$\varepsilon_0 = 8.85 \cdot 10^{-12}\,\text{C}^2/\text{N} \cdot \text{m}^2 \text{ and } \mu = 4 \cdot \pi \cdot 10^{-7}\,\text{T} \cdot \text{m/A}$$

In a vacuum, the electric and magnetic fields are related by:

$$E = c \cdot B$$

And the speed in vacuum is given by:

$$c = \frac{1}{\sqrt{\varepsilon_0 \cdot \mu_0}}$$

Example

Reduce the expression of the energy of the electromagnetic waves to a simpler form using the connection between the electric field and the magnetic field.

Solution

Start with the definition of the energy, and, using the previous expression, try to simplify it.

$$u = \frac{1}{2} \cdot \varepsilon_0 \cdot E^2 + \frac{1}{2 \cdot \mu_0} \cdot B^2$$

$$u = \frac{1}{2} \cdot \varepsilon_0 \cdot (c \cdot B)^2 + \frac{1}{2 \cdot \mu_0} \cdot B^2$$

$$u = \frac{1}{2} \cdot \left(\varepsilon_0 \cdot c^2 + \frac{1}{\mu_0} \right) \cdot B^2$$

$$u = \frac{1}{2} \cdot \left[\varepsilon_0 \cdot \left(\frac{1}{\sqrt{\varepsilon_0 \cdot \mu_0}} \right)^2 + \frac{1}{\mu_0} \right] \cdot B^2$$

$$u = \frac{1}{2} \cdot \left[\varepsilon_0 \cdot \left(\frac{1}{\varepsilon_0 \cdot \mu_0} \right) + \frac{1}{\mu_0} \right] \cdot B^2$$

$$u = \frac{1}{2} \cdot \left[\frac{1}{\mu_0} + \frac{1}{\mu_0} \right] \cdot B^2$$

$$u = \frac{1}{2} \cdot \left[\frac{1}{\mu_0} + \frac{1}{\mu_0} \right] \cdot B^2$$

$$u = \frac{1}{\mu_0} \cdot B^2$$

▶ Practice

8. Ultraviolet waves of $5 \cdot 10^{-8}$ m are produced by the sun. What is the frequency of the waves? What is the time for the waves to travel to Earth? The distance to the sun is $1.5 \cdot 10^{11}$ m.

9. For best performance, an antenna has to have a length half of the wavelength of the received wave. Find the size of an antenna that receives frequencies of 10^8 Hz.

10. A wave is propagating through a vacuum, and the amplitude of the electric field is 200 V/m. Find the energy of the wave and the amplitude of the magnetic field necessary to propagate this wave.

LESSON SUMMARY

This lesson introduces you to the concept of optics and the geometrical analysis of optical phenomena. We will study the concept of light rays, the laws of reflection, the laws of refraction, and the total internal reflection.

▶ Light Rays

The study of light encompasses many fields of physics, from mechanics to quantum mechanics and from classical to modern physics. Isaac Newton explained reflection and refraction phenomena based on particle motion, and Max Planck's particle theory explained radiation. On the other hand, the theories of electricity, magnetism, and waves explained light behavior as a wave, as Christian Huygens and James Maxwell did in their theories. A dual explanation of the properties and processes in which light is involved emerged through history. In this lesson, we will address the particle explanation of light.

The geometrical analysis of light propagation assumes that light travels in a straight line through a medium and between two points. If the optical properties of the medium change, light changes the path of propagation. This is called *geometrical optics* and the propagation of light in a straight line is called *ray approximation*.

▶ Reflection of Light

At the boundary between two media, the light ray will change its direction of propagation depending on the properties of the second medium and on the relative position of the light with respect to the surface of the interface. The light propagating from a source toward a smooth surface will bounce from the surface and return to the medium that contains the source. This phenomenon is called *reflection of light*, the incoming light ray is called the *incident ray*, and the returning light ray is called the *reflected ray*. A diagram of the propagation of light at the interface between two media also defines the important angles we will use to set the laws of reflection: the *incident* and *reflection angles*. Both angles are defined relative to the perpendicular to the interface called the *normal*. The two media are shown differently in Figure 18.1 to enhance the surface of separation where reflection occurs.

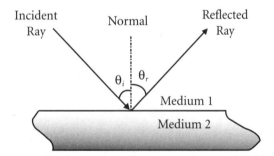

Figure 18.1

Experimental work shows that reflection is governed by the following laws:

- The incident, reflected ray, and the normal are in the same plane.
- The angle of incidence and the angle of reflection are equal:

$$\theta_i = \theta_r$$

If several rays of light are parallel and are traveling toward a smooth surface, after reflection, they will be once again propagating in parallel directions, as in Figure 18.2. This is called *specular reflection* and the reason is that each of the beams will reflect from the same plane surface.

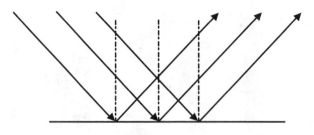

Figure 18.2

If the surface is not smooth, the outgoing set of rays will no longer be parallel because the roughness of the surface means that different rays have different incident and respective reflection angles. This is called a *diffuse reflection*, and the way light is reflected at different angles from the rough surface is shown in Figure 18.3.

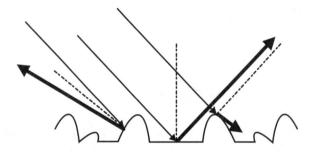

Figure 18.3

The rays represented by thicker lines represent the reflected rays and one can see that their direction is dictated by the normal to the surface, which differs between the three cases (the normal is perpendicular on the tangent to the curve at a certain position).

Example

Two planes are set such that they form an angle of 100° with each other. A light is incident on the first surface at an angle of 60°. Find the angle of the reflected light from the second plane with respect to the normal to that plane.

Solution

First, we need to set our angle diagram and use the laws of reflection to determine the angle of the outgoing ray (see Figure 18.4).

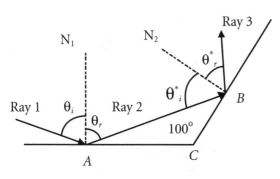

Figure 18.4

In the *ABC* triangle, the angle at *A* can be found from the first law of reflection:

$$\theta_i = \theta_r = 60°$$

And since the triangle totals 180° with *A* at 30°, *C* is 100° and *B* is 50°.

$$\theta_i = 90° - B = 90° - 50° = 40°$$

$$\theta^*_i = 40°$$

Again, we use the law of reflection on the second surface:

$$\theta^*_i = \theta^*_r = 40°$$

Practice

1. In the previous example, find the angle the outgoing ray (Ray 3) makes with the vertical (N_1).

2. Two planes are set such that they form an angle of 90° with each other. A light is incident on the first surface at an angle of 70°. Find the angle of the reflected light from the second plane with respect to the normal to that plane.

3. In Figure 18.5, the propagation of the incident ray is such that the angle of the reflected ray with the horizontal is 25°. Find the incident angle.

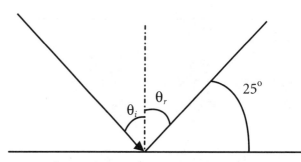

Figure 18.5

▶ Refraction of Light

The examples we studied previously are probably easy to understand if you have performed experiments such as shining a light on a mirror or a shiny metal surface. But what happens when light meets a transparent medium and not an opaque one? We all know that light is transmitted beyond the surface of separation. Light goes through the water in your glass and even through the glass itself. This phenomenon of light propagation from a transparent medium to another transparent medium is called *refraction*. But refraction is affected by the properties of the medium itself, and the direction of propagation is changed by it. The corresponding rays are called *incident* and *refracted* rays, as are the angles. Figure 18.6 shows an incident wave and the refraction on the separation surfaces.

On the far left, we have the incident ray refracting on the surface and propagating inside Medium 2 at an angle smaller than the incident angle:

$$\theta_i < \theta_r$$

This behavior happens when light comes from a medium where the speed of light is larger and

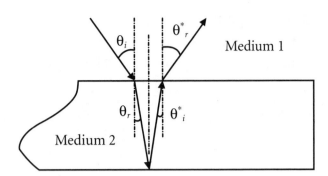

Figure 18.6

propagates into a medium with reduced speed. The light bends toward the normal when

$$v_1 > v_2$$

where v_1, and v_2 are the speed of light in Medium 1 and Medium 2.

On the right side of the picture, we see the light reflecting from the bottom of Medium 2 and refracting at the surface of separation a second time. This time, the angle of refraction is larger than the angle of incidence because the light returns to Medium 1 where the speed of propagation is larger.

$$\theta^*_i > \theta^*_r$$

The light bends away from the normal when

$$v_1 < v_2$$

Analyzing the geometry of the figure and relating to the speed in respective media, one can determine after some calculations a law of refraction relating the angles of incidence and refraction.

The laws of refraction are as follows:

- The incident, refracted ray, and normal are in the same plane.
- The angle of incidence and the angle of refraction are related by

$$\frac{\sin \theta_r}{\sin \theta_i} = \frac{v_2}{v_1}$$

In optics, we also work with a coefficient that relates the speed of light in the specific medium with the speed in vacuum, and it is called the *index of refraction*:

$$n = \frac{\text{speed of light in vacuum}}{\text{speed of light in medium}} = \frac{c}{v}$$

The index of refraction is a unitless quantity and it is material dependent. A few values for the most common substances are given in Table 18.1.

Because the index of refraction is so close to 1 for air, we will consider $n = 1$. One note on propagation in a different medium is that the frequency of the wave

Table 18.1

REFRACTION VALUES OF COMMON SUBSTANCES

MATERIAL	INDEX OF REFRACTION, n
Air	1.00029
Co2	1.00045
Water	1.333
Ice	1.31
Diamond	2.42
Zirconia	2.2
Glass, flint	1.66
Vacuum	1

will remain constant while the wavelength changes with speed.

Returning to the laws of refraction, we will find a second version of the law of the angles by multiplying the right-hand-side fraction with the speed of light in a vacuum:

$$\frac{\sin\theta_r}{\sin\theta_i} = \frac{c}{c} \cdot \frac{v_2}{v_1}$$

and with the definition of the index of refraction:

$$n_1 = \frac{c}{v_1}$$

$$n_2 = \frac{c}{v_2}$$

$$\frac{\sin\theta_r}{\sin\theta_i} = \frac{n_1}{n_2}$$

or separating on the same side factors related to the incident and refracted rays, respectively:

$$n_1 \cdot \sin\theta_i = n_2 \cdot \sin\theta_r$$

This is also known as Snell's law of refraction (Willebroad van Roijen Snell, 1580–1626).

For the purpose of this lesson, we will consider the index of refraction constant, although in reality, n is wavelength dependent. This dependence is the explanation for phenomena such as the dispersion of light through a prism.

Example

Light travels from a vacuum through the medium of an index of refraction of 1.55. Find the speed of light in the second medium and the wavelength in each medium if the frequency is $6 \cdot 10^{14}$ Hz. If the light comes at an incident angle of 30°, what is the refraction angle?

Solution

We want to set all known data and then determine what expressions are useful to determine the unknowns. We know that the first medium is a vacuum and the second is a material that has an index of refraction of 1.55.

$$n_1 = 1$$

$$n_2 = 1.55$$

$$\theta_1 = 30°$$

$$f = 6 \cdot 10^{14}\,\text{Hz}$$

$$v_2 = ?$$

$$\lambda_1 = ?$$

$$\lambda_2 = ?$$

$$\theta_2 = ?$$

From the definition of the index of refraction, we can determine v_2:

$$n_2 = \frac{c}{v_2}$$

$$v_2 = \frac{c}{n_2}$$

$$v_2 = \frac{3 \cdot 10^8\,\text{m/s}}{1.55} = 1.94 \cdot 10^8\,\text{m/s}$$

We remember that $v = \lambda \cdot f$, and that frequency stays the same with refraction. Then:

$$v_1 = \lambda \cdot f$$

$$\lambda_1 = \frac{v_1}{f}$$

And since the first medium is a vacuum, the speed v_1 equals c:

$$\lambda_1 = \frac{c}{f} = \frac{3 \cdot 10^8 \, \text{m/s}}{6 \cdot 10^{14} \, \text{Hz}}$$

$$\lambda_1 = 600 \, \text{nm} \quad \overset{500}{}$$

And in the second medium,

$$\lambda_2 = \frac{v_2}{f} = \frac{1.94 \cdot 10^8 \, \text{m/s}}{6 \cdot 10^{14} \, \text{Hz}}$$

$$\lambda_2 = 323 \, \text{nm}$$

Then to determine the refraction angle, we apply Snell's law:

$$n_1 \cdot \sin \theta_i = n_2 \cdot \sin \theta_r$$

$$1 \cdot \sin 30° = 1.55 \cdot \sin \theta_r$$

$$\frac{1 \cdot \sin 30°}{1.55} = \sin \theta_r$$

$$\sin \theta_r = 0.32$$

$$\theta_r = \sin^{-1}(0.32) = 18.7°$$

▶ Practice

4. Determine the angle of refraction for a light ray that travels from air to water at an angle of incidence of 42°.

5. In Figure 18.7, draw the light ray propagation of the two parallel rays through air, in glass, and back in air.

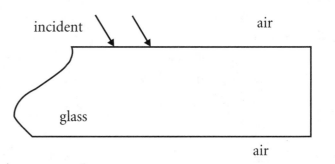

Figure 18.7

6. In Figure 18.8, draw the light ray propagation of the two parallel rays through air in glass and back in air. Consider that inside the glass, the surface is such that, instead of refraction, reflection will occur.

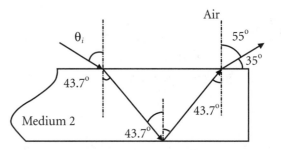

Figure 18.8

7. A light ray propagates from a medium with a small index of refraction to a medium with a larger index of refraction. Is the light going to be bent toward or away from the normal? Explain.

8. For Figure 18.9, fill in the missing numbers and find the index of refraction for the second medium.

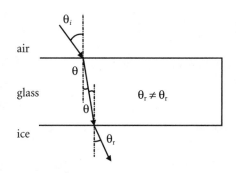

Figure 18.9

9. Imagine a setup where the light has to travel from air to glass and to go out in ice. Draw the diagram representing light propagation through these media and show the angle of incidence and refraction on each surface.

10. For Figure 18.10, find the angle of refraction for the first surface of separation and the angle of refraction for the ray that propagates outside the glass (flint) and into the air again.

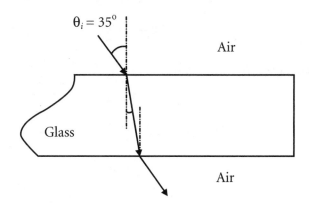

Figure 18.10

11. For Figure 18.11, find the angle of refraction for the ray that propagates outside the glass (flint) and into the air again.

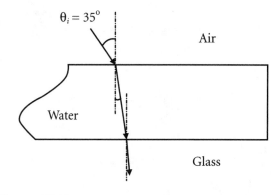

Figure 18.11

▶ Internal Reflection

Let's summarize with a specific case: light rays going from a medium with a large optical density (large n) to a smaller n. In this case, the angle of refraction is larger than the angle of incidence, and so the light will move *away* from the normal. What happens when the light is at 90° from the normal? In this case, the light is no longer transmitted into the second medium but is returned to the first medium. This is the case of *total internal reflection*, and the limit angle of internal reflection can be determined by applying Snell's law (see Figure 18.12).

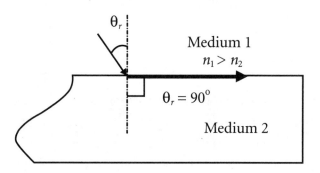

Figure 18.12

$$n_1 \cdot \sin \theta_i = n_2 \cdot \sin \theta_r$$

$$n_1 \cdot \sin \theta_i = n_2 \cdot \sin 90°$$

$n_1 \cdot \sin \theta_i = n_2$

We will call the angle of incidence for which total internal reflection happens a *critical angle* θ_c.

$n_1 \cdot \sin \theta_c = n_2$

$\sin \theta_c = \dfrac{n_2}{n_1}$

$\theta_c = \sin^{-1}\left(\dfrac{n_2}{n_1}\right)$

Example

Can a light ray propagating from air to water suffer total internal reflection at any angle?

Solution

This is a general question that addresses the expression of the critical angle of total internal reflection:

$\theta_c = \sin^{-1}\left(\dfrac{n_2}{n_1}\right)$

and $n > 1$ for any of the two media in the experiment.

If we have Medium 1 to be air, then $n_1 = 1$ and the equation becomes·

$\theta_c = \sin^{-1}\left(\dfrac{n_2}{1}\right)$

$\theta_c = \sin^{-1} n_2$

But $n_2 > 1$ and because the limits for the sine function are between -1 and $+1$, the above equation has no solution. Hence, no critical angle exists for total internal reflection to happen.

▶ Practice

12. A light source is placed at the bottom of a swimming pool, and a light ray directed toward the surface of the water makes an incident angle of 68° with the normal. Find the angle of refraction in air.

13. A light ray has an optical path, as shown in Figure 18.13. Determine if the light will suffer a total internal reflection in the glass or not. The angle between surfaces 1 and 2 is 20°.

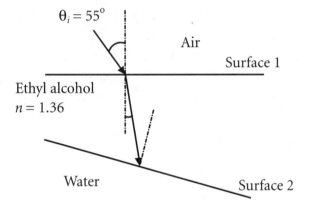

Figure 18.13

19 ▶ Propagation of Light

LESSON SUMMARY

The knowledge of geometrical optics is applied in this lesson to the work of some optical tools such as plane mirrors, curved mirrors, and convergent and divergent lenses. We will determine if an image formed with these tools is real or virtual, straight or inverted, or smaller or larger than the object.

▶ Images in Plane Mirrors

In the previous lesson, we were already exposed to the concept that makes plane mirrors work: reflections from a flat surface. In this case, we will use a plane mirror, investigate the incident and reflected rays, the normal, and their relative positions. A *plane mirror* is an opaque, flat, shiny object that reflects light that propagates toward it. Think of your morning look in the mirror: What do you see? The image of your face staring back at you as if you were copied at an equal distance from the real you into the mirror. But is that an image that is real? In other words, is that an image that you can project on a screen? If you put a screen at the back of the mirror, you will not get an image: The mirror is opaque and light does not propagate through. The image that you see is called a *virtual image*. Figure 19.1 shows how the virtual image is formed. In order to form a point on the image, we need at least two rays (or geometrical projections of two rays) to intersect. The horizontal axis on which the object and the mirror sit will be called the *optical axis*. The quantities in Figure 19.1 are shown in Table 19.1.

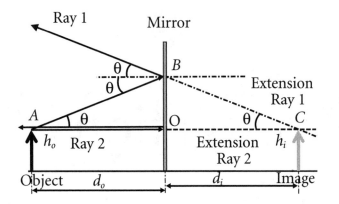

Figure 19.1

Table 19.1

QUANTITIES FOR FIGURE 19.1'S

VIRTUAL IMAGE

d_o	Distance from the object to the mirror
d_i	Distance from the image to the mirror
h_o	Object height
h_i	Image height

We define lateral magnification to be the ratio of the image height to the object height:

$$m = \frac{h_i}{h_o}$$

where

 $m > 0$ if the image is upright

 $m < 0$ if the image is reversed

 $m > 1$ if the image is larger than the object

 $m < 1$ if the image is smaller than the object

The image in the mirror forms at the intersection of two extensions of light rays, and therefore, the image is *virtual*.

Right triangles *ABO* and *BCO* are equilateral triangles having a common side and all angles are equal.

Accordingly, we can determine that the two distances, d_o and d_i, are equal and the height of the object and of the image is the same.

Also, due to light propagation in a straight line, the top of the object corresponds to the top of the image, and object points on the optical axis will have a corresponding image also on the axis.

In conclusion, the image in the previous plane mirror is

- Straight ($m > 0$)
- Virtual (image formed by ray extensions)
- The same size as the object ($m = 1$)
- At the same distance from the mirror as the object ($d_o = d_i$)

Example

A pendulum is suspended 10 cm in front of a plane mirror and above ground at a height of 30 cm. Characterize the properties of the image formed by the mirror.

Solution

We will draw a diagram of the image, and using the previous geometrical analysis, we will find the solution of the problem (see Figure 19.2).

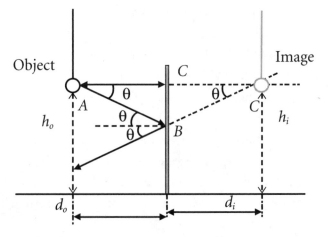

Figure 19.2

As before, right triangles *ABO* and *BCO* are equilateral due to all angles being equal and one common side. The height of the image with respect to the optical axis is the same for both the object and the image, and the distance from the object to the mirror is the same as the distance of the image to the mirror.

Example

Consider two mirrors at 90° with respect to each other and an image in front of them as in the figure. Find the number and position of the images with respect to the mirrors.

Solution

Again, we will start with a diagram of the setup and a geometrical analysis. Image 1 and Image 2 are formed similarly to the images in the previous examples. They will be virtual images, as large as the object, and the object distance and the image distance are the same relative to their respective mirrors.

Image 3 is more complex because it is formed after a double reflection (once on each of the two mirrors). Again, the image is virtual, as tall as the object, and at the same distance from the tip of the two mirrors (see Figure 19.3).

▶ Practice

1. Consider the arrangement of a solar eclipse, and using the ray approximation, draw at least three rays that will show how a solar eclipse happens.

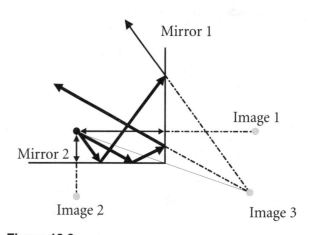

Figure 19.3

You can use as a starting point the planetary arrangement shown in Figure 19.4 (drawing not at scale).

Figure 19.4

2. Consider the arrangement of a lunar eclipse, and using the ray approximation, draw at least three rays that will show how a lunar eclipse happens. You can use as a starting point the planetary arrangement shown in Figure 19.5 (drawing not at scale).

Figure 19.5

3. An object is placed in front of a system of two mirrors, as shown in Figure 19.6. Find the number of images and show the first few images' formation.

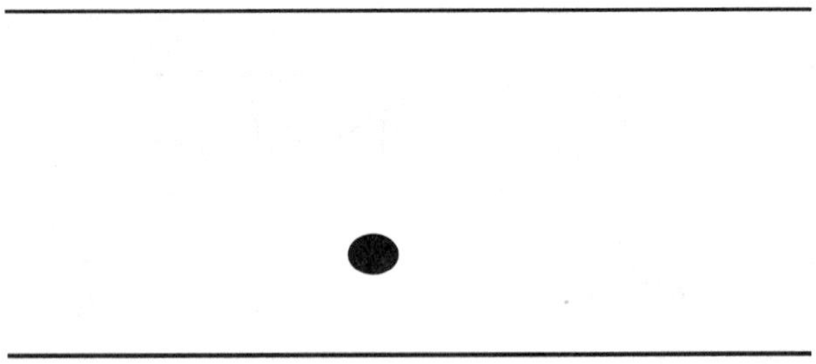

Figure 19.6

4. Consider a person 1.64 m tall from the ground to the level of his or her eyes. The person stands in front of a mirror and the mirror is 0.84 m high, starting from the ground up. Can the person see his or her toes by looking in the mirror? Draw the diagram.

5. An object is placed in front of a mirror and an image is obtained with a d_i equal to 20 cm. The object is displaced from its initial position to a point 30 cm in front of the mirror. What is the distance between the image and the mirror after displacement? What is the distance to the mirror of the object in the first case?

▶ Images in Curved Mirrors

A curved mirror forms an image differently than a plane mirror because the surface is no longer a plane, and every point on the mirror will have a different normal. A curved mirror has a few characteristics, such

as *curvature point* C, *radius* R, *focal point* F, *focal distance* f, the tip of the mirror, and the type of curvature. We will analyze each of them on a diagram.

Figure 19.7 shows two types of mirrors. The one on the left is called concave, and the one on the right is called convex. A *concave mirror* has the reflecting side on the interior of the curvature, whereas *convex mirrors* have the reflecting side on the outside of the mirror.

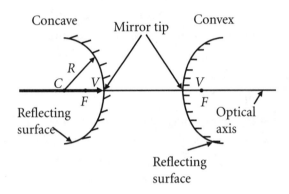

Figure 19.7

A few characteristics of curved mirrors follow.

- The *curvature*, *focal distance*, and *radius* are related by the following expression:

$$CV = R = 2 \cdot f$$

$$R = 2 \cdot f$$

- The *mirror equation* connects the characteristic distances:

$$\frac{1}{d_o} + \frac{1}{d_i} = \frac{2}{R}$$

or

$$\frac{1}{d_o} + \frac{1}{d_i} = \frac{1}{f}$$

- *Magnification* of the image is

$$m = \frac{h_i}{h_o} = -\frac{d_i}{d_o}$$

- h_o and h_i are greater than 0 if the object/image is upright and are less than 0 if inverted.
- d_i is greater than 0 if the image is at the left of the mirror and is less than 0 if at right.
- f is greater than 0 if the focal point is real and is less than 0 if the focal point is virtual.
- m is greater than 0 when the image is upright and is less than 0 when the image is inverted.

■ All parallel light rays passing through the curvature C will be reflected by the mirror on the same path as the incident light (Ray 1 in Figure 19.8).

■ Light passing through the focal point will be reflected by the mirror on a direction parallel to the optical axis (Ray 2). The reverse path is also possible; light parallel to the optical axis is reflected through the focal point.

■ All light rays directed along the optical axis toward the mirror will be reflected back on the same path as the incident light ray (Ray 3).

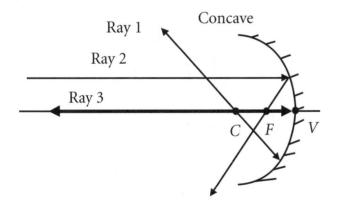

Figure 19.8

■ The focal point is *real* for the concave mirrors and *virtual* for the convex mirrors (see Figure 19.9 as only the extension of the ray passes through the focal point because the mirror is opaque).

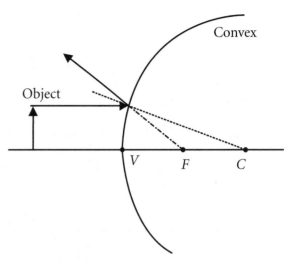

Figure 19.9

Let us use the previous information in an example. Remember that to obtain an image point, you need to intersect at least two rays or extensions of rays.

Example

An object 3 cm high is placed in front of a concave mirror at a distance of 5 cm, and the radius of the mirror is 12 cm. Find the characteristics of the image obtained in the mirror.

Solution

We will convert all measurements in meters, draw the geometric diagram of the experiment, and set up our equations.

$h_o = 3 \text{ cm} = 0.03 \text{ m}$

$d_o = 5 \text{ cm} = 0.05 \text{ m}$

$R = 12 \text{ cm} = 0.12 \text{ m}$

Image characteristics $= ?$

$f = R/2 = 0.06 \text{ cm}$

All three rays were drawn as in the previous example. Without any calculation, we can draw qualitative conclusions on the image (see Figure 19.10):

- Virtual (extension of rays)
- Larger than the object
- Upright

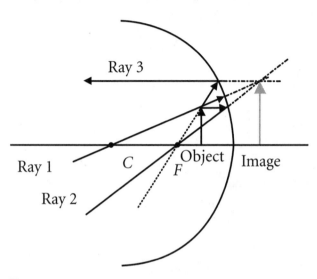

Figure 19.10

The equations defined before will have to agree with the geometry of the setup.

$$\frac{1}{d_o} + \frac{1}{d_i} = \frac{2}{R} = \frac{1}{f}$$

$$\frac{1}{0.05} + \frac{1}{d_i} = \frac{1}{0.06}$$

We solve for d_i:

$$\frac{1}{d_i} = \frac{1}{0.06} - \frac{1}{0.05}$$

$$\frac{1}{d_i} = \frac{0.05 - 0.06}{0.06 \cdot 0.05}$$

$$\frac{1}{d_i} = \frac{-0.01}{0.003}$$

$$d_i = -0.3 \text{ m}$$

Because d_i is negative, it means that the image is at the right of the mirror, and the object will be virtual. Because the mirror is opaque, the light rays cannot pass through it.

$$m = -\frac{d_i}{d_o} = -\frac{-0.3}{0.05} = 6$$

The magnification $m = 6$ ($m > 0$ and $m > 1$) means the image is larger than the object and upright.

▶ Practice

6. An object 3 cm high is placed in front of a concave mirror at a distance of 9 cm, and the radius of the mirror is 12 cm. Find the characteristics of the image obtained in the mirror and draw the image (see Figure 19.11).

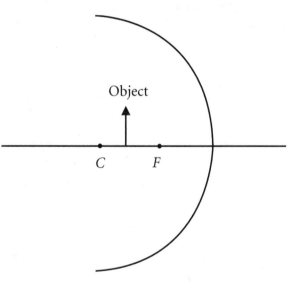

Figure 19.11

7. An object 3 cm high is placed in front of a concave mirror at a distance of 15 cm, and the radius of the mirror is 12 cm. Find the characteristics of the image obtained in the mirror.

8. A convex mirror of focal length 10 cm has an object placed in front of it at a distance of 30 cm. The object is upright and with a height of 10 cm. Find the characteristics of the image.

► Characteristics of Thin Convergent and Divergent Lenses

Now that we have a complex understanding of the light propagation because of opaque objects, let us study some that are transparent to light that we call *lenses*. Although a mirror works mostly through reflection, lenses having light transmitted through their material also deal with refraction. Two types of lenses exist: *convergent,* which gathers together an incoming bunch of light rays (see Figure 19.12), and *divergent,* which spreads apart a bunch of incoming light rays (see Figure 19.13). Both types of lenses are transparent. We consider the lenses thin so that expressions connecting lens characteristics do not depend on the thickness of the lens.

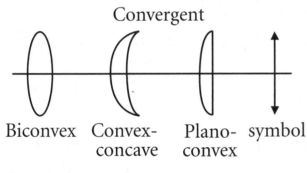

Convergent

Biconvex   Convex-concave   Plano-convex   symbol

Figure 19.12

The *lens equation* is similar to the mirror equation and is

$$\frac{1}{d_o} + \frac{1}{d_i} = \frac{1}{f}$$

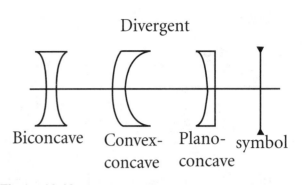

Divergent

Biconcave   Convex-concave   Plano-concave   symbol

Figure 19.13

But in this case, the *focal length* is

$$\frac{1}{f} = (n - 1) \cdot \left(\frac{1}{R_1} - \frac{1}{R_2} \right)$$

where R_1 and R_2 are the radii of the two curvatures (left and right) and n is the index of refraction of the material the lens is made of.

Example

A slab of glass has a plane on both sides. Find the "extreme" focal distance of such a lens and the position of an image formed by the lens.

Solution

We will start with the definition of the focal length and then solve for f:

$$\frac{1}{f} = (n - 1) \cdot \left(\frac{1}{R_1} - \frac{1}{R_2} \right)$$

$$f = \frac{1}{(n - 1)} \cdot \left(\frac{1}{R_1} - \frac{1}{R_2} \right)^{-1}$$

$$f = \frac{1}{(n - 1)} \cdot \left(\frac{R_1 \cdot R_2}{R_2 - R_1} \right)$$

If the "lens" is a glass slab, then both R_1 and R_2 are very large and the focal distance is infinity.

Table 19.2

CONVENTION OF SIGN

QUANTITY	> O	< O
d_o	The object is in front of the lens (real object)	The object is in the back of the lens (virtual object, as the one created by another lens or mirror)
d_i	The image is in the back of the lens (real)	The image is in front of the lens (virtual)
h_i	Image is upright	Image is inverted
f	Convergent lens	Divergent lens
$R_{1,2}$	Curvature is in the back of the lens	Curvature is in front of the lens

The *magnification equation* is identical to the one we defined for mirrors:

$$m = \frac{h_i}{h_o} = -\frac{d_i}{d_o}$$

and the convention of sign is shown in Table 19.2.

Because lenses are transparent and light can travel from both sides, each lens has two corresponding focal points.

Example

Considering the sign conventions and using the lens equation, find the position of an image and its magnification if the object is placed in front of a convergent lens beyond its focal point at a distance of 30 cm. The focal distance is 10 cm.

Solution

The object's distance and focal distance of the lens will be converted first in meters. Then we can determine the image position by setting up the lens equation with considerations on the sign.

$$d_o = +30 \text{ cm} = +0.30 \text{ m}$$

$$f = +10 \text{ cm} = +0.1 \text{ m}$$

$$d_i = ?$$

$$\frac{1}{f} = \frac{1}{d_o} + \frac{1}{d_i}$$

$$\frac{1}{0.1 \text{ m}} = \frac{1}{0.3 \text{ m}} + \frac{1}{d_i}$$

$$\frac{1}{0.1 \text{ m}} - \frac{1}{0.3 \text{ m}} = \frac{1}{d_i}$$

$$\frac{0.3 - 0.1}{0.03 \text{ m}} = \frac{1}{d_i}$$

$$d_i = \frac{0.03 \text{ m}}{0.2}$$

$$d_i = +0.15 \text{ m}$$

The image is in the *back* of the lens and it is *real*.

$$m = -\frac{d_i}{d_o}$$

$$m = -\frac{0.15}{0.3} = -\frac{1}{2}$$

And the image is inverted.

▶ Practice

9. Using the previous example, find the characteristics of an image if the object is placed in front of a divergent lens beyond its focal point at a distance of 30 cm and the focal distance is 10 cm.
10. A plano-convex lens has a radius of 20 cm. What is the other radius of the lens?
11. If a flint glass lens with an index of refraction of 1.66 has equal radii and a focal distance of 20 cm, find the radius of the curvature.

▶ Images in Thin Convergent and Divergent Lenses

As we have drawn diagrams for the plane and curved mirrors, we will check our understanding of image formation by finding the way to construct an image in a thin lens. The same important rays will become handy in this process with the main difference being that, although mirrors are opaque, lenses are transparent, so instead of reflection phenomena, we deal with refraction.

Considering a convergent lens, let's study the light propagation (I will use lens symbols; see Figure 19.14):

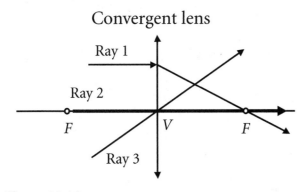

Figure 19.14

- All rays parallel to the optical axis converge beyond the lens and propagate through the focal point.
- All rays propagating along the optical axis continue to propagate in the same direction beyond the lens.
- A light ray passing through the tip of the lens will propagate in the same direction beyond the lens.
- Incoming rays tend to be bent toward the thicker part of the convergent lens.

The following are the characteristics of a divergent lens (see Figure 19.15):

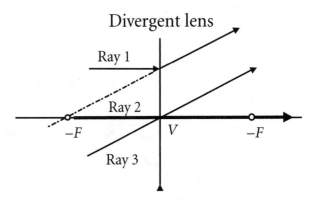

Figure 19.15

- All rays parallel to the optical axis diverge beyond the lens and their extension passes through the virtual focal point.
- All rays propagating along the optical axis continue to propagate in the same direction beyond the lens.
- A light ray passing through the tip of the lens will propagate in the same direction beyond the lens.
- Incoming rays tend to be bent toward the thicker part of the divergent lens top of the lens.

Depending on the relative position of the object to the focal point and the type of lens, image characteristics are different.

Example

In a previous example, you considered the sign conventions and the lens equation in order to find the position of an image and its size if the object is placed in front of a convergent lens beyond its focal point at a distance of 30 cm with a focal distance of 10 cm. Draw the diagram corresponding to this situation and compare it with the quantitative results and conclusions.

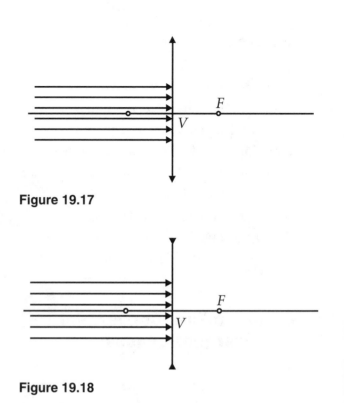

Figure 19.17

Solution

As we see from Figure 19.16, the image is reversed ($m < 0$), real, and at the back of the lens, and the image is also smaller than the object. In addition, the image is beyond the focal point, so it should be positive and larger than 0.10 m (which it is since the result is $+0.15$ m). These conclusions based on the image are the same as the ones we determined based on the lens equation and magnification in the previous example.

Figure 19.18

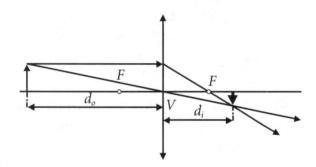

Figure 19.16

▶ Practice

12. An incident fascicle of rays propagates toward a convergent lens, as in Figure 19.17. Continue the ray diagram beyond the lens.
13. An incident fascicle of rays propagates toward a divergent lens, as in Figure 19.18. Continue the ray diagram beyond the lens.

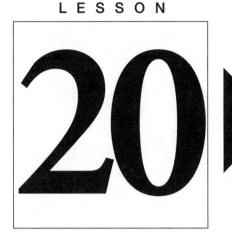

20 ▶ Diffraction and Interference

LESSON SUMMARY

In this lesson, we will address the second approach to the concept of light: waves. We will study the superposition principle, diffraction, Huygens' principle, constructive and destructive interference, diffraction gratings, and polarization.

▶ Superposition Principle

We have studied harmonic motion and the time dependence of perturbation. We will now deepen our understanding of waves by studying their interaction. Because each wave is a time and spatial variation of a perturbation and because the appearance of the wave might be different depending on the relative distance between the point of study and the source, we are looking for an expression that connects all these elements together: time, displacement, and propagation. The expression is

$$y(x, t) = A \cdot \sin(k \cdot x - \omega \cdot t)$$

where A is the amplitude, ω is the angular speed, t is the time, and x is the distance over which propagation occurred in time t, and k is called the *wave number* and is defined as

$$k = \frac{2 \cdot \pi}{\lambda}$$

where λ is the wavelength, and $\alpha = \omega \cdot t$ is called the *phase* and represents an angular displacement. In SI units: x, y, and A are in meters, ω is in radians/seconds, t is in seconds, and k is in m^{-1}.

If a source produces waves at different times, then at the same position in space, there will be differences between the displacements because of the time delay. We call this *initial phase*. An example would be the case of a wave that was produced at time t before the time considered to be the origin, which would be t at 0 seconds. This means that at time 0 seconds, the wave has already reached some displacement, while the second wave starts from 0 meters displacement (see Figure 20.1).

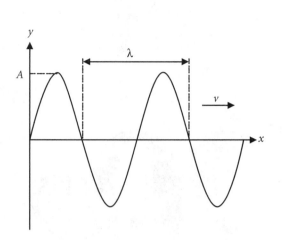

Figure 20.2

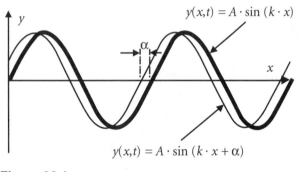

Figure 20.1

The $y(x,t)$ is called the *harmonic wave function* and is a characteristic of all periodic waves, giving the displacement and propagation for a certain moment in time (see Figure 20.2).

In the case of a three-dimensional wave, such as the water ripples in an aquarium or a lake or the waves coming from a light source, we can define a concept helpful for future developments: *wavefront*. Throw a stone in the water, and ripples forming from the source of perturbation will soon be visible. You can see concentric circles propagating out in space. A cross-section through water would show that the surface of the water is displaced up and down. At different positions compared to the source of perturbation, the dis-

placement is the same: as for instance, different points are at maximum displacement (amplitude) at the same time. We call these points *in phase* and the circles that connect these points in phase are called *wavefronts*. The radius from the source to the wavefront is called a *ray*.

Figure 20.3 shows the wave propagation in free space, but what will happen if the space contains more than one source or obstacles? Let us answer the first part of the question. The *principle of superposition* says that when two or more waves are present at the same point in space and at the same time, the result of the superposition is the sum of the individual waves.

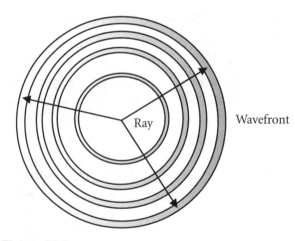

Figure 20.3

Example

Consider two sources emitting waves and two waves meeting in a region of space. The wave diagram is shown in Figure 20.4. What is the result of the superposition of the two waves?

Solution

At each point in the figure, the two displacements are equal and opposite. Because the superposition is an algebraic sum of the two waves, the result will be zero at every point, as shown by the example on the left:

$$A + (-A) = 0$$

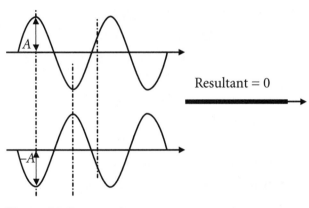

Figure 20.4

▶ Practice

1. Consider two sources emitting waves and two waves meeting in a region of space. The wave diagram is shown in Figure 20.5. What is the result of the superposition of the two waves?
2. Consider the following two waves. What are the amplitude, the frequency, and the wavelength of each wave? Also, find the result when the two waves are at the origin of time and space.

$$y_1 = 20 \text{ cm} \cdot \sin(1.1 \cdot 10^{10} \cdot x - 2 \cdot t)$$

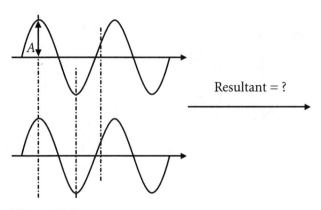

Figure 20.5

and

$$y_2 = 23 \text{ cm} \cdot \sin(0.94 \cdot 10^{10} \cdot x - 0.18 \cdot t)$$

▶ Diffraction and Huygens' Principle

If the lights are turned on in your house and you close your bedroom door, you can still tell the lights are on. How does this happen? If light only propagates in a straight line, then there should be only a small amount making its way through the keyhole or under the door. Is there something more to propagation?

The answer is *diffraction*, which is the bending of waves around obstacles. Bending occurs proportionally to the wavelength of the wave and is inverse proportional to the size of the obstacle. That means that for light waves (which have small wavelengths) and large openings, the ratio of the wavelength to the width (λ/w) will be very small, and the bending will not permit you to see around a corner. If we imagine the same source of waves producing some plane waves that encounter a small and a large obstacle, beyond the obstacle, diffraction will create different patterns of wave propagation, as shown in Figure 20.6. For a large-size aperture ($w \gg \lambda$), no bending is produced, whereas when the two are comparable ($w \sim \lambda$), bending occurs.

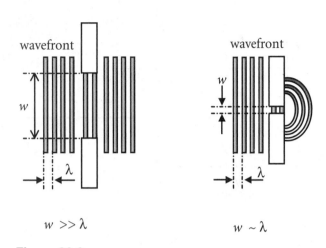

Figure 20.6

The waves we see on the right of Figure 20.6 are actually composed by superimposing many waves produced by different points at the obstacle. *Huygens' Principle* states that every point on a wavefront produces a subset of waves that moves with the same velocity as the incident wave. At a later time, the wavefront is found to be the surface tangent to the propagating subset of waves (see Figure 20.7).

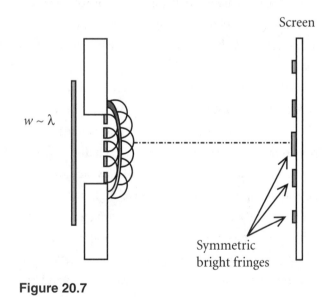

Figure 20.7

Example

Will red light or violet light produce a broader fringe pattern on a screen? (See Figure 20.7.)

Solution

The size of the broadening pattern will be larger when more diffraction will take place. The diffraction pattern is dependent on the wavelength and the width of the opening:

$$\text{Fringe pattern} \sim \frac{\lambda}{w}$$

At the same size of aperture (opening), the red light, which has a larger wavelength, will give a larger diffraction pattern, while violet (at the other end of the spectrum), with a reduced wavelength, will show a less extended fringe pattern.

▶ Practice

3. Two screens each have an aperture; one is 550 nm and the other one is 0.600 μm. Which one will produce on a screen a broader fringe pattern if illumination with a blue light of 430 nm is used?

4. Is it fair to say that no bending of light occurs through an open door, but diffraction occurs when you shine a laser light through the measuring part of a micrometer?

Figure 20.7 not only portrays Huygens' Principle; it also shows the image formed on a screen: a strong central light followed by symmetric fringes of dark and light. Considering the earlier example with the waves that cancel each other, it will make perfect sense to say that at some points on the screen, the two or more waves present at the same time will be in opposite phase. Hence, when superposition adds the waves, the result will be zero: no light. At other positions, the resultant will be a nonzero amount and even reach a maximum when the superposition is among waves that are in phase with each other.

We call the situation when a dark fringe (no light) is obtained *destructive interference,* and con-*structive interference* leads to light. The condition for destructive interference is

$$\sin \theta = m \cdot \frac{\lambda}{w}$$

where m equals 1, 2, 3, and so on depending on which fringe the angle θ is considered for: the first dark fringe from the bright central spot, the second, third, and so on (see Figure 20.8).

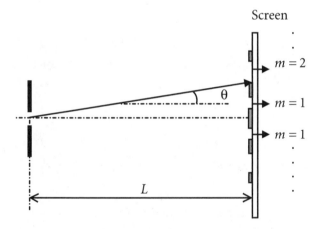

Figure 20.8

Example

The first dark fringe on a screen is 50 cm away from an aperture and is at a height of 5 cm above the center of the bright fringe. Find the width of the aperture (if the wavelength is 600 nm) and the angle that the first dark fringe position makes with the horizontal.

Solution

First, all units need to be converted in SI, we will then draw the diagram, and we will set our equations and solve for the unknowns.

$h = 5\,\text{cm} = 0.05\,\text{m}$

$d = 50\,\text{cm} = 0.50\,\text{m}$

$\lambda = 600\,\text{nm} = 600 \cdot 10^{-9}\,\text{m}$

$w = ?$

$\theta = ?$

From Figure 20.9, one can determine the angle corresponding to the first fringe:

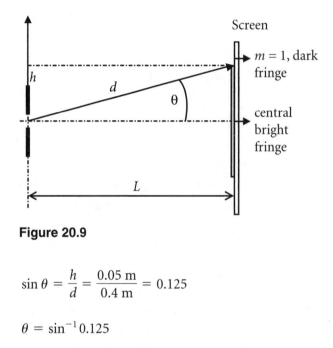

Figure 20.9

$$\sin \theta = \frac{h}{d} = \frac{0.05\,\text{m}}{0.4\,\text{m}} = 0.125$$

$$\theta = \sin^{-1} 0.125$$

$$\theta = 7.2°$$

Using this information and the condition for the first dark fringe ($m = 1$), we can set a new equation:

$$\sin \theta = m \cdot \frac{\lambda}{w} = \frac{\lambda}{w}$$

$$0.125 = \frac{600 \cdot 10^{-9}\,\text{m}}{w}$$

$$w = \frac{600 \cdot 10^{-9}\,\text{m}}{0.125}$$

$$w = 4.8\,\mu\text{m}$$

► Practice

5. A screen is in front of a 0.95 μm aperture. Find the distance to the position of the first dark fringe if a $690 \cdot 10^{-9}$ m light is shone on the aperture and the position of the dark fringe is 20 cm away from the bright central of the image.

6. The width of the bright central fringe on a screen is 18 cm and the light that forms it is a blue 400 nm. The light is shown on a 0.80 μm aperture. Find the distance to the screen.

► Diffraction Gratings

A fringe pattern is not only produced when light encounters an aperture, but also when two or more parallel, thin slits are placed in front of an incident wave. A central bright fringe will form, followed by a first-order fringe on each side of the central one and so on. Both of the first-order fringes are at the same angle with respect to the central fringe, as shown in Figure 20.10.

The fringes where the result of the superposition of all the waves at a point and time is maximum are called the *principal maxima* (constructive interference). The fringes are less bright at other positions as well.

If the source is monochromatic (a single frequency), then the fringes are also monochromatic. If the source is a mixture of lights, then the central fringe will resemble the source, but the subsequent fringes will be split in multiple fringes, one for each of the composite colors. Therefore, a lamp producing a combination of blue and indigo as the output light after the diffraction grating will split into a higher-order, multicolor set of fringes with the blue one ($\lambda_{\text{blue}} > \lambda_{\text{indigo}}$)

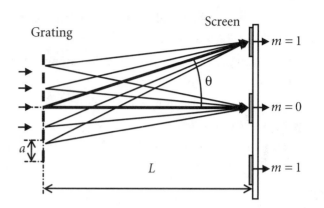

Figure 20.10

being spread farther since the corresponding angle is larger.

The condition to obtain a principal maximum is

$$\sin \theta = m \cdot \frac{\lambda}{a}, m = 0, 1, 2, 3, \ldots$$

Diffraction gratings are characterized by the number of grooves per centimeter or per millimeter. If the number is known, then one can calculate the groove separation a.

► Practice

7. Laser light is a monochromatic light (one color and one characteristic wavelength). For instance, the helium-neon laser produces a 632.8 nm red light and the solid-state green laser 532 nm. Therefore, the fringe pattern will be composed of dark and one-color light fringes. What do you think a white light fringe pattern will look like? Why?

8. White light is directed toward a diffraction grating and that light splits into monochromatic principal maxima. Which color will be closer to the central white?

▶ Polarization

We have studied the propagation of electromagnetic waves and should remember that they are transversal waves with an interdependent variation of electric and magnetic fields (**E** and **B** make a 90° angle and both are perpendicular at the direction of propagation). The direction of the electric field defines the direction of polarization. If a source produces waves that are all oriented such that **E** is directed in a single direction, we call those *polarized waves* (see Figure 20.11). When waves are produced such that an electric field is chaotically spread, the wave is *unpolarized*.

Polarized light

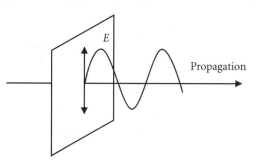

Figure 20.11

If an obstacle of a certain shape is placed in front of a source of electromagnetic waves, then the waves can be polarized. The alternation of the electrical field that sustains the magnetic field and, therefore the propagation of the wave, will not be possible in certain directions. Figure 20.12 shows a polarized wave that can propagate through the groove because the groove and the polarization are in the same plane.

And in the case where the polarization and the slit are at 90°, the light does not propagate farther than the slit (see Figure 20.13).

The light polarized can subsequently change polarization and intensity through a *polarizer* and an *analyzer*. Incoming unpolarized light will be absorbed

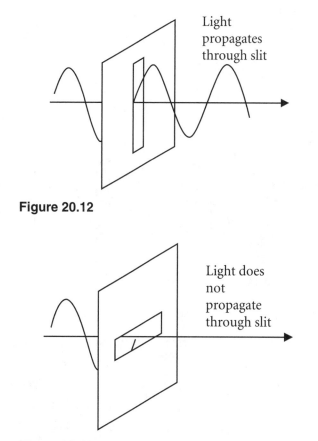

Light propagates through slit

Figure 20.12

Light does not propagate through slit

Figure 20.13

by the polarizer in all directions other than the direction corresponding to the *transmission axis* of the polarizer. The average intensity of light leaving the polarizer is half the intensity of the incident light:

$$\overline{S}_{after \cdot polarizer} = \frac{1}{2} \cdot \overline{S}_0$$

The light output will change further, and emerging light following the analyzer has an average intensity given by Malus' law (Etienne-Louis Malus, 1775–1812):

$$\overline{S}_{after \cdot analyzer} = \overline{S}_{after \cdot polarizer} \cdot \cos^2 \theta$$

where $\overline{S}_{after \cdot analyzer}$ is the average intensity of the outgoing light and $\overline{S}_{after \cdot polarizer}$ is the average intensity of the incident polarized light, while θ is the angle between the incident and outgoing polarization of the wave.

The intensity of light is measured in watt/s². It is proportional to the square of the electric field. Hence, an increase of E by two will increase the intensity by four (see Figure 20.14).

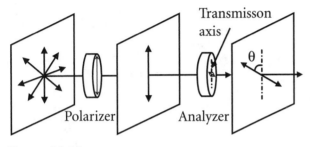

Figure 20.14

Example

Consider a set of a polarizer and an analyzer, and the incident light bringing in an average intensity of 800 W/m². What is the average intensity after the polarizer and then after the analyzer if the analyzer's transmission axis makes a 90°-angle with the axis of the polarizer?

Solution

First, we define the data and then we set the equations needed to solve the problem:

$$\overline{S}_0 = 800 \text{ W/m}^2$$

$$\theta = 90°$$

$$\overline{S}_{after \cdot polarizer} = ?$$

$$\overline{S}_{after \cdot polarizer} = \frac{1}{2} \cdot \overline{S}_0$$

$$\overline{S}_{after \cdot polarizer} = 400 \text{ W/m}^2$$

$$\overline{S}_{after \cdot analyzer} = \overline{S}_{after \cdot polarizer} \cdot \cos^2 \theta$$

$$\overline{S}_{after \cdot analyzer} = \overline{S}_{after \cdot polarizer} \cdot \cos^2 90° = 0$$

Therefore, no light will be coming out of the system.

▶ Practice

9. Is it possible for unpolarized light to "disappear" after it propagates through a system of polarizer and analyzer?

10. Is it possible for unpolarized light to emerge from a system of one polarizer and one analyzer with the same intensity in which it went in?

11. Is the process of polarization characteristic only for light waves? How about the other electromagnetic waves?

12. Incident light is entering a system of three polarizers with an intensity of 2 kW/m². The angles for each of the polarizers are $\theta_1 = 60°$, $\theta_2 = 90°$, $\theta_3 = 30°$. What is the average intensity of the outgoing light?

13. Incident light is entering a system of three polarizers with an intensity of 2 kW/m². The angles for each of the polarizers are $\theta_1 = 60°$, $\theta_2 = 45°$, $\theta_3 = 30°$. What is the average intensity of the outgoing light?

▶ Posttest

If you have completed all 20 lessons in this book, then you are ready to take the posttest to measure your progress. The posttest has 30 multiple-choice questions covering the topics you studied in this book. While the format of the posttest is similar to that of the pretest, the questions are different.

Take as much time as you need to complete the posttest. When you are finished, check your answers with the answer key that follows. Along with each answer is a number that tells you which lesson(s) of this book teaches you about the physics skills needed for that question. Once you know your score on the posttest, compare the results with the pretest. If you scored better on the posttest than you did on the pretest, you should look at the questions you missed, if any. Do you know why you missed the question, or do you need to go back to the lesson and review the concept?

If your score on the posttest doesn't show much improvement, take a second look at the questions you missed. Did you miss a question because of an error you made? If you can figure out why you missed the problem, then you understand the concept and just need to concentrate more on accuracy when taking a test. If you missed a question because you did not know how to work the problem, go back to the lesson and spend more time working that type of problem. Take the time to understand basic physics thoroughly. You need a solid foundation in basic physics if you plan to use this information or progress to a higher level. Whatever your score on this posttest, keep this book for review and future reference.

1. ⓐ ⓑ ⓒ ⓓ
2. ⓐ ⓑ ⓒ ⓓ
3. ⓐ ⓑ ⓒ ⓓ
4. ⓐ ⓑ ⓒ ⓓ
5. ⓐ ⓑ ⓒ ⓓ
6. ⓐ ⓑ ⓒ ⓓ
7. ⓐ ⓑ ⓒ ⓓ
8. ⓐ ⓑ ⓒ ⓓ
9. ⓐ ⓑ ⓒ ⓓ
10. ⓐ ⓑ ⓒ ⓓ

11. ⓐ ⓑ ⓒ ⓓ
12. ⓐ ⓑ ⓒ ⓓ
13. ⓐ ⓑ ⓒ ⓓ
14. ⓐ ⓑ ⓒ ⓓ
15. ⓐ ⓑ ⓒ ⓓ
16. ⓐ ⓑ ⓒ ⓓ
17. ⓐ ⓑ ⓒ ⓓ
18. ⓐ ⓑ ⓒ ⓓ
19. ⓐ ⓑ ⓒ ⓓ
20. ⓐ ⓑ ⓒ ⓓ

21. ⓐ ⓑ ⓒ ⓓ
22. ⓐ ⓑ ⓒ ⓓ
23. ⓐ ⓑ ⓒ ⓓ
24. ⓐ ⓑ ⓒ ⓓ
25. ⓐ ⓑ ⓒ ⓓ
26. ⓐ ⓑ ⓒ ⓓ
27. ⓐ ⓑ ⓒ ⓓ
28. ⓐ ⓑ ⓒ ⓓ
29. ⓐ ⓑ ⓒ ⓓ
30. ⓐ ⓑ ⓒ ⓓ

1. The Great Wall of China is 3,946 miles long. Find the length in km.
   - **a.** $6.349 \cdot 10^6$ km
   - **b.** $6.349 \cdot 10^3$ m
   - **c.** 6.349 km
   - **d.** $6.349 \cdot 10^3$ km

2. A light-year (distance traveled by light in one year's time) is $9.46 \cdot 10^{12}$ km. Convert this length to miles.
   - **a.** $5.87 \cdot 10^9$ miles
   - **b.** $5.87 \cdot 10^{12}$ miles
   - **c.** $5.87 \cdot 10^6$ miles
   - **d.** $5.87 \cdot 10^3$ miles

3. The Farad (F) is a unit for capacitors, but it is an unusually large unit for usual capacitors. Convert a pF into F.
   - **a.** 10^{-12} Farad
   - **b.** 10^{-15} Farad
   - **c.** 10^{-9} Farad
   - **d.** 10^{-3} Farad

4. Light emitted by the sun takes 8.31 minutes to reach us at a speed of $3.00 \cdot 10^8$ m/s. Find the distance the light travels in that time.
   - **a.** $1.5 \cdot 10^8$ m
   - **b.** $1.5 \cdot 10^9$ m
   - **c.** $1.5 \cdot 10^{11}$ m
   - **d.** $1.5 \cdot 10^{12}$ m

5. You have measured the size of an object's diameter three different times, and you have the following values: 22.2, 22.7, and 23.4 cm. What is the average measurement expressed with the correct number of significant figures?
   - **a.** 22.5 cm
   - **b.** 23 cm
   - **c.** 22 cm
   - **d.** 22.8 cm

6. Write the following quantities in scientific notation:
   55.5 mi/h; $149.6 \cdot 10^6$ km; 0.001408 kg/cm^3; 286.1°
   - **a.** $5.55 \; 10^2$ mi/h; $1.496 \cdot 10^8$ km; $1.408 \; 10^{-3}$ kg/cm^3; $2.861 \cdot 10^{20}$
   - **b.** $5.55 \; 10^1$ mi/h; $1.496 \cdot 10^8$ km; $1.408 \; 10^{-3}$ kg/cm^3; $2.861 \cdot 10^{20}$
   - **c.** $5.55 \; 10^1$ mi/h; $1.496 \cdot 10^8$ km; $1.408 \; 10^{-2}$ kg/cm^3; $2.861 \cdot 10^{20}$
   - **d.** $5.55 \; 10^1$ mi/h; $1.496 \cdot 10^8$ km; $1.408 \; 10^{-3}$ kg/cm^3; $2.861 \cdot 10^{30}$

7. Perform the following additions to the correct number of significant figures:
   $25.22 + 0.0225 + 1,000.2 + 100 = ?$; $1,234.56 + 0.02 = ?$
   - **a.** 1,125.44; 1,234.6
   - **b.** 1,125; 1,234.58
   - **c.** 1,125.44; 1,234.58
   - **d.** 1,125; 1,235

8. Calculate the magnitude of the vector in each case. The first pair gives you the start point of the vector; the second pair is the tip: (0,0) and $(3,-2)$; AND (0,0) and $(-4,8)$.
   - **a.** 4 AND 9
   - **b.** 3 AND 9
   - **c.** 3 AND 8
   - **d.** 4 AND 8

9. The mass of the electron is $9,109.38188 \cdot 10^{-35}$ kg. Write the mass in scientific notation.
   - **a.** $9.10938188 \cdot 10^{-30}$ kg
   - **b.** $9.10938188 \cdot 10^{-31}$ kg
   - **c.** $9.10938188 \cdot 10^{-33}$ kg
   - **d.** $9.10938188 \cdot 10^{-32}$ kg

10. Consider two objects acted on by the same force and their final accelerations are 2.50 m/s^2 and 3.00 m/s^2. If the mass of the first object is 1.25 kg, find the force and the mass of the second object.

   a. 4.04 kg and 3.13 N

   b. 1.04 kg and 4.13 N

   c. 1.04 kg and 3.13 N

   d. 1.04 N and 3.13 kg

11. The acceleration of a 5.0 kg object is $a = (15; 10)$ m/s^2. Find the magnitude of the net force acting on the object.

   a. 9 N

   b. 90 N

   c. 90 kg

   d. 900 N

12. A car of mass 2,500 kg starts from rest and travels 8 m in 2 s. What are the values of the acceleration and of the net force assuming uniform acceleration?

   a. 4 m/s^2 and 10,000 N

   b. 4 m/s and 10,000 N

   c. 40 m/s^2 and 10,000 N

   d. 4 m/s^2 and 1,000 N

13. A book is moved on a table with constant velocity. The book has a mass of 1 pound. Find the weight and the normal force in newtons.

   a. $W = 4.5$ N

   b. $W = N = 4.5$ N

   c. $N = 4.5$ N

   d. $W = 4.5$ N and $N = 0$ N

14. For the system represented below, draw the free body diagram for each of the objects.

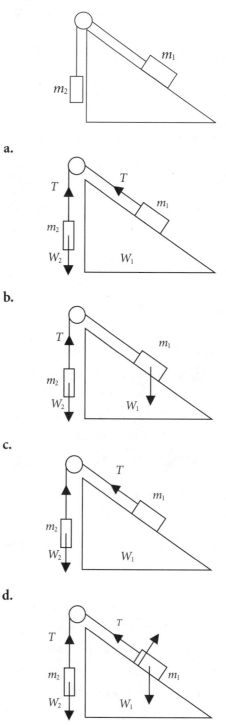

a.

b.

c.

d.

15. An object of 1,550 g mass moves on a surface with the coefficient of kinetic friction of 0.3230. Find the force of friction acting on the object.

    a. 50.06 kg

    b. 50.06 N

    c. 5.006 N

    d. 5.006 kg

16. Two different objects have the same momentum but one object is three times smaller in mass than the other ($m_1 < m_2$). How do the two velocities compare? Consider one-dimensional motion.

    a. $m_1/m_2 = v_2/v_1 = 1/3$

    b. $m_1/m_2 = v_2/v_1 = 3$

    c. $m_1/m_2 = v_1/v_2 = 3$

    d. $m_2/m_1 = v_2/v_1 = 1/3$

17. Two objects of masses 40.0 and 4.00 kg collide elastically head on. Object 1 is at rest initially and the other one is moving at a speed of 1.50 m/s. After collision, the second object will recoil at a speed of 1.20 m/s. What is the speed of the heavy object? There is no external force acting on the system.

    a. 27 m/s

    b. 2.7 m/s

    c. 0.27 m/s

    d. 0.027 m/s

18. Consider a car collision in which one car is driving east at 18 m/s speed and the other is moving north at 20 m/s. The cars are of similar mass, 1,500 kg. Find the velocity immediately after the collision if the collision is inelastic.

    a. $v = (9; 20)$ m/s

    b. $v = (18; 10)$ m/s

    c. $v = (18; 20)$ m/s

    d. $v = (9; 10)$ m/s

19. A car needs to be pushed for a short distance. You apply a force of 1,110 N and move it for about 1,080 cm. What is the work done?

    a. 1.2 J

    b. $1.2 \cdot 10^4$ J

    c. $1.2 \cdot 10^2$ J

    d. $1.2 \cdot 10^6$ J

20. An object is slowing down to a final speed two times smaller than the initial speed. What is the ratio of the final and initial kinetic energies?

    a. $1/4$

    b. $1/2$

    c. $1/8$

    d. $1/16$

21. An object at the end of a string is moved around in a circle of radius 80 cm. Between two close instances, the arc length is 10.0 cm, and the time is 0.2 s. Find the average angular speed of the object.

    a. 6.2 rad/s

    b. $6.2 \cdot 10^{-2}$ rad/s

    c. $6.2 \cdot 10^2$ rad/s

    d. $6.2 \cdot 10^{-4}$ rad/s

22. A force of 25,400 N is exerted on the 25 cm piston of a hydraulic press. Find the force needed to be applied on the 10 cm diameter for the press to be in equilibrium.

    a. $4.1 \cdot 10^1$ N

    b. $4.1 \cdot 10^2$ N

    c. $4.1 \cdot 10^3$ N

    d. $4.1 \cdot 10^4$ N

23. Find the value of 32° F in Kelvin degrees.

   a.   0 K

   b.   273.15 K

   c.   100 K

   d.   300 K

24. Water is boiling in a container in your kitchen. What is the temperature doing in the process?

   a.   remaining constant

   b.   increasing

   c.   decreasing

   d.   remaining at 0°

25. Consider the PV-diagram below. Find the work for the process.

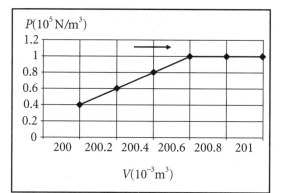

   a.   58 J

   b.   5.8 J

   c.   0 J

   d.   −58 J

26. How is the decrease of the distance between the two parallel plates of a capacitor affecting its capacitance?

   a.   decreasing

   b.   increasing

   c.   staying the same

   d.   capacitance becoming zero

27. A current is passed through a wire. What is the ratio of the magnetic fields produced at a distance of r and at $3 \cdot r$ from the wire?

   a.   1

   b. $1/2$

   c. $1/3$

   d. $1/9$

28. Determine the amplitude A of an oscillatory motion if the displacement is 12.0 cm between times $t_0 = 0$ seconds and time $t = T/4$, where T is the period of oscillations.

   a.   24.0 cm

   b.   12.0 cm

   c.   6.0 cm

   d.   1.0 cm

29. A microwave oven works based on microwaves that have wavelengths between 30 cm and 10^{-3} m. Find the range of frequencies if the speed is $3 \cdot 10^8$ m/s.

   a. 10^6 and $3 \cdot 10^{11}$ Hz

   b. 10^7 and $3 \cdot 10^{11}$ Hz

   c. 10^9 and $3 \cdot 10^9$ Hz

   d. 10^9 and $3 \cdot 10^{11}$ Hz

30. Consider two sources emitting waves and two waves meeting in a region of space. The wave diagram is shown in the figure below. What is the result of the superposition of the two waves?

a. same frequency and amplitude

b. same frequency wave with amplitude two times larger

c. same amplitude wave with frequency two times larger

d. same frequency wave with amplitude four times larger

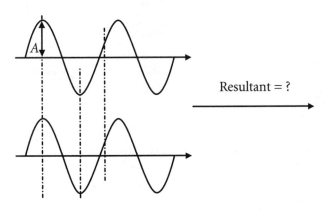

Resultant = ?

▶ Answer Key

▶ Pretest

1. b. 441 yd and 403 m; 18 yd and 16 m (Lesson 1)

2. a. Lesson 1

3. d. $4.0225 \cdot 10^8$ m (Lesson 1)

4. a. $7 \cdot 10^8$ miles/hour (Lesson 1)

5. c. $1.4 \cdot 10^{11}$ m (Lesson 1)

6. c. 3.4 cm (Lesson 1)

7. b. $3.4 \cdot 10^{-2}$ kg, $1.234 \cdot 10^2$ in, $1.5 \cdot 10^3$ N, $1.013 \cdot 10^5$ N/m² (Lesson 1)

8. d. 1,430.63 and 1,234.88 (Lesson 1)

9. b. Lesson 2

10. b. Lesson 2

11. a. 1.62 kg and 6.5 N (Lesson 5)

12. d. 0.187 kg (Lesson 5)

13. c. 5 m/s² and 7,500 N (Lessons 3 and 5)

14. c. $W = N = 5.5$ N (Lesson 5)

15. a. Lesson 5

16. c. 0. 15 N (Lesson 5)

17. d. $m_1/m_2 = v_2/v_1 = 10$ (Lesson 6)

18. a. 1,350 N (Lessons 3 and 5)

19. b. 0.54 m/s (Lesson 6)

20. c. $v = \frac{1}{2}(11k + 9j)$ m/s (Lesson 6)

21. b. 0 J (Lesson 7)

22. a. $\Delta KE = W = -(50 \cdot m)$ J (Lesson 7)

23. b. 14.14 m/s² (Lesson 8)

24. d. $5 \cdot 10^3$ Pa (Lesson 10)

25. a. Lesson 11

26. a. -10^2 J (Lesson 12)

27. d. $+2.88 \cdot 10^{-16}$ Coulombs; 1,800 electrons (Lesson 13)

28. c. 4 (Lesson 15)

29. b. $1.94 \cdot 10^8$ m/s (Lesson 18)

30. b. Lesson 19

► Lesson 1

1. You need a ruler or a tape measure to measure the length, width, and height of your oven. The volume is a derived quantity, obtained by multiplying together these three fundamental quantities (lengths).

2. Density's unit is a derived unit.

3. We use another quantity, the length of the mercury column, to express it. Therefore, there is a pretty good chance that pressure will be a derived unit (which is the case indeed).

4. Some bulbs use the light emitted by a filament, while others (so called eco-bulbs) are more efficient and use the light of a glow discharge. As long as the light-generating mechanism and its efficiency may be the same, the electrical power used by the bulb may be (and it was) used as a rough measure of the light you expect from such a bulb. But as soon as you have bulbs with different efficiencies, you may find that an eco-bulb rated at 30 W shines brighter than a conventional bulb rated at 60 W, and therefore, the electrical power used by the bulb is no longer an accurate measure of the brightness of the bulb. The "geek units," lumens, refer exactly to the light intensity and therefore are more appropriate to characterize all the bulbs.

5. In order to define the radian, you have to measure a length; therefore, it is a derived unit.

6. $1.32 \cdot 10^{25}$ lbs and $2.11 \cdot 10^{25}$ oz, respectively (keeping only significant figures)

7. 3.3 liters

8. The area is 85 square feet or 7.9 m^2.

9. $1.02 \cdot 10^3$ ft^3 or 29 m^3

10. Degree kelvin. Kilogram.

11. 10.58 oz

12. To two significant figures, 3.7 gallons of gas

13. 62.1 mi/3.7 gal = 16.78 mi/gal. Therefore, it is a light truck or SUV.

14. b.

15. c.

16. b.

17. b.

18. c.

19. b.

20. 83.491 g (and keep only five significant figures)

21. The five-digit display limits your accuracy to five significant figures.

22. $1.66 \cdot 10^4$ cm^3. We have still only three significant figures.

23. $1.11 \cdot 10^2$ V or 111 V. The result has only three significant figures.

24. b.

25. c.

26. In scientific notation:

    1 kg = $6.852 \cdot 10^{-1}$ slug

    1 mi/hour = $1.60 \cdot 10^3$ m/h

    1 N = $2.448 \cdot 10^{-1}$ lb

    Planck's constant = $6.626 \cdot 10^{-34}$ J · s

    Acceleration due to gravity = $3.22 \cdot 10^{+1}$ ft/s^2

    Sun's mass = $1.99 \cdot 10^{30}$ kg

27. The same rules apply for scientific notation numbers, only that they are easier to apply.

28. $1.54 \cdot 10^{-25}$ kg

► Lesson 2

1. $r = 6.71, \theta = 63.4°$

2. $PQ = 5$

3. $r = 10.3, \theta = 60.94°$

5. $\theta = 53.13°$

5. $OQ = 10.3$

6. $x = 2.598, y = 1.5, z = 5$

7. $OP = 5.83$

8. $r = 7.12, \theta = 119.445°$

9. 8.37 m and 57.66 N

10. No, see relation for magnitude:

$$A^2 = A_x^2 + A_y^2 + A_z^2$$

11. $A = F$

12. $C = -13\,k$

13. $A \cdot B = 0$; therefore, the vector's directions are perpendicular to each other.

14. Same as for problem 13

15. $A + B = 5.0\,i + 1.0\,j$ and $B - A = 1.0\,i - 5.0\,j$. Both magnitudes equal 5.1.

16. The directions are perpendicular, as the scalar product of the vectors is zero.

17. The magnitude is 13.

▶ Lesson 3

1. 1,980 m

2. -0.2 m/s^2

3. 4 m

4. 2.192 m/s

5. 1.1×10^4 m/s^2

6. 0.625 s

7. 8 m/s or 28.8 km/h

8. 4 m/s^2

9. 1 m/s

10. 0.636 m/s

11. 0.25 m/s

12. 0.034 m/s^2

13. 0.005 m/s^2

14. 0.055 m/s^2

15. 6.705 m/s^2

16. 53.64 m

17. $a = 5.046$ m/s^2 and 17.81 m

18. 96.95 m

19. 71.43 s

20. 24,489.8 m

21. 51.756 m

22. Let $t = 3.25$ s and let $t_s = $ time for sound propagation. Obviously, one condition is that $t_s < t$ (from causality). Let the depth of the well be d, and let v_s be the speed of sound in air. We have

$$d = \tfrac{1}{2}g(t - t_s)^2$$

$$d = v_s t_s$$

Eliminating d and solving for t_s, we find $t_s = 0.142$ s, and therefore $d = 47.428$ m. Neglecting the finite sound speed introduces a 9.125% error.

23. 4.9 m

24. $4.9\,(9 - 4) = 24.5$ m

25. 54.221 m/s

▶ Lesson 4

1. Although displacement is zero, since the person returns to the same place where the motion started from, distance is not zero.

2. The resultant is (15.7, 5.7) cm or 16.7 cm and 20° north of east.

3. The distance is 18 cm, while displacement is 16.7 cm.

4. No, although the magnitude might stay constant, as in the case of a car, the object might move on a curve and then, due to the change in direction, velocity changes, too.

5. Displacement is (40,30) m or 50 m and 37° north of east. Average velocity is (16,12) m/s or 20 m/s at 37° north of east.

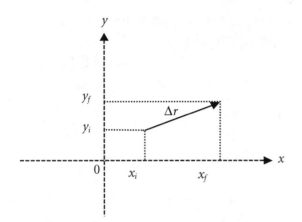

6. I will choose two far away points for clarity:

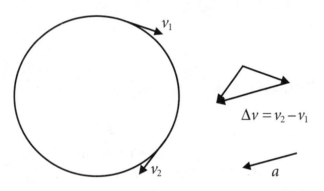

7. $v_r = 41$ m/s due north

8. $v_r = 11.2$ m/s at 10.3° downward

9. 80° west of south (if we consider downward direction south)

10. It's nonzero since on the x-axis, the object moves with constant velocity all the time.

11. At no time, because the acceleration due to gravity is constantly nonzero

12. $R = 10.2$ m and $h = 2.55$ m

▶ **Lesson 5**

1. $5.98 \cdot 10^{27}$ g

2. More, mass is a measure of inertia.

3. Less, 0.004 kg $<$ 10 kg

4. No, speed will change.

5. Yes, the one put out by the engine.

6. No, it will decelerate (slow down) because the engine was overcoming friction. Without the engine, friction converts the energy of the car into heat.

7. No, the forces might cancel each other out.

8. No, because net force zero means that acceleration is zero, so there is no change in speed.

9. No, the object might be at rest.

10. No, because force is proportional to acceleration and acceleration is the change in velocity, not the velocity itself.

11. No, the larger the object, the smaller the acceleration: $a = F/m$.

12. 5 m/s² and 10,000 N

13. (0.5; 4.9) N

14. 9.85 m/s² and 4.9 N

15. $\alpha = 5.9°$ west of south

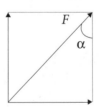

16. $a_1/a_2 = {}^4/_3$

17. Yes, the net force is the result of *all* forces acting on the object, not only one.

18. Net force $= -90$ N and $a = -450$ m/s²

19. 0 N and 0 m/s²

20. 10 cm/s² $= 0.1$ m/s² and $F = 15$ N

21. Action is the student's force of 25 N and acts on the strings. Reaction is the elastic force in the string that wants to return the string to its initial situation and that force is -25 N and it's caused by the string on the student.

22. Yes, with an equal and opposite force.

23. No, because of friction acting differently on objects.

24. Yes, because there is only gravity and the acceleration of gravity is a constant.

25. No, mass does not influence the acceleration when friction is absent.

26. $W = 25$ N

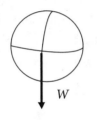

27. 3:2 ratio also

28. 200 N. The system can be regarded as one single object with 20 kg mass.

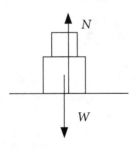

29. See diagram.

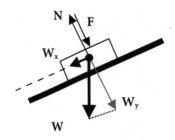

30. 140 N

31. No, cases such as the inclined plane in problem 29 or the object in problem 30 show that the normal force is a result of action.

32. Tension and weight are the forces acting on the three objects.

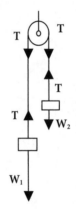

33. Case (a) $a = g/4$

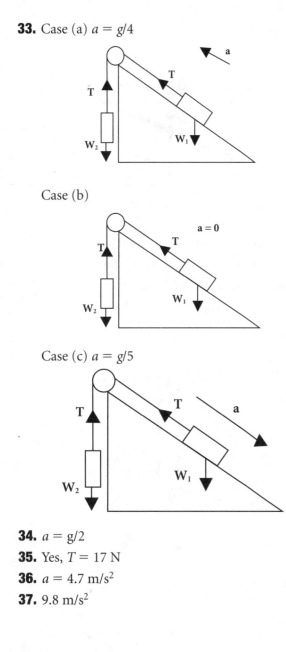

Case (b)

Case (c) $a = g/5$

34. $a = g/2$
35. Yes, $T = 17$ N
36. $a = 4.7$ m/s^2
37. 9.8 m/s^2

▶ Lesson 6

1. No, speed could be zero or very small.
2. Only when speed is zero, because there can be no zero moving mass.
3. Yes, if the velocity is in the negative direction.
4. They are the same.
5. No, since impulse also considers the time of interaction.

6. No, the time of interaction can be negligible and then the impulse tends to zero.
7. 225 N · s
8. Longer since the force then would be smaller.
9. Because on the carpet, the time of interaction is longer and the force of impact is smaller.
10. No, momentum is a quantity of state, while impulse measures a state change.
11. When the object stops
12. If the object moves at a constant speed, there is no change in momentum, so no impulse.
13. $F = 1,800$ N
14. The momentum being constant means that when we consider momentum a vector both the magnitude and the direction of the momentum have to be the same in the initial and final states.
15. Since momentum is a vector, you can have the following situation:

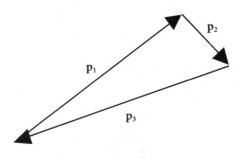

16. Throw the ball in a horizontal direction.
17. Yes, it would have more momentum.
18. Yes. Because speed changes direction before and after collision and velocity, momentum and impulse will consider direction also.
19. $v_{2\ after\ collision} > v_{1\ before\ collision}$
20. $v_f = (v_1 + v_2)/2$
21. The speed of the bike will almost be unchanged and at most decrease by a small amount.
22. Equal and opposite, because the final momentum has to be equal to the initial momentum, which was zero.
23. Equal in magnitude, opposite in direction.

24. No, the resultant immediately after collision is nonzero.

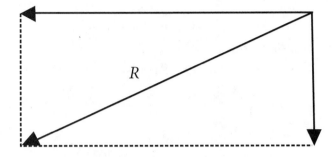

25. Yes, if the momenta of the two cars are equal and opposite.

26. $v_{1x} = 120$ m/s and $v_{1y} = 50$ m/s

27. Before explosion: $(-10.6; 10.6)$ m/s or 15 m/s at 135° with respect to the x-axis
After collision, the first piece moves at $(120; 50)$ m/s or 130 m/s at 23° with respect to the x-axis. The second moves at $(-10; 0)$ m/s or 10 m/s at 180° with respect to the x-axis, and the third piece moves at $(0; 12)$ m/s or 12 m/s at 90° with respect to the x-axis.

28. 0.05 kg, 0.25 kg, and 0.5 kg

▶ Lesson 7

1. $7.2 \cdot 10^2$ J
2. $-2 \cdot 10^5$ J
3. 0 J and 5.4 J
4. 0 J and -5.4 J
5. $7.93 \cdot 10^2$ watts
6. On the small wheel ($F \cdot v = $ constant)
7. Yes, since time is the same.
8. $8 \cdot 10^{-2}$ hp
9. The object is slowing down; work is done by the object on the surroundings.
10. $1/9$
11. Yes, large speed

12. As much as the work lost by friction
13. 10 m/s
14. $5.6 \cdot 10^{-1}$ m
15. 1.5 kg and 15 N
16. 2 m
17. KE is decreasing.
18. No, if the process is conservative, that just means the PE is decreasing.
19. No, friction is not a conservative force.
20. Lower it on the ground.
21. 37.5 J
22. 11.3 m
23. 51 J, 8.1 J, 59 J
24. 10.2 m
25. 6 J, 6 J
26. 4 m/s

▶ Lesson 8

1. No, direction changes.
2. Yes, since acceleration is the time change of velocity.
3. No, trajectory is not linear.
4. 347 degrees
5. $9.06 \cdot 10^5$ km
6. Equal
7. 60 s and $1/60$ Hz
8. $7.5 \cdot 10^{-1}$ m/s
9. $4.7 \cdot 10^{-1}$ m/s
10. $2.32 \cdot 10^{-1}$ s
11. 32.5 m/s
12. ω stays the same and v is changing, increasing if the distance decreases and vice versa
13. Decreasing
14. Increasing
15. $7.27 \cdot 10^{-5}$ rad/s and 4.64 km/s
16. $3.4 \cdot 10^8$ m/s^2 and $2 \cdot 10^{12}$ N

17. The same angular speed. The object with larger mass has a larger centripetal force.

18. 1.3 Hz, 0.75 s, 34 m/s^2

19. 34 N, 44 N, 24 N

▶ Lesson 9

1. A longer one since $I \sim L^2$

2. Closer to the massive end so that the distance to the axis of rotation is smaller and the bat has less inertia.

3. The cylinder, since it has less inertia.

4. The double diameter one has a moment of inertia four times larger.

5. $^1/_4$ since the one rotating around the center has a moment of $m \cdot L^2/_{12}$ and the other is $m \cdot L^2/_3$

6. 0.5 m

7. By the door knob, since torque is then larger, and the effect on the door is larger, too.

8. Perpendicular to the door plan.

9. Apply force on the pivot point or along the lever arm.

10. Apply them in different directions so that the torques cancel each other out.

11. 1,625 N · m = 1,600 N · m

12. 2.5 m and 5 m

13. The one with the steering wheel in part B.

14. Torque is associated with interaction, while work is associated with energy carried by an object.

15. Yes, if one pushes farther from the pivot point than the other.

16. Because they both act on the pivot point.

17. Net torque is zero, so the system is in equilibrium.

18. No, there is a net torque of 51 N · m.

▶ Lesson 10

1. $^9/_{16}$

2. No, the scale measures the force acting on the spring inside the scale, not the pressure.

3. $7.5 \cdot 10^{-4}$ Pa and 10^{-1} Pa or N/m^2

4. 5,600 N/m^2

5. $10.3 \cdot 10^6$ Pa

6. 5 kg

7. $^4/_{11}$

8. $^4/_{11}$

9. $1.07 \cdot 10^8$ Pa and atmospheric pressure is about 1,000 times smaller.

10. Due to the increase in the height of the water column, the pressure increases, too.

11. 2.1 kPa

12. Is the atmospheric pressure and the oil: $1.02 \cdot 10^5$ Pa.

13. Will rise since the weight is smaller than the buoyant force

14. The board is 0.6 m in water.

15. $F^{net}/V = 19,500$ N/m^3

16. $F_1/F_2 = {}^1/_9$

17. 0.67 m

▶ Lesson 11

1. 61° C

2. 311.8 K

3. No, since the data cannot be fitted with a linear equation.

4. 11° C

5. 11 K; they are the same.

6. $t(°\text{Fake}) = \frac{4}{5}t(°\text{C}) + 55$

7. Pressure, density, volume, etc.

8. Work

9. Slowing down since the object loses energy

10. Stays the same since the interaction is similar

11. Heat is transferred through both radiation and conduction to the pot and then transferred to the (bottom layer of) water through radiation and conduction through c on to the top layers.

12. At the bottom closer to the heat source

13. The large specific heat object heats up slower at half the rate.

14. No, because the water will take a lot of heat to change its temperature slightly.

15. Then energy is not conserved and you have to take losses to the surroundings into account.

16. 10.6 Celsius or kelvin degrees

17. $t^i = 6.1°\,C$ and $t^f = 16.7°\,C$

18. Stays the same

19. No, all heat is used to change the state.

20. It warms it up.

21. 2 grams

22. The longer one expands three times more than the shorter one.

23. The longer one increases its volume nine times.

24. It's easier for long objects.

25. $L_0 = 0.15$ m and $L_f = 0.15$ m $+ 165$ μm

the system is positive since it is performed on the system.

5. $\Delta V = 16.1 \cdot 10^{-3}$ m^3, $V_i = 1$ m^3, and $V_i = 0.2$ m^3

6. $W = -2.9 \cdot 10^2$ J

7. No, since the pressure is not constant along the whole process.

8. Yes, due to the difference in sizes.

9. Larger because the temperature increases at constant volume and then the pressure has to increase.

10. $W = +157$ J and it is performed on the system since it is positive.

11. Negative heat means the system releases heat to the surroundings.

12. It doesn't since internal energy has to be constant.

13. $W = -150$ J and the system is expanding.

14. 768 cm^3

15. Yes, $W = -270$ J.

16. The initial and final temperatures are the same. Hence, the change in internal heat is zero and $W = -Q$; then $Q = 270$ J.

17. The system absorbs heat through this process since $Q > 0$.

▶ Lesson 12

1. Of process, since it relates to a mechanical change.

2. Decrease by the same ratio as the volume increases since the P, V product is constant.

3. We will consider that all work done by the external force is used upon compressing the piston and so the work is $W = P \cdot \Delta V = (F/area) \cdot \Delta V = 16$ J.

4. The work done by the force is negative since it's done on the outside, and the work received by

▶ Lesson 13

1. Half the charge from the charged metal object will transfer to the neutral object once contact is established.

2. 60 electrons and $-96 \cdot 10^{-19}$ C

3. The insulator will charge with a charge of $96 \cdot 10^{-19}$ C.

4. $F = 3 \cdot F_1 = 3 \cdot 28.8 \cdot 10^{-23}$ N $= 86.4 \cdot 10^{-23}$ N

5. $F^* = F/100 = 86.4 \cdot 10^{-23}$ N$/100 = 0.864 \cdot 10^{-23}$ N and $F^*/F = 1/100$

6. $F_{BA} + F_{CA} = 57 \cdot 10^{-27}$ N

7. $F_{BA} - F_{CA} = 35 \cdot 10^{-27}\,\text{N}$

8. $F_x = -2.8 \cdot 10^{-3}\,\text{N}$, $F_y = 22 \cdot 10^{-3}\,\text{N}$, $F_{resultant} = 22.2 \cdot 10^{-3}\,\text{N}$

9. Not necessarily, since now we will have different charges and different distances in between.

10. The field will be four times smaller since E $\sim$ $1/r^2$,

$$E = k \cdot \frac{q}{4 \cdot r^2}$$

11. The field decreases by 3 since E $\sim$ q,

$$E = k \cdot \frac{q/3}{4 \cdot r^2}$$

12. Since $E \sim 1/r^2$, the smaller the distance, the larger the field.

13. Since $E \sim 1/r^2$, the larger the distance, the smaller the field.

14. $E = 1.2 \cdot 10^{-3}\,\text{N/C}$

15. The electric field is a vector and three vectors can be added to create no result.

16. $W = 40 \cdot 10^{-19}\,\text{J}$

▶ **Lesson 14**

1. Decreases to $-1.6 \cdot 10^{-2}\text{A}$

2. Reverses but absolute magnitude will be the same

3. The longer one has a resistance three times longer.

4. The one with the larger diameter has a resistance of $(2.5)^2 = 6.25$ times smaller.

5. $I_{Al}/I_{Fe} = R_{Fe}/R_{Al} = 1/3$

6. 10.8 pC

7. The capacitance increases by three and so does the charge: $C = 3.6$ pF and $q = 32.4$ pC.

8. 5.72 mA

9. A voltage of 645 mV has to be supplied.

10. Through resistances R_1 and R_2, the current is 1.69 mA; through R_3 is 3.31 mA and through R_4 is 5 mA.

11. $V_1 = 37.4$ mV, $V_2 = 109$ mV, $V_3 = 145$ mV, $V_4 = 500$ mV

12. $R_{series} = 100\Omega$, $R_{parallel} = 9.7\Omega$

13. $59.67\Omega \sim 60\Omega$

14. $I = 0.2$ A

15. $I_1 = 0.097$ A, $I_2 = 0.064$ A, $I_3 = 0.039$ A

16. $V_1 = V_2 = V_3 = 2$ V, $V_4 = 6$ V, $V_5 = 4$ V

▶ **Lesson 15**

1. $F = 0$ since the angle between the field and the speed is zero.

2. When the field and the velocity are either in the same or opposite directions

3. $F_S/F_{magnet} = 9\ T/10$ gauss $\sim 10^4$

4. The force is in the $-y$ direction and the trajectory will be curved as shown in the figure.

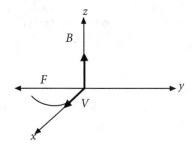

5. $12°$

6. $30°$

7. The two have to make a 90° angle.

8. The two have to make a 0° angle.

9. $10^{-3}\ T$

10. The force will be oriented toward the wire.

11. The wires will repel each other since the fields are in the same direction (as N and N would do).

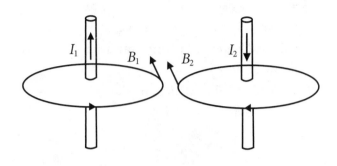

12. The force between the wires is inverse proportional with the distance between, so the force would be half when the two wires are at twice the distance.

13. F/L = 0.3 N/m

14. $11 \cdot 10^{-6}$ T

15. $0.5 \cdot 10^{6}$ A

► **Lesson 16**

1. $\Delta x = 12.5$ mm

2. The two forces weight and elastic force are equal in magnitude and opposite in direction.

3. 2.6 rad/s = 150 deg/s

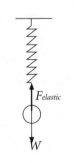

4. 0.42 Hz, $\pi/2 = 90°$, $2 \cdot \pi/3 = 120°$, $\pi = 180°$, $2 \cdot \pi = 360°$

5. $a(t) = \omega \cdot A \cdot \sin(\omega \cdot t)$ and $a_{max} = \omega \cdot A$ when $t = T/4$ and $v(T/4) = 0$ m/s

6. Displacement is $x(t) = 1.2$ m $\cdot \sin(5 \cdot t + 30°)$ and $v(t) = 6$ m/s $\cdot \cos(5 \cdot t + 30°)$ and acceleration is $a(t) = -30$ m/s$^2 \cdot \sin(5 \cdot t + 30°)$

7. At $t = 0$ s, angular displacement is $\theta(0\text{ s}) \cdot = 5 \cdot t + 30° = 30°$, initial displacement is $x(0\text{ s}) = 1.2$ m $\cdot \sin(5 \cdot t + 30°) = 0.6$ m and initial speed is $v(0\text{ s}) = 6$ m/s $\cdot \cos(5 \cdot t + 30°) = 5.2$ m/s.

8. $v = 2 \cdot E/m \cdot A^2 = 15$ m/s

9. $v = \omega^2 \cdot A$, $\omega \cdot = (v/A)^{1/2} = 22$ rad/s

10. $T = 8$ s, $f = 0.125$ Hz, $\omega \cdot = 0.785$ rad/s

11. $PE_{max} = KE_{max} = E = 31$ J

12. The kinetic energy of the oscillator will decrease by the same amount the PE increases: $\Delta PE = Ef - Ei = 3 \cdot Ei - Ei = 2 \cdot Ei$, but E = constant so $\Delta PE = -\Delta KE \cdot$ Hence, $\Delta KE = -2 \cdot Ei$.

13. The oscillator moving with a larger amplitude will have a total mechanical energy four times larger.

► **Lesson 17**

1. $\lambda = V/f = 3 \cdot 10^4$ m and the period is $T = l/f = 10^{-4}$ s

2. $f = 10$ cycles/6 s = 1.7 Hz, $T = 1/f = 0.6$ s, $v = 10$ cm/s = 0.1 m/s

3. $v_{heavy}/v_{light} = (1/2) < 1$ hence $v_{heavy} < v_{light}$

4. 5,040 m/s in steel and $4.7 \cdot 10^4$ m/s in air; both much larger than the speed of sound in air

5. v is proportional to $\rho^{1/2}$ s$^{\circ}$ with increasing density the speed decreases.

6. Both ice and steam have $-\frac{1}{2}$ lower density than liquid water, hence the speed will be smaller in water, but larger in ice and steam.

7. Because v_{ice} is larger than v_{water} and at constant frequency speed is proportional to wavelength then $\lambda_{ice} > \lambda_{water}$

8. The time of travel is $t = d/c = 500$ s and the frequency of the waves is: $f = c / \lambda = 6 \cdot 10^{15}$ Hz

9. $L = \lambda/2 = v/2 \cdot f = 1.5$ m

10. $E = c \cdot B$ hence the magnetic field will be $B = E/c = 6 \cdot 10^{-5}$ T and the energy is $u = B^2/\mu_0 = 3 \cdot 10^{-7}$J

▶ Lesson 18

1. $10°$ west of the normal N_1

2. $20°$ with respect to the normal on the second mirror

3. $\theta_i = 65°$

4. $r = 30°$

5. The light rays will encounter two surfaces of separation and refraction will happen at the outside of glass and inside. The refracted light rays are parallel to the incident ones.

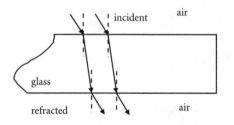

6. The light rays will suffer refraction, reflection, and refraction back into air. The light returns to air at the same angle as the incident angle but shifted toward right due to the path covered in glass.

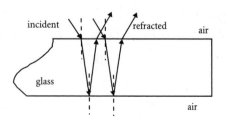

7. Because the product of the index of refraction to the sine of the angle is constant and sine is a function increasing with angle between $0°$ and $90°$, then a decrease in the index of refraction means an increase in the refraction angle, so the refracted light will be bent away from the normal.

8. We apply Snell's law and find the index is: $n = \sin 55°/ \sin 37° = 1.4$.

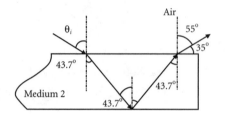

9. There are two refraction processes in between three different media, so the angles made by the light with the normals are going to be different according to the index of refraction:

MATERIAL	INDEX OF REFRACTION
Air	1.00029
Glass	1.66
Ice	1.31

So, from air to glass, the light bends toward the normal, whereas from glass to ice, it bends away from normal but less than it would bend in air. According to the incidence angle, there also can be total internal reflection at the surface between glass and ice.

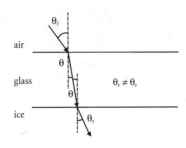

10. The angle of refraction on the first surface is 20°, and the angle of refraction at the second surface is the same as the angle of initial incidence 35°.

11. The angle of the outgoing ray is 20°.

12. The light ray will totally reflect water because the first term of Snell's law can not be reproduced in air regardless of the angle of refraction: $n_{water} \cdot \sin \theta = $ constant and $1.33 \cdot \sin 68° = 1.23$. Because the light ray is supposed to travel in air, $n = 1$, then the $\sin \theta_r$ would have to be greater than 1!

13. The light will be refracted into the water at an angle of refraction of 60° with respect to the second surface of separation.

▶ Lesson 19

1. The light rays will go in straight lines from the sun toward the moon-Earth system and from the shadow of the moon on the earth (umbra) and the penumbra.

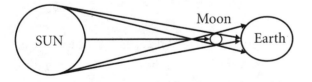

2. The same procedure as in the example below will be employed in this case.

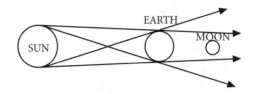

3. The number and position of the images is found by applying the laws of reflection to the parallel mirrors: Each image is an object for the next mirror. There will be an infinite number of images formed in the system of two parallel mirrors.

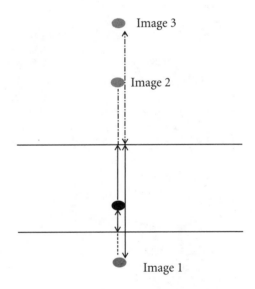

4. Yes

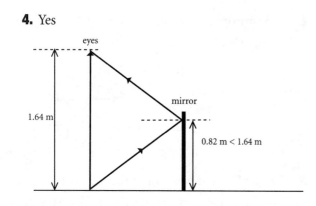

5. $d_i = 30$ cm, $d_o = 20$ cm

6. $d_i = 18$ cm, $m = -2$, $h_i = -6$ cm, image is real, inversed, and larger than the object

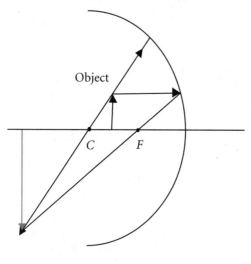

7. $d_i = 10$ cm, $m = -2/3$, $h_i = -2$ cm, image is real, inversed, and smaller than the object

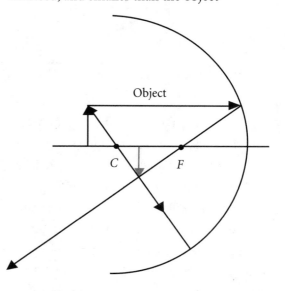

8. $d_i = -7.5$ cm, $m = 0.25$, $h_i = 2.5$ cm, image is virtual, straight, and smaller than the object

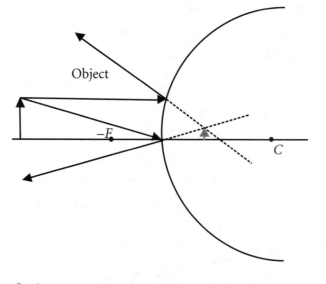

9. $d_i = -7.5$ cm, $m = 0.25$, $h_i < h_0$, the image is virtual, smaller than the object, and upright

10. The other radius is infinity because the plane will be part of a huge sphere of radius infinity.

11. $R = 26.4$ cm

12. All rays will bend toward the focal point and will pass through the focal point.

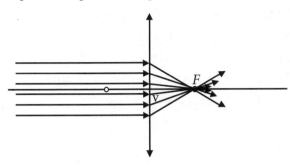

13. The light is spread by the lens, and the back extension of the light will pass through the focal point.

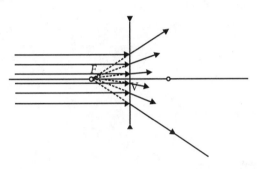

▶ Lesson 20

1. A wave with the same frequency and double amplitude

2. $A_1 = 20$ cm, $A_2 = 23$ cm, $\lambda_1 = 5.7 \cdot 10^{-10}$ m, $\lambda_2 = 6.7 \cdot 10^{-10}$ m, $f_1 = 0.32$ Hz, $f_1 = 0.03$ Hz, $y_1 + y_2 = 43$ cm

3. The 550 nm will give a larger diffraction pattern.

4. Yes, the size of the door opening is so much larger than the wavelength of light while a micrometer can open a few micrometers (or the equivalent of a hundred nanometers, the range of light wavelength).

5. $d = 27$ cm

6. $L = 16$ cm

7. Each component color of light will diffract differently because the bending is directly proportional to the wavelength: the central is a bright white followed by the rainbow colors bright maxima and in between the dark fringes.

8. The one with least diffraction: violet

9. Yes, if the transmission axes are perpendicular on each other.

10. As noted in the lesson: The average intensity of light leaving the polarizer is half of the intensity of the incident light.

11. For all electromagnetic waves, we can define polarization because the same principle of electrical current variation applies to all.

12. It will be zero because the second polarizer is at 90° with respect to the first one.

13. $S = 0.375$ kW/m^2

▶ Posttest

1. **d.** $6.349 \cdot 10^3$ km (Lesson 1)

2. **b.** $5.87 \cdot 10^{12}$ miles (Lesson 1)

3. **a.** 10^{-12} Farad (Lesson 1)

4. **c.** $1.5 \cdot 10^{11}$ m (Lesson 3)

5. **d.** 22.8 cm (Lesson 1)

6. **b.** $5.55 \cdot 10^1$ mi/h; $1.496 \cdot 10^8$ km; $1.408 \cdot 10^{-3}$ kg/cm^3; $2.861 \cdot 10^{20}$ (Lesson 1)

7. **c.** 1125.44; 1234.58 (Lesson 1)

8. **a.** 4 and 9 (Lesson 2)

9. **d.** $9.10938188 \cdot 1\ 0^{-32}$ kg (Lesson 1)

10. **c.** 1.04 kg and 3.13 N (Lesson 2)

11. **b.** 90 N (Lesson 2)

12. **a.** 4 m/s^2 and 10,000 N (Lesson 5)

13. **b.** $W = N = 4.5$ N (Lesson 5)

14. **d.** (Lesson 5)

15. **c.** 5.006 N (Lesson 5)

16. **a.** $m_1/m_2 = v_2/v_1 = 1/3$ (Lesson 6)

17. **c.** 0.27 m/s (Lesson 6)

18. d. $v = (9; 10)$ m/s (Lesson 6)

19. b. $1.2 \cdot 10^4$ J (Lesson 7)

20. a. $1.2 \cdot 10^4$ J (Lesson 7)

21. b. $6.2 \cdot 10^{-2}$ rad/s (Lesson 8)

22. c. $4.1 \cdot 10^3$ N (Lesson 10)

23. b. 273.15 K (Lesson 11)

24. a. Is constant (Lesson 12)

25. d. -58 J (Lesson 12)

26. a. Decreases (Lesson 13)

27. c. $^1/_3$ (Lesson 15)

28. b. 12.0 cm (Lesson 16)

29. d. 10^9 and $3 \cdot 10^{11}$ Hz (Lesson 17)

30. b. Same frequency wave with an amplitude two times larger (Lesson 20)

APPENDIX

Glossary of Terms

acceleration   vector showing the time rate of change of the velocity

action and reaction forces   forces showing up during interaction of two or more objects

adiabatic process   process where no heat is exchanged

alternative current (*ac*)   the current flows half of the time in one direction and the other half of the time in the opposite direction

amplitude   the maximum displacement from the equilibrium position

angular displacement   the angle between two positions of the object on the circular path

angular frequency 2π times the frequency

angular speed   time rate of change of the angular displacement

average velocity   change in displacement over time

buoyancy   upward force exerted on an object immersed in a liquid

calorimetry   study of heat exchange in systems that are thermally isolated from their surroundings

capacitance   the measure of an object's ability to store electrical charge

Cartesian coordinates   coordinates with respect to a reference frame made of reciprocally perpendicular axes

Celsius temperature scale   scale based on a 0° C temperature when water freezes and 100° C when water boils at normal atmospheric pressure

centripetal acceleration   acceleration due to the change in the direction of the tangential velocity

centripetal force   the net force on an object moving in a circular trajectory

compression   regions of increased pressure and density

concave mirror   a mirror that has the reflecting side on the interior of the curvature

conductor   material through which a flow of electrical charge can be easily established

conduction   charge movement inside a material

conservation of energy   energy is constant

conservation of mechanical energy   the total mechanical energy of an isolated system stays the same

conservation of momentum   momentum stays the same before and after collision

constructive interference   interference that produces a wave with more intense characteristics (increased amplitude)

convergent lens   a lens that gathers together an incoming bunch of parallel light rays

convex mirrors   mirrors that have the reflecting side on the outside of the mirror

coordinates   set of numbers that uniquely specify the position of a point with respect to a frame of reference

Coulomb's law   the electrical force between two point-like particles is proportional to each of their charges and inversely proportional to the square distance between them

critical angle   angle above which total internal reflection occurs

d_o distance from the object to the mirror

d_i distance from the image to the mirror

density   mass per unit volume of a given substance

destructive interference   interference that produces no resultant wave

divergent lens   lens that spreads apart a bunch of incoming parallel light rays

dielectric constant (of a material)   the factor by which a parallel-plate capacitor's capacitance increases when the gap between its plates is filled with that material

diffuse reflection   a fascicle of parallel light ray reflects from a surface and forms a fascicle of chaotically reflected light rays due to surface roughness

diffraction   bending of the waves around obstacles

displacement   change in position of a point-like object or particle

direct current (dc)   constant electric current

elastic force   force proportional to the displacement from the equilibrium position and directed such that it tries to reestablish equilibrium

electric charge   property associated with an electric force of attraction between oppositely charged objects or an electric force of repulsion between same-charge objects

electric current   electrical charge flowing in the unit time through a cross-sectional area of a conductor

electrical field   properties of the space around electrically charged objects that measure the strength of electrical interaction with a small test-charge

electrical resistance   the ratio of the voltage applied to the current established at the terminals of an electrical object

electrical resistivity   electrical resistance of a material of unit length and unit cross-sectional area

electron   the smallest negative electric charge in existence

electromagnetic spectrum   gamma, X-ray, ultraviolet, visible infrared, microwave, and radio waves

electromagnetic wave   fluctuation of a magnetic and electric field

electromotive force   maximum potential difference given out by a battery

energy of electromagnetic field   energy carried by the electric and magnetic fields

equilibrium   a state where the net force on an object or a system of objects is zero

equation of state   a relation between the state variables of a given thermodynamic system

external forces   forces coming from outside a system or an object

Fahrenheit temperature scale   scale based on a 32° F temperature when water freezes and 212° F when water boils at normal atmospheric pressure

fixed frame of reference   rectangular system of axis considered at rest

focal distance $\frac{1}{2}$ of the radius

focal length of a mirror   proportional to the radii of the two spherical surfaces and the index of refraction of the material the lens is made of

focal point   point through which the rays coming parallel to the optical axis are reflected

frequency   number of revolutions made during a second

friction   force oriented against the direction of motion showing up when two surfaces come into contact

fringes   alternation of light and dark spaces due to superposition of waves

fundamental quantity   quantity that cannot be derived from measuring other quantities

fundamental unit   unit of a fundamental quantity

fusion   phase change between liquid and solid phase

geometrical optics   analysis of light based on the ray approximation

gravitational potential energy   energy due to position or configuration in the gravitational field of Earth

h_o object height

h_i image height

harmonic motion   periodic oscillatory motion around an equilibrium position

harmonic wave function   displacement equation for a wave that connects the x and y displacement with time

heat   energy exchanged with the surrounding by an object that changes only its temperature

heat capacity   the heat absorbed (or released) to increase (or decrease) the temperature of the system or object by one unit

heat engine   a device that converts internal energy into work using heat flowing from one high-temperature source to another low-temperature source

heat transfer   energy transferred through heat

Huygen's principle   every point on a wavefront produces a subset of waves that move with the same velocity as the incident wave; at a later time, the wave front is found to be the surface tangent to the propagating subset of waves

ideal gas law   the equation of state for an ideal gas of noninteracting particles

inelastic collision   after collision, the objects move together, some mechanical energy is converted into heat while momentum is conserved

impulse a measure of the effect of a force during a given time interval

incident ray the incoming light

incident angle angle made by incident ray and normal

index of refraction the ratio of the speed of light in a vacuum and the speed of light in a medium

inertia tendency to preserve the same state of motion or of rest

induction local charge distribution created by another neighboring charged object

internal energy sum of kinetic and potential energy of a grand collective of particles constituting the system under thermodynamic study

International System of Units system based on seven fundamental units, the most usual ones being the meter, kilogram, and the second

instantaneous velocity velocity at a given instant of time

insulator material capable of keeping the electrical charge localized

internal forces forces occurring inside a system or object

isolated system system of objects with no external forces acting

Kelvin temperature scale a temperature scale independent of a thermometer's working substance, offset of the Celsius scale by 273.15 degrees

latent heat heat absorbed during a phase change (no change in temperature)

lens a curved transparent medium

linear momentum a measure of a body's inertia equal to its mass times velocity

linear motion motion along a straight line

longitudinal wave the disturbance and the wave propagation are parallel to each other

kinetic energy energy due to motion

magnification the ratio of the height of the image and the height of the object

magnetic field field characterizing interaction between permanent magnets or electrical currents

magnetic force force exerted on an electrical charge moving in a magnetic field

magnification equation calculates the ratio of the image size to the object size or the image distance to the object distance

maximum height the height reached by an object thrown upward (vertical velocity is zero while the component of the velocity on the horizontal is nonzero in the case of projectile motion)

mechanical energy the sum of potential and kinetic energy

mirror/lens equation establishes a connection between the distance to the object, to the mirror, and the focal distance

moment of inertia a measure of the rotational inertia around a certain axis of rotation

multimeter instrument capable of measuring voltage, current, electrical resistance, and other electrical quantities (i.e., capacitance)

normal perpendicular to the surface of separation

normal force force of reaction from the surface of support

optical axis the horizontal line perpendicular to the surface of the mirror or going through the tip of the mirror

period time to complete a revolution

periodic waves exhibits periodic behavior (that is, period, frequency, and angular displacement)

perfectly elastic collision collision conserving the total kinetic energy and the momentum of the bodies involved in the collision; after collision, the bodies move separate

phase angular displacement

phase change transformation from one phase to another, for example, from solid to liquid by melting

plane mirror an opaque, flat, shiny object that reflects light that propagates toward it

polar coordinates coordinates with respect to a polar axis

polarization the direction of the electric field defines the direction of polarization

polarized wave a source producing waves that are all oriented such that E is directed in a single direction

potential energy energy due to position or configuration

power the work performed on an object in a unit of time

pressure force exerted upon a unit area of a surface

principle of superposition concludes on how the wavefronts add to each other when present in the same place at the same time

principal maxima bright central fringe

process variables variables describing a transition (process) between two equilibrium states

projectile motion motion of an object with constant velocity on the horizontal and accelerated motion on the vertical

PV-diagram graph of pressure versus volume

radius the radius of the sphere of which the concave/convex mirror is part off

range the horizontal displacement of an object in a symmetric projectile motion

rarefaction regions of diminished pressure and density

ray the radius from a source of wave to the wavefront

ray approximation light traveling in a straight line in a medium between two points

real image image that you can obtain on a screen

reflection angle angle made by the reflected light and the normal

reflection laws the law stating the equality between the angle of incidence and angle of reflection and the fact that all light rays in a reflection phenomena are part of the same plane

reflection of light light propagating from a source toward a smooth surface that will bounce from the surface and return to the medium that contains the source

reflected ray the outgoing light ray

reference frame an origin and a set of reference axes to help specify position in space

refracted angle angle made by the refracted light ray and the normal

refraction light propagation from a transparent medium to another transparent medium

refraction laws the law stating the relationship between the angle of incidence and the index of refraction to the angle of refraction and the index of refraction in the second medium and the fact that all light rays in a refraction phenomena are part of the same plane

refracted ray   the light ray that passes in the second medium

refrigerator   a device that transfers heat from a low-temperature source to another high-temperature source using mechanical work in the process

relative velocity   the resultant vector measuring the velocity of an object in a fixed frame

resultant force   net sum of all forces acting on the object

revolution   one rotation

right-hand-side rule (or corkscrew rule)   rule to find out the direction of the magnetic force

rigid objects   objects that keep their shape and form while under external influence

rotational equilibrium (about a given axis)   a state with no net external force and no net torque (about that axis)

rotational inertia   tendency to preserve the same state of rotational motion

scalar   quantity completely specified by its value

scalar   (1) (**dot**) **product** of vectors **A** and **B**;   (2) scalar quantity given by A · B · cos (**A,B**)

significant figure   figure that when dropped or left out of a calculation, negatively impacts the precision of the calculation

simple thermodynamic process   a process where one parameter is fixed (for example, isobaric process, at constant pressure; isochoric process, at constant volume; isothermal process, at constant temperature)

sound wave   a mechanically created wave that needs a solid, liquid, or gaseous medium to propagate

specific heat   the heat absorbed (or released) by one unit of mass to increase (or decrease) the temperature of the system or object by one unit

speed   magnitude of velocity

speed of a wave   is the ratio of the wavelength to the period

slope   ratio of ordinate to abscissa separations for a linear graph

specular reflection   a fascicle of parallel light rays reflects from a surface and forms a fascicle of parallel reflected light rays

state variables   variables completely describing the state of a thermodynamic system (for example, pressure, volume, and temperature)

sublimation   phase change between solid and gas state

torque   a measure of a force's ability to rotate an object about some given axis

total internal reflection   beyond a certain angle of incidence, the light might not be able to refract in a second medium and remains in the medium where it was produced

tangential velocity   component of the velocity along the tangent to the circle at the object's position

temperature   quantity describing average internal energy of a large collection of particles

tension force   the force in cables and ropes in response to a pulling force

thermal equilibrium   a system whose temperature stays the same and has no heat exchanges between its parts

thermodynamic cycle   a chain of repeatable thermodynamic transformations that eventually brings the system back to its initial state after a finite time

thermodynamic work   work performed by a system due to thermal interactions with its surroundings

thermal expansion   increase in size and volume of a solid object due to heating

time of flight   describing a projectile motion, the time an object is in the air

transversal wave   have the disturbance and the wave propagation perpendicular to each other

two-dimensional motion   motion described by both $x(t)$ and $y(t)$ dependence

uniform circular motion   motion of an object traveling at a constant speed on a circular path

unit prefixes   factors used to name subunits that multiply up or divide down the unit

unit vector   unit magnitude vector defined along one of the Cartesian axes of a reference frame

unpolarized waves   when waves are produced such that electric field is chaotically distributed

vaporization   phase change between liquid and gas state

vector   quantity specified by both its value and direction

vector components   (along a set of axes)   projection of a vector along the directions of the unit vectors of a reference frame

vector   (1) **(cross) product** of vectors **A** and **B**;   (2) a vector with direction defined by the *right-hand rule* and magnitude $A \cdot B \cdot \sin(A, B)$

velocity   vector showing the displacement change rate

virtual image   image that you cannot obtain on a screen

voltmeter   instrument that measures potential differences

wave   a disturbance propagated through the material with no bulk flow of matter but the propagation of the energy from one position to another

wavefront   the surface of points having the same phase

wavelength   the distance between two identical positions the wave has reached

wave number   inverse proportional with the wavelength

weight   force exerted by Earth's gravity

work   a measure of the effect of a force on the system's energy equal to the scalar product of the force to the displacement along the force

work-energy theorem   the work done on an object is equal to the change in its kinetic energy

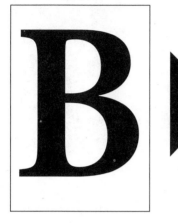
Physical Constants, Conversion Factors, and Prefixes

▶ Physical Constants

NAME	SYMBOL	SI VALUE	SI UNIT
Atomic unit of mass	u	1.66067×10^{-27}	kg
Electron mass at rest	m_e	9.109×10^{-31}	kg
Elementary charge	e	1.602×10^{-19}	C
Standard free fall acceleration	g	9.8	$m \cdot s^{-2}$
Normal atmospheric pressure	1 atm	1.013×10^5	$N \cdot m^{-2}$
Planck's constant	h	6.625×10^{-34}	$J \cdot s$
Boltzmann's constant	k_B	1.380×10^{-23}	$J \cdot K^{-1}$
Universal gas constant	R	8.314	$J \cdot K^{-1} \cdot mol^{-1}$
Avogadro's number	N_A	6.022×10^{23}	mol^{-1}
Speed of light (in vacuum)	c	3.00×10^8	$m \cdot s^{-1}$
Permitivity of free space	ε_0	8.85×10^{-12}	$C^2 \cdot N^{-1} \cdot m^{-2}$
Coulomb constant	$1/(4\pi\epsilon_0)$	8.99×10^9	$N^1 \cdot m_2 \cdot C^{-2}$
Permeability of free space	μ_0	$4\pi \times 10^{-7}$	$T \cdot m \cdot A^{-1}$

▶ Conversion Factors

Length

1 inch = 2.54 centimeters

1 foot = 12 inches = 30.48 centimeters

1 yard = 3 feet = 91.44 centimeters

1 mile = 1.609 kilometers

1 kilometers = 0.621 mile

Volume

1 liter = 1,000 centimeters^{-3}

1 quart = 946 milliliters = 0.946 liters

1 gallon = 4 quarts = 3.784 liters

Speed

1 kilometers/hour = 0.2778 meters/second

1 meters/second = 3.5997 kilometers/hour

1 mile/hour = 0.447 meters/second

Mass

1 slug = 14.59 kilograms

1 pound (lb) equivalent mass = 0.4536 kilogram

1 μ = 1.66067 × 10^{-27} kilogram

Time

1 minute = 60 second

1 hour = 60 minutes = 3,600 seconds

1 day = 24 hours

1 year = 365.242 days

Angle

180 degrees = p rad

1 radian = 57.30 degrees

1 degree = 60 minutes

Pressure

1 atmosphere (atm) = 1.01325 × 10^5 N · m^{-2}

1 Pascal (Pa) = 1 N · m^{-2}

1 pounds/square inch (psi) = 1 lb/in^2 = 6.8947 × 10^3 Pa

1 unit of pressure (torr) = 1 millimeter mercury (mmHg) = 133.322 Pa

Force

1 newton (N) = 0.2248 lb = 10^5 dynes

1 lb = 4.448 N

Work and Energy

1 Joule (J) = 10^7 erg = 0.738 ft · lb = 0.239 calories (cal)

1 cal = 4.186 J

1 British thermal unit (Btu) = 252 cal = 1.054 × 10^3 J

1 kilowatts/hour (kWh) = 3.60 × 10^6 J

Power

1 horse power (hp) = 550 ft · lb/s = 746 watts (W)

1 Btu/h = 0.293 W

SI Prefixes

10^{24} = yotta = Y	10^{-24} = yocto = y
10^{21} = zetta = Z	10^{-21} = zepto = z
10^{18} = exa − E	10^{-18} = atto = a
10^{15} = peta = P	10^{-15} = femto = f
10^{12} = tera = T	10^{-12} = pico = p
10^9 = giga = G	10^{-9} = nano = n
10^6 = mega = M	10^{-6} = micro = μ
10^3 = kilo = k	10^{-3} = mili = m
10^2 = hecto = h	10^{-2} = centi = c
10^1 = deka = da	10^{-1} = deci = d

C ▶ Additional Resources

▶ Books

Cutnell, J.D., and K.W. Johnson. 2001 and 2004. *Physics*, 5th and 6th eds. New York: John Wiley & Sons.

Das, B. 2004. *Mathematics for College Physics*. New Jersey: Pearson Prentice Hall.

Hecht, E. 2003. *Physics Algebra/Trig*. Stamford, CT: Thomson Brooks/Cole.

Hewitt, P.J. 1998 and 2004. *Conceptual Physics*, 8th and 9th eds. Reading, MA: Addison Wesley.

LearningExpress. 2005. *Algebra Success in 20 Minutes a Day*, 2nd ed. New York: LearningExpress.

Serway, R.A., J.S. Faughn, C. Vuille, and C.A. Bennett. 2006. *College Physics*, 7th ed. Stamford, CT: Thomas Brooks/Cole.

Serway, R.A., and J.W. Jewett. 2004. *Physics for Scientists and Engineers*, 6th ed. Stamford, CT: Thomson Brooks/Cole.

Shipman, J.T., J.D. Wilson, and A.W. Todd. 2003. *An Introduction to Physical Science*, 10th ed. Boston, MA: Houghton Mifflin Co.

▶ Internet

For web resources, a large number of educational websites provide simulations that can add to the experience of learning physics. One that is repeatedly used at this level of presenting the material is www.physicsclassroom.com.